Mac® OS X Programming

Contents At a Glance

Mac® OS X Programming

Dan Parks Sydow

New Riders

www.newriders.com
201 West 103rd Street, Indianapolis, Indiana 46290
An Imprint of Pearson Education
Boston • Indianapolis • London • Munich • New York • San Francisco

Mac® OS X Programming

Trademarks

Warning and Disclaimer

Publisher
David Dwyer

Associate Publisher
Stephanie Wall

Production Manager
Gina Kanouse

Managing Editor
Kristy Knoop

Development Editor
Jill Batistick

Product Marketing Manager
Stephanie Layton

Publicity Manager
Susan Nixon

Project Editor
Todd Zellers

Indexer
Cheryl Lenser

Manufacturing Coordinator
Jim Conway

Book Designer
Louisa Klucznik

Cover Designer
Brainstorm Design, Inc.

Cover Production
Aren Howell

Proofreader
Sossity Smith

Composition
Barb Kordesh

Media Developer
Michael Hughes

TABLE OF CONTENTS

About the Author

Dan Parks Sydow is a software engineer and writer based in Milwaukee, Wisconsin. He has written over twenty computer-related books, including a dozen Macintosh programming books. Whether it's by way of a beginner-level book, such as *Mac Programming for Dummies 3rd Edition* (IDG Books Worldwide, 1999), or an advanced-level text, such as *The Metrowerks CodeWarrior Professional Book* (Ventana, 1997), Dan welcomes the opportunity to help others master the art of Macintosh programming. When functioning in the real world (that is, when working in business as opposed to writing), he has worked on Macintosh programs that performed tasks such as the manipulation of hear magnetic resonance (MR) images, and he has designed complex fourth dimension databases that interface Macs to mainframe computers.

About the Technical Reviewers

These reviewers contributed their considerable hands-on expertise to the entire development process for *Mac OS X Programming*. As the book was being written, these dedicated professionals reviewed all the material for technical content, organization, and flow. Their feedback was critical to ensuring that *Mac OS X Programming* fits our reader's need for the highest-quality technical information.

Dennis Groves was born and raised in Seattle, Washington. While a sophomore in high school, Dennis began his career as a software engineer for a well known CADD company. It was there that he discovered UNIX and began to run a multi-user BBS with Usenet news feed. Since that time he has advised clients on the large scale implementation of systems and network administration software with a focus on security. Dennis also has over six years with system administration, network administration, integrating heterogeneous platforms and information security. He has spent the last five years pen-testing high profile websites, and web application security consulting for many significant companies in the financial arena.

Since graduation, **Bill Larson** has worked for software vendor companies in the semiconductor and security software industries. He has worked with the Macintosh since Mac OS 6.5 and UNIX since Solaris 2.2. He is currently working on security consulting projects and with an application security company. His newest toy is Mac OS X 10.1 with OpenBase, PHP 4.0, Apache, and XDarwin. He's starting to explore the new changes with Project Builder and Interface Builder and to write wrapper GUI's for open source security tools using the Mac OS X development tools. Bill lives in Phoenix, Arizona with his wife, Karen, and three children. He has an AA in Applied Science Electronics Technology and a BS in Electrical Engineering.

Acknowledgments

I'd like to thank Stephanie Wall, Ann Quinn, and the rest of the New Riders staff for making this book happen. Thanks to Jill Batistick for numerous helpful suggestions and for cleaning up my prose. Finally, a tip of the hat to Dennis Groves for an insightful technical review.

Tell Us What You Think

As the reader of this book, you are the most important critic and commentator. We value your opinion and want to know what we're doing right, what we could do better, what areas you'd like to see us publish in, and any other words of wisdom you're willing to pass our way.

As the Associate Publisher for New Riders Publishing, I welcome your comments. You can fax, email, or write me directly to let me know what you did or didn't like about this book—as well as what we can do to make our books stronger.

Please note that I cannot help you with technical problems related to the topic of this book, and that due to the high volume of mail I receive, I might not be able to reply to every message.

When you write, please be sure to include this book's title and author as well as your name and phone or fax number. I will carefully review your comments and share them with the author and editors who worked on the book.

Fax: 317-581-4663
Email: stephanie.wall@newriders.com
Mail: Stephanie Wall
          Associate Publisher
          New Riders Publishing
          201 West 103rd Street
          Indianapolis, IN 46290 USA

Introduction

With Mac OS X, Apple is assured of assuming leadership in operating system market share. Alright, maybe not. However, the winds of change are certainly in the air. The Mac finally has an operating system that lays claim to *all* the key buzzwords. Take a deep breath, and then repeat after me: Mac OS X includes preemptive multitasking, protected memory, dual-processor support, multithreading, superior stability, and advanced virtual memory management, and is industrial-strength, UNIX-based, and open source. Anyone who in the past had a Mac will want Mac OS X—and a few people and businesses who didn't have Macs will too. Its UNIX underpinnings will capture the curiosity of many UNIX programmers, and it will make the Macintosh a realistic choice for many UNIX-based businesses too. Cool, lower-priced Apple hardware running Mac OS X, such as the iMac desktop computers and the iBook portable computers, keep Macs, and now Mac OS X, in the educational market.

What does all this glowing praise, and possible market expansion, mean to you, the computer programmer? Opportunity! Whether you want to develop freeware to make a name for yourself, write shareware to make some money on the side, port existing code to Mac OS X, or simply be able to include "Macintosh programming" on your resume, now is the time to learn (or improve on your existing) Macintosh programming techniques. Whether you're an old hand at Mac programming or new to the platform, this book will help you learn to program in Mac OS X.

Target Audience

If you've never programmed before, this book is not for you. If, however, you're interested in developing Mac OS X applications and you know C or C++, and if you have written (even very basic) programs for *any* platform, this book will serve as an excellent resource.

If you're coming from a Mac OS programming background, this book will fill you in on all the new technologies that come with Mac OS X, and it will help you make the transition from using the original Macintosh Toolbox API to using the Carbon API. If you're coming from a different platform, such as UNIX or Windows, this book will quickly bring you up to speed on the basics of Mac OS X programming. It then will propel you into the realm of developing real-world, full-fledged Mac OS X applications.

Necessary Software

To get the most from this book, you'll need a Macintosh computer running any version of Mac OS X. You'll also want to have Apple's Project Builder integrated development environment (IDE) software to create and edit source code files and to compile and build applications. In addition, you'll want to have Apple's Interface Builder software to create and edit interface elements such as menus and windows.

Here's the really good news: If you have Mac OS X, you have both Project Builder and Interface Builder. They're on the Developer Tools CD that comes with every copy of Mac OS X.

Organization of This Book

This book consists of eleven chapters organized in such a way that they should be read sequentially. The first chapter provides a broad overview of the new Mac OS X system software. The second chapter introduces basic Mac OS X programming concepts and software tools and has you developing several, albeit simple, Mac OS X applications from start to finish. Chapters 3 through 7 deal with events, windows, controls, menus and graphics, respectively, and provide a foundation for any and all the programs you'll write. The remaining chapters deal with slightly more esoteric, though still important, topics such as readying your program for other languages, QuickTime movies, application icons, and porting older code to Mac OS X. Additionally, at the end of each chapter you find a "For More Information" section, which provides additional resources related to topics discussed in the individual chapters.

Chapter 1, "System Components and Programming Technologies," presents an overview of the layout of the Mac OS X system software. Aqua is the name of the new user interface, but Mac OS X consists of much more than a pretty face. Here you read about the conceptual layers of system software such as the application environments (including Carbon and Cocoa), application services (such as Quartz and QuickTime), core services (such as Apple Events and Open Transport), and the kernel environment (which includes Mach and BSD).

Chapter 2, "Overview of Mac OS X Programming," examines the IDEs (integrated development environments) available to Mac OS X programmers. Here the focus is on Apple's Project Builder IDE and Interface Builder interface layout software. Both applications are free from Apple, so you're all set to follow along with this chapter's short, straightforward examples. Here you see the basic code common to all Mac OS X applications, and you compile and build applications that display functioning windows, menus, alerts, and graphics.

Chapter 3, "Events and the Carbon Event Manager," covers a set of API (application programming interface) routines that are entirely new to Mac OS X. Mac programs always have been event-based. A user action such as a click of the mouse generates an event to which the program responds. Now, with the new Carbon Event Manager, setting up your program to recognize and handle various events is easier than ever. For a programmer, this is very powerful stuff.

Chapter 4, "Windows," contains all the information you need to implement fully functional windows. Here you see how your program supports multiple windows of the same type, multiple windows of different types, and how your program can let the system handle basic window management tasks (such as closing a window) or how you can alternatively take control and add special behavior to the handling of these tasks.

Chapter 5, "Controls," shows how your program's windows include controls. The subject of controls, including push buttons, radio buttons, checkboxes, and text input fields, is an important one because it is one of the two primary means by which a user interacts with your program. The other user-input system is the subject of the next chapter.

Chapter 6, "Menus," shows you how your program fully supports menus and menu items. Here you see how to add and remove menus and menu items, implement hierarchical menus (submenus) and pop-up menus, and change the characteristic of menus and menu items (by enabling, disabling, or altering the font of menus or items).

Chapter 7, "QuickDraw Graphics," demonstrates how your program draws text and graphics to windows. QuickDraw is simply a set (albeit a *large* set) of drawing routines that make it easy to draw stylized text (words that appear in a font, typeface, and size of your choosing) and to draw a variety of 2-D shapes including lines, ovals, and rectangles. Here you'll also see how to add patterns and colors to any shape you draw.

Chapter 8, "Text and Localization," explains how your program can be properly set up so that translation of its text to another language becomes an easy task. Don't think your program will ever ship to foreign markets? Don't be so sure! If it happens, you want to have the language translation require minimal effort. Even if your application is suited only for customers of one language, you'll want to read this chapter. It explains how you can store all your program's text in one easy-to-edit file and how your program can make use of that text on demand.

Chapter 9, "QuickTime Movies and File Handling," covers the details of how your program can open a window and play any QuickTime movie within that window. Where does that movie come from? It comes from a file on the user's disk. Thus, this chapter also covers the details of Navigation Services, which is the set of routines that make it easy for your application to display the standard Open window that let's a user navigate through folders and select a file.

Chapter 10, "Bundles and Icons," exposes the details of how your program is packaged and how your program can display its own icon on the desktop. When you build an application, you're actually bundling several files together in a directory. Although hidden from the user, they're all there on the user's desktop. Here you see how your application's files are organized. You also get tips and information on creating an icon and the low-down on associating that icon with your application.

Chapter 11, "Porting Mac OS 8/9 Code to Mac OS X," deals with the process of moving an existing code base from Mac OS 8 or 9 to Mac OS X. Here you see how to determine which routines need to be replaced or modified, and you read about techniques and caveats for porting an application so that it runs native under Mac OS X.

Appendix A, "Carbon API Summary," lists and describes the calling convention for many commonly used Carbon API routines. Developing a Mac OS X program means knowing, and making use of, many of the thousands of Apple-written routines that comprise the Carbon API. This book discusses well over a hundred of these routines. This appendix serves as a handy reference to many of those functions.

Appendix B, "UNIX and the Terminal," explains the basics of UNIX. Yes, the underpinnings of the Macintosh operating system are now really, truly Unix. This book does not rely on your knowing how to be a UNIX end user or a UNIX programmer, but if you're neither, your curiosity may get to you! Here you see how to navigate through directories and write and compile a very simple program, all from the command line through the Terminal application.

Conventions Used in This Book

This book uses the following conventions:

- **Italics:** Used to emphasize new terms and important ideas when they're first introduced.

- **Constant width font:** Used to represents code, such as names of variables, functions, arguments, and so on.

- **Abbreviations and acronyms:** Used freely throughout the book, but each is written out when it is first introduced in a chapter.

1

System Components and Programming Technologies

THE ORIGINAL MACINTOSH OPERATING SYSTEM (OS) was introduced in January 1984. Since then, the OS has been modified, enhanced, and nipped and tucked to bring it from version 1 to version 9. More than a decade and a half of work has brought about numerous look-and-feel improvements, but core system changes have been minimal. Mac OS X put an end to that. Not only has the graphical user interface (GUI) taken on a dramatic new look, the OS core itself has been completely revamped. For the first time, UNIX powers the Macintosh OS.

> **Note**
> Although the name is "Macintosh," you'll see plenty of references to "Mac" in this book and elsewhere. It's an accepted shorthand.

Whether you're an experienced Mac software developer or a first-time Mac programmer, you need to become familiar with the new components and technologies of Mac OS X. In this chapter, you'll read about the OS software, and you'll see how this code is conceptually divided into layers. When it comes time to start looking at the higher-level code for building applications (you need only wait until Chapter 2, "Overview of Mac OS X Programming," for that), this overview of the system software will help you understand what application code is intended to do. In this chapter, you also read about the pros and cons of Carbon and Cocoa, which are the two primary means of creating a Mac OS X application, and why the focus of this book is on Carbon.

System Software Layers

The components, or technologies, that make up the Macintosh OS are illustrated in Figure 1.1.

Moving from an upper layer to a lower layer in the OS model pictured in Figure 1.1 takes you from more directly accessible code to less directly accessible code. For instance, the code in the highest layer, the User Interface, produces Aqua—the interface with which a Mac user interacts directly. Conversely, the code in the lowest layer, the Kernel Environment, produces Darwin—the core OS that is most often accessed only by code in the layer just above it (the Core Services layer).

In Figure 1.1, the lines that leave the bottom of the Classic box and the line that leaves the bottom of the BSD box ("BSD" stands for Berkeley Software Distribution) hint that code in one layer can interact with code in a non-adjacent layer (more on this later in this chapter). However, it's a more likely scenario that code within one layer interacts with code in an adjacent layer. Figure 1.2 provides an example of this.

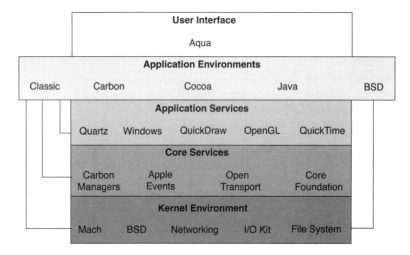

Figure 1.1   An overview of the five layers of Mac OS X.

On the left side of Figure 1.2, a user clicks a Draw button in a window. The code that's responsible for the display of the button that is a part of the Aqua interface is in the User Interface layer. A click on the button results in the application invoking a function in the Carbon API (which is code in the Application Environments layer). That function in turn accesses QuickDraw code (which exists in the Application Services layer) to perform the drawing of a shape (refer to the right side of Figure 1.2).

The representation shown in Figure 1.1 is a simplification of the enormous complexity of the code that makes up the Macintosh OS—but this figure does provide a means of understanding the roles different components play and how these various components interact with one another. The next several pages describe the five layers. As you read these pages, you'll want to frequently refer back to Figure 1.1.

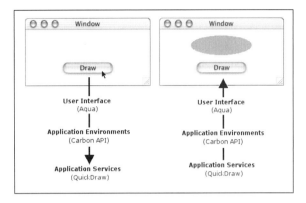

Figure 1.2   An example of the interaction of code in different layers.

User Interface

In Mac OS X, the GUI has been given the name Aqua. To the average end-user, Aqua is Mac OS X. Figure 1.1 reveals just how much more there is to Mac OS X, but that information can be kept among us programmers! If an application you develop has the Aqua look, a user of your application is satisfied, he or she won't be the least bit interested in technologies such as Carbon and QuickDraw.

Fortunately, and of course, by no accident, Apple has made the Aqua interface easy to integrate into any Mac OS X application that a programmer develops. A program's interface elements, such as windows and menus, can be visually designed using one software tool, while the program's source code can be written in another software tool. When it comes time to build the application, the source code file gets compiled and the resulting compiled code gets linked with the interface elements.

Figure 1.3 shows a window being constructed using Apple's Interface Builder program (a free application included with every copy of Mac OS X and an application discussed throughout this book). In Interface Builder, a programmer simply uses drag-and-drop to copy interface elements such as buttons, sliders, and text boxes from a palette to a window. After saving the Interface Builder file, its contents can easily be used in a program. Note in Figure 1.3 that the elements that are displayed in Interface Builder all have the look of Aqua. When it comes time to write the code that displays the window, there's no need to write any special Aqua code.

When a Mac OS X program runs, it automatically displays the Aqua interface. This is true even if you use an older interface-designing tool that hasn't been updated for Mac OS X. Apple's resource editor ResEdit is one such tool. Before Interface Builder arrived, ResEdit was the interface design software most commonly used by Macintosh programmers. A programmer still can use ResEdit to design a program's interface, even though ResEdit runs in the Classic (Mac OS 9) environment.

At the top of Figure 1.4, an alert is being laid out in ResEdit where it will be saved to a file (note the non-Aqua look of the title bar of the window holding the alert, as well as the non-Aqua look of the OK button in that window). When a Mac OS X program is built using the contents of this file, the running of the program results in the alert taking on the Aqua look—as shown in the bottom of Figure 1.4.

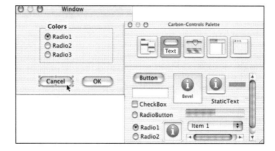

Figure 1.3   Using Interface Builder to define an Aqua interface for a program.

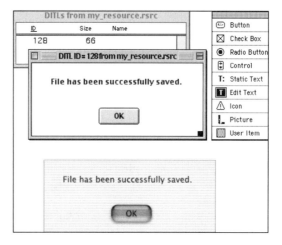

Figure 1.4   Using ResEdit to define an Aqua interface for a program.

Chapter 2 includes a walk-through of the process of creating a simple Mac OS X application. There you'll see a detailed example of how interface elements are created and made use of by source code.

Application Environments

Just under the User Interface layer are the Application Environments (see Figure 1.1). In other Mac OS X documentation, you might have seen a more abbreviated version of Figure 1.1 that displayed only three application environments: Classic, Carbon, and Cocoa. This is done because Apple's emphasis has been on those three. The following is a brief introduction to these environments. Later in this chapter, we cover them—and two additional environments—in greater detail.

Classic

The Classic environment exists for one specific reason: backward compatibility. A Mac user with a computer running Mac OS X most likely owns at least one application that hasn't been upgraded to become a native Mac OS X application. Such a program isn't capable of displaying the Aqua look and it won't support Mac OS X enhancements such as protected memory. To enable Mac users to preserve their investment in Mac OS 8 and OS 9 applications, Apple has included the Classic environment as a part of Mac OS X. When the user runs an older Mac program, that program runs in the Classic environment, where it displays the look and feel of a program running in Mac OS 9.

You might have heard the Classic environment referred to as a "Mac OS 9 emulator." That's not quite right. For a Mac user running Mac OS X to launch an older program, that user's Mac must have a copy of Mac OS 9.1 installed. Mac OS 9.1 can be installed either on the same drive as Mac OS X, though on a different partition, or on a different drive altogether. In any case, for Classic to work, the user's Macintosh must have two complete, separate OSs installed: Mac OS 9.1 and Mac OS X.

When a program runs (on any computer), it is a *process*. The OS sets aside a block of memory devoted to that one process. If you double-click the TextEdit program icon on your Mac, for example, Mac OS X considers it a process and loads the TextEdit code into a block of memory. If you then run Internet Explorer, Mac OS X considers that another process, and it loads the Internet Explorer code into a separate block of memory. To make use of the Classic environment, Mac OS X runs Mac OS 9.1 as if the OS itself were a process. It's as if one OS (Mac OS 9.1) is functioning within another (Mac OS X).

The Classic environment is a wonderful bit of technology and trickery that makes Mac OS X all the more useful. Because of Classic, just about any Mac program written within the last few years—and some older applications as well—can be run on a Macintosh sporting Mac OS X. As nifty as Classic is, though, Apple strongly discourages programmers from writing applications specifically designed to run in Classic. In other words, don't get an older copy of an integrated development environment (IDE), sit down at a Mac running Mac OS 8 or OS 9, and set about developing a program that runs on that machine. Rather than expending effort developing a program that is immediately dated (won't run native on Mac OS X), you should devote the same effort to developing a Macintosh program that runs native on Mac OS X. In certain circumstances, you can create such a program that also can execute on a computer running Mac OS 8 or OS 9. To do that, you'll make use of the Carbon environment.

Carbon

For years programmers wrote Mac programs using the Macintosh Toolbox. The Macintosh Toolbox is an application programming interface (API), which is a set of thousands of functions that relieves a programmer of much of the busy work of writing the code most programs need. The Macintosh Toolbox still exists, and it's still possible for a programmer to use it to write what is now called a Classic program. However, there's no reason for a programmer to do this. With Mac OS X, Apple has created the Carbon API, which is an enhanced subset of the Macintosh Toolbox API. The term *enhanced subset* is one that I've just coined, and it requires a little explanation!

Why Carbon API is an Enhanced Subset

As Apple was developing Mac OS X, it was modifying the Macintosh Toolbox. The result was the Carbon API. Apple examined each of the thousands of Macintosh Toolbox functions and eliminated the ones that could not be adapted to work in Mac OS X. The Carbon API includes about 70 percent of the functions of the Macintosh Toolbox; this is the reasoning for calling it a subset of the Toolbox. Of the thousands of functions that were salvaged, many had to have some of their code rewritten to work properly in Mac OS X; this is why Carbon is an enhancement.

Fortunately for Mac programmers, most of the code changes Apple made to Macintosh Toolbox functions are kept hidden. For instance, the Macintosh Toolbox API FrameOval function exists by the same name in the Carbon API, and it is invoked by a programmer in the same way now as in the past. In both cases, the result of making a call to FrameOval is—you guessed it—the drawing of a framed oval. Exactly what does the code that comprises the FrameOval function look like? A programmer didn't know that information when using the Macintosh Toolbox API, and he or she doesn't know that information now when using the Carbon API. To make use of a Carbon API function, a programmer need only know how to invoke the function. The "internals" of the function are unimportant.

There are some features of Mac OS X that aren't present in Mac OS 9. These features are not addressed by any function in the original Macintosh Toolbox. To address this issue, Apple has added a number of new routines to the Carbon API. These routines didn't exist in the original Macintosh Toolbox API (which is another reason for saying that Carbon is an enhanced version of the Toolbox).

When you develop a Carbon application, you're creating a program that runs native in Mac OS X. Building this application under certain conditions in certain development environments (namely including the CarbonLib library in a Metrowerks CodeWarrior project) enables this same program to run on a computer that's running Mac OS 8 or 9. Such a program won't, however, have the Aqua look when running under Mac OS 8 or 9. For a programmer with an existing body of Mac code, Carbon is the way to go. The effort to port code from Mac OS 8/9 to Mac OS X through the Carbon API is minimal. For a programmer new to Mac programming, Carbon again might be the best bet. Cocoa is a good programming environment, but it is an object-oriented framework that must be programmed in Objective-C or Java. If you aren't experienced in the techniques of object-oriented programming, the Cocoa learning curve might be too steep for you.

Cocoa

The Cocoa environment is an environment that exists specifically to run native Mac OS X applications. When Apple bought NeXT, Apple used much of the NeXT OS in Mac OS X. Apple also used much of the NeXTSTEP object-oriented framework as the basis for Cocoa. A programmer uses the Cocoa object-oriented programming framework to create programs that run native on Mac OS X. A program designed as a Cocoa application runs native in Mac OS X, but does not run at all on a Macintosh running Mac OS 8 or OS 9.

Carbon or Cocoa?

Cocoa and Carbon are the two primary environments for creating native Mac OS X applications, and a programmer who sets out to develop a program capable of running native on a Mac OS X computer needs to choose between environments. The choice is based on a combination of factors, including the programming background of the programmer and the version of the Mac OS that is expected to represent the majority of the target customers.

One key issue in choosing a programming environment is the learning curve associated with the chosen environment. A programmer with a procedural programming background (namely the C language) should consider Carbon. A programmer with a strong object-oriented programming background might consider Cocoa. Here's why:

- A Carbon application can be written in an object-oriented language such as C++, but it is typically written in C. Most Macintosh programming books (including this one) use the C language in explanations and example source code listings. Almost all of Apple's thousands of pages of online Carbon documentation use C, as do the Apple-supplied Carbon header files.

- A Cocoa application, on the other hand, is created using an object-oriented framework, and is written in an object-oriented language: either Objective-C or Java. If a programmer has little or no object-oriented experience, it might make the sense to choose Carbon over Cocoa. If a programmer has previous Macintosh programming experience, it again makes sense to consider Carbon. The Carbon API looks familiar to a programmer who's worked with the Macintosh Toolbox API, which serves as the foundation of the Carbon API. If a programmer is strong in object-oriented programming, making use of the power of an object-oriented framework makes Cocoa a likely choice.

Another factor in choosing a programming environment is the projected OS makeup of the target audience. If a programmer expects a hefty percentage of intended users to be running Macs that *aren't* running Mac OS X, Carbon becomes the environment to use. It's the one to use because it's possible to build a Carbon application that can run native on a Mac OS X computer and on a computer equipped with Mac OS 8 or Mac OS 9. The same is not true of a Cocoa-built application. It can run only on a Mac OS X computer. A Cocoa-built application does not launch if it's installed on a computer without a running Mac OS X. At this writing, Mac OS X is just being introduced. Although Mac OS X now is being included on all new Macintosh computers, the phase-in period might still take some time (considering that new Macs will also ship with a version of Mac OS 9, and because many owners of older Macs won't immediately [or ever] upgrade to Mac OS X).

Application Services

Directly beneath the Application Environments layer is the Application Services layer, as shown in Figure 1.1. The main system services that exist in this layer—Quartz, Windows, QuickDraw, OpenGL, and QuickTime—are primarily graphics-related. These system services are available to, and crucial to, all application environments except BSD. As you'll see later in this chapter and in Chapter 2, BSD is an environment used to write UNIX programs that run in a Terminal window. As such, these applications don't require access to the graphics-related services.

Quartz and Windows

The primary contributions of the Application Services layer are the drawing of graphics and the implementation of windows. Both services are made possible largely by Quartz—system software that's new to the Macintosh OS. Quartz is made up of a graphics rendering library (Core Graphics Rendering) that supports two-dimensional shapes, and a windows component (Core Graphics Services, which can be referred to as Quartz Windows Server) that's responsible for the graphical display of windows. Figure 1.1 shows how the Application Services layer fits into the overall hierarchy of system software. Figure 1.5 shows a more detailed look at just the Application Services layer.

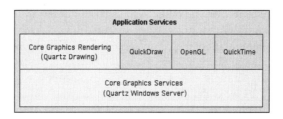

Figure 1.5   A detailed look at the Application Services software layer.

Figure 1.1 generalizes things a bit by showing Quartz and Windows side-by-side. Here in Figure 1.5, you see that the software that services Windows is part of Quartz and that it extends under the other graphics components of Mac OS X. The implication is that, to varying degrees, these other "non-Quartz" graphics components work with the Core Graphics Services (or Quartz WindowsServer) portion of Quartz.

Quartz, like QuickDraw, is graphics rendering software for two-dimensional shapes. Unlike the older QuickDraw software, though, Quartz is based on PDF (Portable Document Format). Being built on PDF gives Quartz the capability to offer programs features such as automatic PDF generation (save-as-PDF), high-quality screen display, and on-screen graphics previews.

The interrelationships and dependencies of the graphics systems (Quartz Core Graphics Rendering, QuickDraw, OpenGL, and QuickTime) and the Quartz Core Graphics Services is a tricky business. Fortunately, you don't need to know the details. Once again, it's the application environment you use (such as Carbon) that shields you from the technical aspects of how your program does what it should do (such as enable a user to drag a window and have that window properly update when the user finishes the drag operation). Quartz is an important part of the system software that makes windows work in your application!

QuickDraw

Both the Quartz and QuickDraw sets of system software include the capability to render two-dimensional shapes. Quartz is used primarily by other system software, and much of the Quartz software isn't directly accessible to programmers by way of function calls. QuickDraw too is used by other system software. An application uses QuickDraw indirectly when interface elements such as windows, controls, and menus need to be drawn. Unlike Quartz, though, the full functionality of QuickDraw is readily available to programmers. This is achieved through a huge set of routines that were a part of the original Macintosh Toolbox API and that now are a part of the Carbon API.

As you'll see throughout this book, including QuickDraw graphics in your own program is relatively easy. All that's needed is the knowledge of which QuickDraw functions to use and the calling conventions for those functions. A function's *calling convention* is the format of the function call, such as its return type and parameter types. For instance, if your program needs to draw the frame of a rectangle in a window, you need to know that the SetRect function defines the boundaries of a rectangle and the FrameRect function draws the frame of a rectangle specified by the just-defined rectangle. Here's the information you need to know about these two QuickDraw routines:

```
SetRect( Rect * r, short left, short top, short right, short bottom )
FrameRect( const Rect * r )
```

To define the boundaries of a rectangle, pass SetRect a pointer to a variable of type Rect along with the pixel coordinates (relative to the top-left corner of the window in which the rectangle will exist). A call to SetRect defines a rectangle, but doesn't draw it. To actually draw the frame of this rectangle, call FrameRect and pass a pointer to the rectangle to draw. The following is a code snippet that does just that. Figure 1.6 shows the results of executing this code.

```
Rect    theRect;

SetRect( &theRect, 50, 20, 250, 120 );
FrameRect( &theRect
```

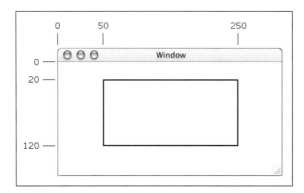

Figure 1.6   Using QuickDraw routines to frame a rectangle.

Figure 1.6 shows the result of running the code snippet. For clarification, I've added a few references to pixel coordinates. This figure should make clear that the QuickDraw frames a rectangle with a width of 200 pixels (extending from pixel 50 to pixel 250) and a height of 100 pixels (extending from pixel 20 down to pixel 120). This brief example isn't intended to give you a comprehensive picture of how your program creates a window and draws it—you are, after all, only in Chapter 1! It does show, however, that your program needs very little code to draw graphics and that the code is fairly easy to comprehend (provided you're shown the format of how to use it).

QuickDraw is very important to Mac programmers. I'll have a lot to say about QuickDraw in this book. In fact, an entire chapter (Chapter 7, "QuickDraw Graphics") is devoted to using QuickDraw to include graphics in your own applications. To summarize, QuickDraw is a set of system routines that provide programmers with the ability to define and draw two-dimensional shapes and text.

OpenGL

Mac OS X relies primarily on Quartz and QuickDraw for the rendering of two-dimensional graphics. For three-dimensional graphics, Mac OS X makes use of OpenGL. OpenGL is new to the Mac OS, but this software library itself isn't new. OpenGL was introduced in 1992, and since then, it has become the industry standard for three-dimensional graphics.

OpenGL is an API designed to make it possible for programmers to include sophisticated graphics (such as texture mapping and special effects) in their programs. All programs don't need the functions that make up the OPENGL API. They're designed for graphics-intense programs such as animation-rich games and medical imaging software.

OpenGL programming is beyond the scope of this book. However, the Mac programming knowledge you gain from this book enables you to set up a program that is ready to support OpenGL. That is, after reading this book, you can create a program that includes menus, QuickTime movie playing capabilities, multiple windows, and controls in those windows. With these foundations, you then can focus on adding OpenGL three-dimensional functionality to your application.

QuickTime

QuickTime is the name of the system software that provides applications with the capability to include several multimedia capabilities. Most notably, QuickTime enables an application to play back QuickTime movies. QuickTime, however, also gives a program the capability to play music, display animations, and compress and expand files.

For programmers, Apple has made the inclusion of QuickTime functionality easy. The original Macintosh Toolbox API, and now the Carbon API, includes a huge number of QuickTime-related routines. These routines are conceptually divided into categories within the Carbon API—the two most notable categories being the Movie Toolbox and the Component Manager.

Although the number of QuickTime functions is large, accomplishing a single QuickTime-related task requires the knowledge of just a few routines. For instance, if you want your own application to have the capability to play an existing QuickTime movie in a window that displays standard QuickTime controls (such as the play and stop buttons), you need add only a couple dozen lines of code to your program. That code includes all the function calls your program makes to do the following:

- Open the file that holds the QuickTime movie
- Load the movie data from the file on disk into memory
- Create a window in which the movie is to play
- Play the movie from start to finish

Take a look at this snippet to get a short preview of what QuickTime code looks like:

```
Movie   theMovie;

do {
  MoviesTask( theMovie, 0 );
} while ( IsMovieDone( theMovie ) == false );
```

The Carbon API function MoviesTask plays one frame of the specified movie, so this routine is called repeatedly until the movie is finished playing. Another Carbon API function, the very appropriately named IsMovieDone, is called after each call to MoviesTask to verify whether the specified movie has finished playing. When IsMovieDone returns true, the program knows that movie play has completed and that there is no need to again call MoviesTask.

This book exists primarily to get a programmer up to speed in creating an application that runs native on Mac OS X. As such, Mac OS X programming basics are thoroughly covered. The Macintosh OS is anything but basic, so why should this book stick to just the basics? Well, you'll note that an entire chapter—Chapter 9, "Playing QuickTime Movies"—is devoted to the techniques necessary to include movie-playing capabilities in your own applications. With some good code snippets and plenty of detailed explanations on the use of key Carbon API QuickTime-related functions, even someone new to Mac programming will find that it's not too challenging to spice up an application with QuickTime movie-playing features.

Other Application Services

Figure 1.1 shows the primary components of the Application Services layer, but there are other, lesser, components as well. A cursory mention of some of these will help define terms that appear elsewhere in this book and in other Mac OS X documentation.

The first technology is the *Process Manager*. It manages the processes executing in Mac OS X. Each running application has its own execution environment consisting of its own protected area of memory. This environment—referred to as a process or an *execution context*—is maintained by the Process Manager system software. The Process Manager is responsible for launching an application and then scheduling the CPU time used by the executing application.

Another Application Services technology is the Event Manager. In a Mac program, an action is referred to as an *event*. For instance, when the user clicks the mouse button, the program interprets that action as an event. However, an event is more than simply an action. It is the composite of an action *and* additional information that's descriptive of the action. For example, *where* the cursor was located at the moment the user clicked the mouse button is information that's encoded in a *mouse-down event*. In Chapter 3, "Events and the Carbon Event Manager," you'll read about events and how your program makes use of the functions that comprise the Event Manager portion of the Carbon API. In that chapter, *Event Manager* refers to a set of API functions that a programmer can use. The other use of the term "Event Manager" describes the actual event-handling system software in the Application Services layer.

Another Application Services technology is the Clipboard. If you've used a Macintosh running Mac OS 9 or earlier, you know about the Clipboard. The Clipboard is the behind-the-scenes software utility that makes it possible to copy one element (such as selected text or graphics) from a document and paste that element elsewhere in the document—or even into a document belonging to another application. In Mac OS X, the Clipboard is referred to as the Pasteboard, and the system software that handles this data transferring exists in the Application Services layer.

Core Services

Under the Application Services layer is the Core Services layer, as shown back in Figure 1.1. Moving deeper into the system software means moving into system code that has little or no effect on the user interface. Unlike components of the Application Services layer (such as QuickDraw and QuickTime), components of the Core Services layer don't produce results that a user can see or hear. Instead, this system software handles more mundane (but important) tasks such as memory management and file system management. We discuss each in turn next.

Carbon Managers

When your application invokes a Carbon API function, the code that actually carries out the function's task might be located in the Core Services layer. In this layer, you find that code for several Carbon Managers, including Alias Manager, Component Manager, File Manager, Memory Manager, Resource Manager, and Thread Manager. As the names of some of these managers hint, their low-level services are available to, and used by, most applications.

Apple Events

An *Apple event* is a high-level event that an application can make use of to communicate with the Finder, another application, or itself. One type of Apple Event that most applications support is the Quit Application event. A Mac user who chooses the Restart or Shut Down menu item from the Finder will notice that the computer won't turn off until each running application quits. This graceful shutdown process is achieved through the use of the Quit Application event. When an Apple Event occurs, it's Core Services code that gets executed. The Core Services layer holds the Apple Event system software.

Open Transport

When a Mac user connects to the Internet, it is the Open Transport code in the Core Services layer that's being executed. Open Transport is the networking and communications system software that was used in Mac OS 9 and that is now a part of Mac OS X. Open Transport enables simultaneous networking systems (such as a program's use of AppleTalk to communicate with a printer and TCP/IP to make an Internet connection). Open Transport also enables a user to create different networking profiles (such as a set of 56K modem settings and a set of cable modem settings) and then switch among them.

Core Foundation

Core Foundation is the Core Services layer code that supports basic services used by most applications. For instance, the Utility Services code offers date and time computations that a program can use, while String Services code provides string manipulation and conversion services that many programs find useful.

A programmer, by way of the Carbon API, can indirectly access much of the code that makes up the Core Foundation. In particular, the API functions that are grouped and that fall under the same heading (Core Foundation) offer a programmer an easy and useful means of including strings, dates, and numbers in his or her applications.

Kernel Environment

The lowest level of the Mac OS X system software—the true core of the OS—is the Kernel Environment. As shown back in Figure 1.1, the Kernel Environment's five major components are Mach, BSD, Networking, I/O Kit, and the File Systems. Collectively this software is the Kernel Environment. You'll also hear this same set of system software referred to as Darwin (with the reference being to the idea that this core software is the origin of the "life" of Mac OS X).

Darwin itself is a complete OS. What Apple has done is enhance its UNIX code and add layers of software to it to lead to the Aqua interface that Mac OS X users experience. Darwin is an interesting, exciting, reliable, and stable foundation for the complete Mac OS X package. The components of Darwin support advanced memory protection and management, multiprocessing and multithreading, and multiple file system support.

Mach

Any OS requires core software that handles the system's most basic and most critical functions. For Mac OS X, this core software is named Mach. Mach technology is new to the Macintosh OS, but the code itself isn't entirely new—Mach itself has been around for well over a decade. The version of Mach that is at the core of Mac OS X is based on code from a combination of the original Mach, Apple's years-old MkLinux project, Mac OS X Server software, and the NeXT OS (NeXT having been bought by Apple a few years ago).

Like the rest of the components of Darwin, the tasks that Mach carries out are all behind the scenes. The details of how Mac OS X handles services such as memory management and protection, schedule handling, and interprocess communication (the act of one running application communicating with another) are unimportant. The Mach code takes care of these tasks in a manner transparent to both the programmer and the end user.

Every previous version of the Macintosh OS has of course had core software, so what's so exciting about the Mach software that serves as the heart of Mac OS X? Mach doesn't simply handle the mundane system-level OS tasks. It carries them out with vast improvements over the methods used by the core software of previous versions of the Mac OS. Consider the following core-level features that Mach implements:

- For the first time, the Macintosh OS has true *protected memory*—a memory scheme that denies a single application the power to crash the entire system. An OS can be stable only when the OS places each process in its own area of memory and then enforces the concept that each process must not write data to the memory area of another process. The Mach software does this, which means that even if one application crashes, other processes are unaffected.

- Today's OSs enable several applications to run concurrently. How efficient an OS is at *multitasking*, or sharing CPU time, can vary quite a bit, though. Mac OS 8 and 9 did only a fair job of multitasking. The Mach code of Mac OS X uses *preemptive multitasking* to do a much better job of allocating CPU resources. Mach includes sophisticated algorithms that rank the importance of various tasks and then prioritize CPU time to ensure that each process runs smoothly and efficiently.

- Mac OS X, like Mac OS 8 and 9, makes use of virtual memory. In a system using virtual memory, physical memory (such as RAM) and storage space (such as a hard drive's disk space) are used in conjunction to provide the effect of almost unlimited memory. For instance, a system that includes 128MB of RAM and a large capacity hard drive can act as if it had several gigabytes of RAM. The Mach code in Mac OS X takes the implementation of virtual memory to a higher level, making it more efficient than virtual memory in previous versions of the Macintosh OS.

BSD

Earlier in this chapter (in Figure 1.1 and elsewhere), you saw that BSD is one of the five application environments. A programmer uses an application environment (such as Carbon or BSD) to access system code. The BSD application environment enables access to BSD system code. The Mach kernel is the foundation of Mac OS X. It provides the lowest-level services, such as memory allocation and process management. Mach, however, doesn't provide the OS with all the basic services. For other low-level services, such as device input and output (I/O), networking, and file system support, the OS kernel relies on BSD.

An OS *can* use BSD UNIX as its entire kernel. That is, BSD is capable of handling all low-level OS services. Apple has opted to *not* have BSD handle all the low-level tasks of Mac OS X. Instead, Apple modified FreeBSD (itself a version of BSD) and combined it with Mach. Together Mach and Apple's version of BSD handle the chores that BSD handles alone in some OSs. Although this separation of duties might seem a little more complex, Apple feels that segregating some of the core level duties makes for a more robust operating system. In Figure 1.1, Mach and BSD are shown in the Kernel Environment layer. If the Kernel Environment layer were to be further subdivided, it would be redrawn with a BSD layer on top of a Mach layer.

Networking

The Kernel Environment includes advanced networking support, and Mac OS X takes full advantage of that support. Included in the Networking component of the Kernel Environment layer are Network Kernel Extensions (NKEs). An NKE offers a means of dynamically extending (modifying) the networking abilities of the Networking component.

I/O Kit

The Kernel Environment is where drivers are supported. A driver is the software that enables a hardware device (such as hard drive or CD drive) and the OS to communicate with one another. The I/O Kit of the Kernel Environment includes an object-oriented development framework that assists programmers in the creation of new drivers. Although driver development can be viewed as a mundane programming task (and one well outside the scope of this book), it is a topic of great importance to the success of an OS. The more third-party devices an OS supports, the more popular the OS can become. In addition, it's unlikely that a computer user will want to purchase an OS that won't work with the user's existing hardware or with much of the new, state-of-the-art hardware that the user plans on buying.

File Systems

If you're a Mac user, you might be familiar with the terms HFS (Hierarchical Filing System Standard) and HFS+ (Hierarchical Filing System Extended). These two filing systems are the ones used by the last several versions of the Macintosh OS. Of course, Mac OS X supports these file systems, but this OS also supports numerous other file systems, including UFS (UNIX file system, the standard file system of BSD), NFS (networked file system, the industry-standard for file systems that are a part of a network), and ISO 9660 (the quality management standard of the International Organization for Standardization, used primarily for CD-ROMs).

Application Environments and Programming Languages

For the remainder of this chapter, the focus is on going further into one layer—the Application Environments layer. From a programmer's perspective, this makes sense. It's the application environment that defines which API a programmer uses and, possibly, which development tools the programmer uses as well.

If you've read all the preceding pages, don't feel as if you've wasted your time. A little extra knowledge of the other system software layers is of benefit. In fact, knowing the system code that your program is accessing enhances your understanding of how your program is doing what you intend it to do!

Classic

This is a compatibility environment that enables programs initially designed to run in Mac OS 8 or 9 to run on a machine running Mac OS X. A non-native Mac OS X program runs in Classic, and does not take on the Aqua look of Mac OS X and does not inherit the many enhancements found in Mac OS X, such as protected memory.

BSD

This environment is a shell that enables a Mac OS X user to use a typical UNIX command line interface to execute BSD commands and programs. The BSD environment will be of benefit to UNIX programmers who are used to moving about in a command line interface, but this environment is of much less interest to a programmer intent on writing Mac OS X applications that sport the Aqua look and that behave as typical Macintosh applications.

Carbon

The Carbon environment is of great interest to Mac programmers. A program running in the Carbon environment has the Aqua look and takes full advantage of the features of Mac OS X. This same program, when built under certain conditions, will execute on a Macintosh running Mac OS 8 or 9 (though it then won't take on the Aqua look). A Carbon application is created using the Carbon API, which is an enhanced version of the Macintosh Toolbox API. A programmer who has familiarity with pre-Mac OS X programming should strongly consider using the Carbon API because the learning curve will not be steep.

Cocoa

This is another environment of interest to Mac programmers. Like a program running in the Carbon environment, a program running in the Cocoa environment has the Aqua look and takes on the improvements associated with Mac OS X. A Mac OS X end user will not be able to distinguish between a Carbon and Cocoa application (that is, the user won't know which environment was used to develop the application). A Cocoa-developed application will not, however, run at all on a computer running Mac OS 8 or 9. Cocoa is an object-oriented application framework that is an excellent environment for a programmer with a strong object-oriented background.

Java

This environment is of interest to Mac programmers who are knowledgeable in the Java programming language and who are looking to create portable applications or applets.

   With the environment summary complete, let's take a longer look at each of the five environments.

BSD

At the core of Mac OS X is BSD UNIX. This means that a programmer working on a computer running Mac OS X can develop and execute a UNIX application. From the Terminal application, a programmer can use standard BSD tools, utilities, and scripts, just as if the programmer were working in a shell on a "typical" UNIX machine. From the command line, a programmer can edit source code files, run the gcc or g++ UNIX compilers, and execute UNIX programs.

   Because a Mac programmer that's interested in creating a true Mac OS X application (one that sports the Aqua interface) will most likely use an Apple API such as Carbon or Cocoa rather than BSD, this book touches lightly on UNIX and the BSD environment. However, because UNIX is new to the Macintosh, I've tried to satisfy the curiosity many readers will have by walking through the command line development of a very simple UNIX application in Chapter 2. If you've never worked in a UNIX environment, you might want to first read through Appendix B, "UNIX and the Terminal," to see how to use the Terminal command line shell application that's included on every Macintosh running Mac OS X. Using the Terminal, you can execute UNIX commands to move about the directory hierarchy and run programs (such as a text editor or a C or C++ compiler).

Classic

This is where it all started. The Classic environment is based on the Macintosh Toolbox, which is an API that has existed (and has been continually upgraded) since the inception of the Macintosh computer. If an application is developed using the Macintosh Toolbox API, and that application is launched on a Macintosh running Mac OS X, the application runs in the Classic environment. Classic is a compatibility environment only. It is Mac OS 9 running *within* Mac OS X. Classic is a wonderful supplement to Mac OS X in that it enables users to preserve their investments in older software. However, because an application developed using the Macintosh Toolbox API can't run native in Mac OS X, no programmer developing a new application should use the Macintosh Toolbox API. If the desired result of a new programming project is a native Mac OS X application that is capable also of executing on a Macintosh running Mac OS 9 or 9, Carbon is absolutely the route to take.

Carbon

The vast majority of programmers developing native Mac OS X applications will do so using either Carbon or Cocoa. The focus of this book is the Carbon environment and the Carbon application programming interface (API).

Carbon API

Apple has expended considerable resources to modify the functions of the Macintosh Toolbox API so that they work on Mac OS X. The result of this effort is a revamped Toolbox API that is now referred to as the Carbon API. Thus, the API used to develop a program that runs in the Carbon environment is a derivative of the API used to develop a program that runs in the Classic environment. In upgrading the Macintosh Toolbox, Apple preserved roughly 70 percent of the original Toolbox functions. The *body* of such a salvaged function (the code that makes up the function itself) might have required change, but the interface to the function (the calling convention to invoke the function) remained static. This useful trick of hiding code changes from programmers means that programmers knowledgeable in using the Macintosh Toolbox will be able to keep most of their existing code and be able to make use of much of their existing knowledge of the Macintosh Toolbox.

Although Apple was able to port thousands of the Macintosh Toolbox routines to run under Mac OS X, many routines had to go. To regain the functionality of these lost routines, and to add programmer support for the new functionalities accompanying Mac OS X, Apple needed to add a number of new routines to the Carbon API. This book includes coverage of many of these routines, with emphasis on the ones that are a part of the much-changed Event Manager (the Event Manager being the name of the large set of event-related routines that we describe in Chapter 3).

In the original Macintosh Toolbox, routines were conceptually grouped into managers. A manager is simply a category of related routines. Managers exist mostly as an organizational tool for programmers. For instance, if a programmer needs to add some new window-related functionality to a program, the programmer knows that to determine how to add that functionality, he or she should search through the descriptions of the routines that are said to be a part of the Window Manager. The Carbon API retains this organizational scheme. Throughout this book (and in any other Macintosh programming documentation), you'll find references to various managers.

Experienced Mac Programmer

The porting of Macintosh Toolbox routines and the addition of new routines has, for the most part, not affected the naming of managers. For instance, the original Macintosh Toolbox API had a Window Manager, a Menu Manager, and a File Manager—and the Carbon API does too. In a few cases, changes to a manager were so large that Apple renamed the manager by prefacing its name with Carbon. Be aware that the Event Manager, the Printing Manager, and the Help Manager now are named the Carbon Event Manager, the Carbon Printing Manager, and the Carbon Help Manager.

Programming Languages and Carbon

The Carbon application programming interface includes different sets of header files so that a programmer can use C, Pascal, or assembly language to develop Carbon applications. Because C is a far more popular language than Pascal or assembly, and because almost all of Apple's thousands of pages of documentation provide C language examples, C is the language of choice for most Mac programmers who use the Carbon API. Because C is so popular with Mac programmers, examples throughout this book will be in the C language.

Object-oriented programmers aren't excluded from using the Carbon API. If you know C++, you'll find that you too can develop a Carbon application. In short, to do this, your program will make calls to C language Carbon API functions from within the body of a C++ class member function. The major difficulty a C++ programmer faces is finding good documentation on programming the Macintosh using object-oriented techniques.

Cocoa

Carbon and Cocoa are the major programming resources for Mac OS X developers. Cocoa is an object-oriented framework. Using Cocoa, a developer creates an application that runs native on Mac OS X, but will not run at all on Mac OS 8 or 9. Because most Mac programmers use a procedural programming language rather than an object-oriented language, and because Cocoa applications don't run on non-Mac OS X computers, the focus of this book is on Carbon rather than Cocoa.

Cocoa API

The Cocoa application environment is based on two object-oriented frameworks: the Foundation framework and the Application Kit framework. The classes that make up the Foundation framework provide an application with core-level services, which are not related to the user interface. The classes of the Application Kit framework supply an application with user interface elements such as windows and menus.

Programming Languages and Cocoa

The Cocoa frameworks (Foundation framework and Application Kit framework) are written in Objective-C. Although Cocoa is object-oriented, you can't use just any object-oriented language to develop Cocoa applications. Instead, you must use either Objective-C or Java (C++ can't be used). The original Cocoa API is Objective-C, but Apple has added a Java API as well (with the Java classes simply "translating" to their Objective-C counterparts).

Like C++, Objective-C is an extension of the C language. Because Objective-C is an extension of ANSI C, and because its additions to C are relatively few, C programmers might find learning Objective-C easier than learning C++. With that said, moving from a procedural language such as C to an object-oriented one (whether it is C++ or Objective-C) can be difficult for many programmers. This book teaches Macintosh programming techniques rather than a programming language. It makes the assumption that the reader knows a programming language; that language is assumed to be C. If you'd like to learn both a new programming language and a new Macintosh development method, you'll need to study both Objective-C and Cocoa.

Java

The previous section, Cocoa, mentioned the Java programming language. The Cocoa frameworks are written in Objective-C and offer a Java "wrapper" to that code so that Java programmers can make use of the frameworks. A Java programmer doesn't have to use the Cocoa framework, though. For Java programmers, Apple provides the Java application environment.

Like the other application environments, the Java environment is for both creating applications and running applications. The Java environment is based on the Java Development Kit (JDK) and the Java virtual machine (VM). This is the industry standard. Any other PC that supports Java includes this type of Java environment as well. This means that a Java application or applet developed in Mac OS X is portable to any other PC that supports the industry standard Java.

A Java application or applet can be created from the BSD command line (using the Mac OS X Terminal application) to run Java tools such as the Java compiler, debugger, and appletviewer. Alternately, a programmer who prefers to work in a graphical interface can use Apple's Project Builder IDE (discussed throughout this book) to develop Java applications and applets.

To make Java development possible, Apple includes an application framework that contains the classes (such as Swing and the Abstract Windowing Toolkit [AWT]) needed for building Java applications and applets.

For More Information

For extra information about any of the topics covered in this chapter (or, for that matter, in this book), you're best bet is to search the web. For more information on the system software that makes up Mac OS X, consider these sites:

- **Darwin:** `http://www.opensource.apple.com`
- **UNIX and Mac OS X:** `http://arstechnica.com/reviews/01q2/macos-x-final/macos-x-15.html`
- **Objective-C:** `http://www.stepwise.com`

2

Overview of Mac OS X Programming

CHAPTER 1, "SYSTEM COMPONENTS AND PROGRAMMING TECHNOLOGIES," described the Mac OS X system software and the application environments and programming languages that can be used to create applications that run on this system software. Now it's time to move from the theoretical to the application of that theory. In this chapter, you'll read about the integrated development environments (IDEs) available to Mac OS X programmers. In particular, you'll learn about two software development applications from Apple: Project Builder and Interface Builder. This pair of software tools enables you to graphically design the elements of your application's user interface (windows, menus, and so forth), write the code that makes use of those interface elements, organize all your files, and build a standalone native Mac OS X application.

In this chapter, you'll walk through the creation of four applications—each one a variation of the Hello World program that typically serves as a programmer's introduction to a new programming language or a new operating system (OS). Although at first glance each example might seem trivial, the discussion of the code that makes up each program provides you with an understanding of many concepts common to all Mac OS applications—including programs far more complex than the ones introduced here. Included in this chapter, you'll find coverage of the organization of source code files, resource files, and libraries in a project, the design and creation of menu and window resources, the purpose and power of events and the event loop, the implementation of error-handling, and simple techniques for adding alerts and pictures to any of your applications.

Before jumping into our four examples, we'll go through some background on development environments.

Development Environments

From Chapter 1, you know that there are a variety of application environments in which a Mac OS X application runs. Carbon, Cocoa, and Java are the three application environments that enable the running of native Mac OS X applications. For a programmer to create an application that runs in one of these environments, some software programming tools are needed. In particular, a resource editor, text editor, compiler, and linker are the tools that make interface layout, source code editing, and application building take place. It's possible to carry out these activities using individual tools, but more typically, a Macintosh programmer uses just two programming applications: a resource editor and an IDE.

A resource editor is used to create and edit resources that are the interface elements of a program, such as menus, windows, and controls that appear in windows. The IDE is a single application that integrates all other facets of developing a program. From the IDE, a programmer edits source code, compiles that code, and links the compiled code with the resources created in the resource editor to build a standalone application.

There are a few IDEs from which a programmer can choose. However, the vast majority of Mac OS X programmers will pick from the two best offerings: Metrowerks CodeWarrior and Apple Project Builder. Both of these tools use the concept of a project—a file that serves as a programmer's command center of sorts—in place of a makefile and command line application building.

Metrowerks CodeWarrior

Metrowerks' IDE is named CodeWarrior. Introduced several years ago for Macintosh program development, it now runs on several major platforms, including Mac OS, Windows, and Solaris. CodeWarrior comes with a number of compilers to give programmers a choice of languages: C, C++, Object Pascal, Java, and Objective-C are all supported.

CodeWarrior Projects

CodeWarrior is a project-based IDE. To develop a program, you create a single project file that holds the files that collectively become an application. Typically, a project file holds source code files, resource files, and libraries.

CodeWarrior walks you through the two-step process of creating a new project. In Figure 2.1, you see that CodeWarrior lets you choose a category of stationery for the project. Stationery is like a template that tells which starter files CodeWarrior should place in the new project. Letting CodeWarrior decide which files to include in the new project saves you the effort of determining the appropriate libraries that are necessary for the type of program you're developing.

In Figure 2.1, I'm choosing Mac OS C Stationery because I'll be developing a program using the C programming language. After naming the project and setting a disk location for the project, it's on to the second new project window—the one shown in Figure 2.2. Here I get to specify the environment for my application. I'll choose MacOS Toolbox Carbon. Figure 2.3 shows the new project that results from my stationery choices. The new project is a window that lists the files that comprise the project.

From the project window, it's easy to add or remove files, edit source code files, or start up a resource editor to edit resource files. It's also easy to compile code and build and debug executables. A new project starts with a source code file and resource file that enable the building of a very simple application.

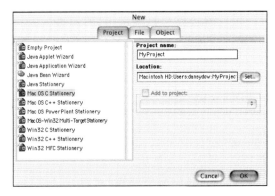

Figure 2.1   Choosing stationery for a new CodeWarrior project.

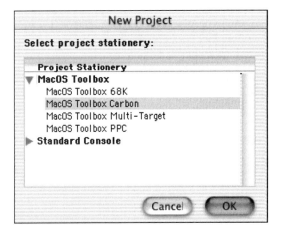

Figure 2.2   Specifying the Mac OS stationery in CodeWarrior.

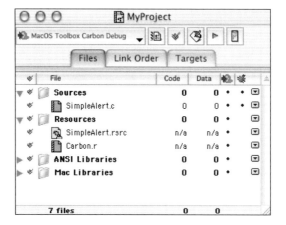

Figure 2.3 The project window of a new CodeWarrior project.

To build and run an executable, choose Run from the Project menu. Figure 2.4 shows that the resulting application displays an alert that includes an icon, text, and a button. Clicking the OK button dismisses the alert, ends the program, and returns you to the project window.

To view or edit the source code file, you double-click the file's name in the project window. Double-clicking the SimpleAlert.*c* source code filename opens a window like the one shown in Figure 2.5.

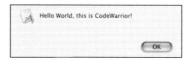

Figure 2.4 The alert displayed by the application built from a new CodeWarrior project.

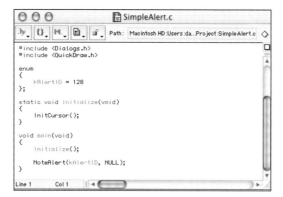

Figure 2.5 The source code file from the new CodeWarrior project.

CodeWarrior and Resources

You can display the contents of a resource file by double-clicking the file's name. The CodeWarrior IDE doesn't have a built-in resource editor, so double-clicking a resource filename results in the file being opened by a separate resource editor. This editor is typically Apple's ResEdit resource editing application. Figure 2.6 shows how the SimpleAlert.rsrc file looks when opened by ResEdit.

A *resource* is code that defines an interface element. As you see in Figure 2.6, a resource can define the size and screen position of an alert as well as the items in the alert (such as text and a button). Resources typically are used to define interface elements. Interface elements are visual entities, so it's of great help to a programmer to have a tool that enables him or her to design and lay out an application's visually. ResEdit is such a tool.

When working with a program such as ResEdit, it becomes easy to think of a resource as some sort of special object. It really isn't. A resource is simply a data structure comparable to a C language `struct`. The interesting thing about a resource isn't that the resource itself is special, but that software tools exist to display the resource code in a manner that's visually appealing and easy for humans to work with. Before tools such as ResEdit existed, a Mac programmer had to create a resource by using code. Some programmers still prefer that method—they use Apple's Rez language to define resources in a text file.

Consider the alert pictured in Figure 2.4. In Figure 2.6, you see the alert (a resource of the type `ALRT`) and dialog item list (a resource of the type `DITL`) resources that define the alert and its items. Example 2.1 shows how the same alert pictured in Figure 2.4 could be defined in code using the Rez language.

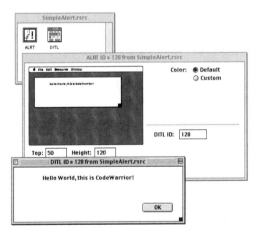

Figure 2.6 The ResEdit resource file from a new CodeWarrior project.

Example 2.1   **Alert Resource Source Code**

```
#include <Dialogs.r>

resource 'ALRT' (128, purgeable) {
   {50, 50, 170, 430},
   128,
   {
      OK, visible, silent,
      OK, visible, silent,
      OK, visible, silent,
      OK, visible, silent,
   },
   alertPositionMainScreen
};

resource 'DITL' (128, purgeable) {
   {  {80, 300, 100, 360},
      Button {
            enabled,
            "OK"
      },
      {15, 70, 85, 350},
      StaticText {
            disabled,
            "Hello World, this is CodeWarrior!"
      }
   }
};
```

A resource file that is created using a graphical resource editor such as ResEdit is usually given a *.rsrc* extension. The SimpleAlert.rsrc file is an example of such a file. A resource file that is created in a text file is usually given a *.r* extension. If the code in Example 2.1 were saved in a text file, the filename of SimpleAlert.r would be appropriate. If one removed the SimpleAlert.rsrc file from the project shown in Figure 2.3 and replaced it with a file that held the code shown in Example 2.1, the application that results from a build of the project would be the same. Running the new version of the application would again result in the display of an alert like the one shown in Figure 2.4.

A Macintosh programmer *could* take the time to learn the syntax of defining resources in code. However, a comparison of Figure 2.6 to Example 2.1 should convince you that for most people, a graphical resource editor is the easier method for creating and editing resources.

Apple Project Builder and Interface Builder

Apple's IDE is Project Builder. Project Builder is designed specifically to generate native Mac OS X applications. Programmers who use Project Builder can program in

C, C++, Java, or Objective-C. As of this writing, Project Builder and its companion resource editor, Interface Builder, are free applications that are bundled with every copy of Mac OS X. Again, as of this writing, these tools don't come preinstalled; they exist on a companion developer tools CD. After they are installed, the tools will be in the Applications folder located in the Developer folder. The examples in this book use Project Builder and Interface Builder.

Project Builder Projects

Like Metrowerks' CodeWarrior, Apple's Project Builder is a project-based IDE. An application begins as a project file that organizes the source code files, resource files, and libraries that are compiled, linked, and combined into a standalone application. Project Builder enables you to set up a new project by prompting you for the type of application you'll be building (see Figure 2.7). The examples in this book are created from projects that make use of nib files (which are discussed just ahead in this chapter), so the Carbon Application (Nib Based) option is the project type with which you'll become familiar.

After you select a project type, Project Builder asks that you enter a project name (to which Project Builder will append a .pbprj extension) and the path for the folder in which the new project should be placed (as shown in Figure 2.8). You won't need to create a new folder to hold the new project and its associated files—Project Builder automatically handles that task.

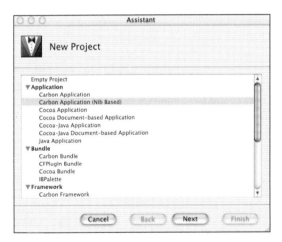

Figure 2.7   Choosing a project type in Project Builder.

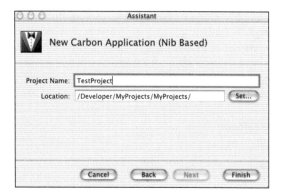

Figure 2.8 Naming the new Project Builder project and specifying its location.

Selecting a project type tells Project Builder which files to include in the new project. This saves you the work of determining the proper libraries that are needed to support the type of application you'll be developing. In Figure 2.9, you see the window that appears when a new project is created.

The project window is the place from which you manage your project. Here it's easy to add or delete files, edit and compile source code, and build and debug executables. To build and run an executable, choose Build and Run from the Build menu. You can do this immediately upon creating a new project because Project Builder adds a simple source code file (main.c) and resource file (main.nib) to any new project. The resulting application displays an empty window that can be moved, resized, minimized, and closed.

A Project Builder project organizes files into groups. In Figure 2.9, you see the group headings are Sources, Resources, External Frameworks and Libraries, and Products. Project Builder supplies a new project with files of each type—these are the files that are needed to create a basic application of the specified type (such as a nib-based Carbon application). Your programming efforts will primarily focus on the files in the Sources and Resources groups.

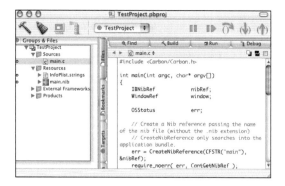

Figure 2.9 The project window of the new Project Builder project.

The Sources group is where you store the source code files you write. Project Builder starts a project with a very simple main.c source code file. You're free to edit this file, or remove it and replace it with one or more .c files of your own making. Clicking a filename in the Sources group (such as main.c) displays the contents of that file in the area on the right side of the Project Builder window. If you'll be writing .h header files, it makes sense to include those files in the Sources group as well.

The Resources group is where you store the resource files that define the interface of your program. Of most interest here is the main.nib file that Project Builder places in the new project. A .nib file is one that is created and edited using Apple's Interface Builder programming tool. Interface Builder, nib files, and the nib resources within these files are discussed throughout the remainder of this chapter.

To view or edit a .nib file (such as main.nib), you double-click the file's name. The double-clicking opens the file in Interface Builder. If your project has other types of resource files, you'll store them here in the Resources group. For instance, a .r Rez file or a .rsrc resource file could be placed in this group.

> **Note**
> The .r file type (created as a source code file using the Rez programming language) is discussed in the "Metrowerks CodeWarrior" section of this chapter.

An example of the creation of a .rsrc file type (as created in ResEdit or some other program) appears in this chapter's HelloWorldPict example program.

The External Frameworks and Libraries group holds libraries and frameworks (a framework being simply a different type of library). When you create a new project, Project Builder places the necessary files in this group, and you will seldom need to add any other files here.

The Products group holds the targets of your project. A target is the result of performing a build and is typically a standalone application. Each example project in this book has just one target, but it is possible to have more than one target associated with one project. An example of this would be having two similar versions of a program: one that includes special error-checking code for debugging purposes and one production-quality program that's stripped of all debugging code.

Interface Builder and Resources

As described in the "Metrowerks CodeWarrior" section of this chapter, a resource is code that defines an interface element such as a menu or window. The same resource can be defined either textually in source code (see Example 2.1) or graphically in a resource file (see Figure 2.6). In the past, resources defined graphically were typically done so using Apple's ResEdit resource editor application. With Mac OS X, programmers have a new way of working with resources—Interface Builder.

Interface Builder is an Apple programming tool that enables a programmer to create and edit interface elements such as menus, windows, and the items in windows in a graphical manner. Interface Builder is an adaptation of an older tool developed by NeXT. When Apple acquired NeXT and the NEXTSTEP OS, they also acquired Interface Builder.

Interface Builder was initially designed as a tool for developing the interface elements for NeXT applications. A file created with Interface Builder is given an extension of .nib, with the *n* in nib standing for NeXT. A nib file is a NeXT Interface Builder file. Figure 2.10 shows how Interface Builder displays the contents of a nib file that holds a menu bar resource and a window resource.

Interface Builder is like ResEdit in that it too displays resource information graphically, but stores that same information as text. Although ResEdit stores resource information in Rez source code, Interface Builder stores resource information in extensible markup language (XML) format. XML is a markup language for documents containing structured information. Unlike Hypertext Markup Language (HTML), which has fixed tag semantics and a fixed tag set, XML enables programmer-defined tags and tag relationships. Just as you don't need to know the Rez language if you're defining resources in ResEdit .rsrc files, you don't need to know XML if you're defining resources in Interface Builder .nib files.

This book's example programs use Project Builder projects and Interface Builder nib files. If you've never used either of these programming tools, you'll want to look over the four example programs in this chapter. They provide a good introduction to working with Project Builder, Interface Builder, and nib files.

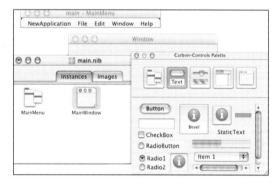

Figure 2.10   The Interface Builder resource file from a Project Builder project.

HelloWorld: Walking Through a Simple Example Program

Just about any tutorial-style programming book I've ever read included a very simple introductory program, typically named something akin to HelloWorld. This is a tutorial-style book as well, and who am I to buck tradition? In this section you'll walk through the creation of a standalone Mac OS X application named HelloWorld. If you've never programmed the Mac, or have programmed the Mac but have never used Apple's programming tools (Project Builder and Interface Builder), you won't want to skip this material. As simple as HelloWorld is, it covers a number of fundamental issues that arise throughout the rest of this book.

Creating the HelloWorld Project

Before creating a new project, you might find it convenient to make a new folder in which you'll store all your projects. Many developers choose the Documents folder as the directory that's to hold their projects, so that's what I'll do. Mac OS X provides a Documents folder off the root folder (the drive on which Mac OS X is installed). Within that folder is a nice place to store all your projects. Within my Documents folder, I've created a folder cleverly named MyProjects. You might want to do the same.

Run the Project Builder application (it's located in the Applications folder in the Developer folder). Now choose New Project from the File menu. Doing that displays the window shown in Figure 2.11. As shown in Figure 2.11, click the Carbon Application (Nib Based) list item located under the Application heading. Then click the Next button.

Figure 2.11   Selecting a new Project Builder project type for the HelloWorld project.

Now supply the new project with a name and a location. In Figure 2.12, I've named my project HelloWorld. Don't bother adding an extension to the name. Project Builder will automatically append a .pbproj extension to the name you supply. Now click the Set button to specify the folder into which this project should go. The window that appears lets you click your way through the folder hierarchy until you reach the folder to which you want the new project saved. Click that folder's name, and then click the Choose button. For my new project, I chose the MyProjects folder in my Developer folder.

In Figure 2.12, you see that Project Builder then automatically created a new folder with the same name I gave my project (HelloWorld) and placed that new folder in the selected folder (the MyProjects folder). Now click the Finish button to tell Project Builder to finish the process of creating the new project.

Now Project Builder opens a window that displays the newly created project. Figure 2.13 shows the window for the HelloWorld project. On the left side of the window I've clicked each Group heading (Sources, Resources, and so forth) to display the files that Project Builder has automatically placed in each group. Project Builder determines the files that are to appear in this project based on the type of project selected (which was Carbon Application [Nib Based], as shown back in Figure 2.11).

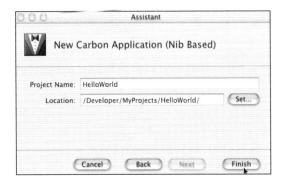

Figure 2.12   Naming the new Project Builder project.

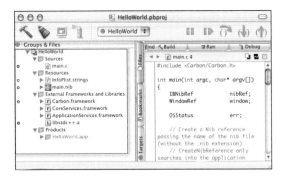

Figure 2.13   The project window of the HelloWorld project.

For most projects, your interest will be with the main.c source code file and the main.nib Interface Builder nib resource file. To start you out, Project Builder supplies a new project with a little source code in the main.c file. Project Builder also includes a few nib resources in the main.nib file it includes with a project. I'll make a few changes to each file to demonstrate the process of editing source code and nib resources and to provide an example of how source code and resource changes affect the application that I'll soon build.

Nib Resources and the main.nib File

As mentioned earlier in this chapter, a nib file is one that holds the definitions for interface elements such as menus and windows, and it is editable using Apple's Interface Builder program. If you use Apple's programming tools, you use Interface Builder to create your program's interface elements and Project Builder to write your program's source code. There is no *required* order to carrying out these tasks, but it typically makes the most sense to first use Interface Builder to design your program's interface.

When you create a new nib-based project (as I've done here with the HelloWorld project), Project Builder adds a nib file to the new project. You can double-click the main.nib filename in the project window to open that file in Interface Builder. Figure 2.14 shows how Interface Builder displays the main.nib file that is used in each new Project Builder project.

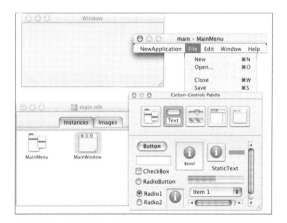

Figure 2.14   The main.nib file that's part of the HelloWorld project.

Nib File Windows

Figure 2.14 shows that Interface Builder displays four windows. You'll want to become familiar with these windows, as they'll be present in just about any nib file with which you work.

The following bulleted list contains the name of each window, followed by the window's title (as it appears in the window's title bar) and a description.

- **Nib file window (main.nib):** In the lower left of Figure 2.14 is the window titled main.nib. This window displays a thumbnail view of the main (top-level) elements in the nib file. In this example, the nib file holds one menu bar and one window. The Instances tab (active in the figure) is used to display the thumbnail view of the main interface elements. The Images tab is used to display images that can be used by window elements.

  Double-clicking a thumbnail image in the main.nib window results in the full-sized display of that element within its own window. For instance, clicking the image above the MainMenu title displays an actual-size view of the menu bar that the thumbnail image represents, as shown in the upper-right corner of Figure 2.14.

- **Menu editor (main – MainMenu):** Each element in the main.nib window can be edited within its own window. Double-click the menu bar thumbnail image (labeled MainMenu in the main.nib window) to display the menu bar. In Figure 2.14, that window has a title of main – MainMenu. In the Menu Editor, you have full control over the content of your program's menu bar.

  You can view the items in the menu of a menu bar by clicking the menu name. Doing that drops that menu down to reveal the items in the menu, just as if the menu were a functional menu in a program. The main.nib file that is the basis of each Project Builder nib-based project includes a menu bar that holds a number of menus and menu items common to most programs.

  Although a menu item *might* automatically have the functionality that accompanies its name (the Quit item in the File menu is functional, for instance), most menu items need source code support to work. Consider the File menu shown in the main – MainMenu window in Figure 2.14. Among its menu items is New. Building an application that makes use of this nib file will result in a program that includes a File menu with a New menu item, but it won't result in this menu item actually doing anything. To add functionality to menu items, you need to supplement the menu items created in Interface Builder with menu-handling source code in Project Builder (we'll do that throughout this book). Although Interface Builder isn't a miracle solution that stamps out a fully functional program, it is a superior programming tool that makes it easy to quickly design the menus and menu items (and, as you're about to see, the windows) that your program will use.

- **Design window (Window):** Just as double-clicking a menu bar thumbnail image in the main.nib window displays a full-sized, editable menu bar, double-clicking a window thumbnail image in the main.nib window displays a full sized, editable window. This window represents the window your program will display when it's launched. In Figure 2.14, that window has a title of Window. As shown in that figure, the window that's provided for you in the main.nib file is initially empty. When Project Builder added the main.nib file to your new nib-based project, it took a guess as to what menus and menu items your program might need. That's not too daunting of a task. Many menus (File, Edit, and so forth) and menu items (Quit, Copy, Paste, and so forth) are common to most Macintosh programs. When it comes to windows, though, Project Builder won't make much of an attempt to guess your program's needs because window content is often the heart of a program, and it varies tremendously from one program to another. Thus, the main.nib file simply includes one empty window as a starting point. As you'll soon see, adding the items (buttons, text edit boxes, and so forth) that your program's window needs is a simple task.

- **Palette (Carbon-Controls Palette):** Did I mention how easy Interface Builder makes it for you to add items to a window? The window titled Carbon-Controls Palette holds just about every type of window-related feature you might want to include in your program's windows. To add an item (such as a push button) to a window, you simply click the item in the palette window and drag and drop it onto the main window (the window titled Window in Figure 2.14). The exact title of this palette window changes depending on which of the five buttons is currently selected from the row of five buttons along the top of the window.

Editing the Menu Bar

The HelloWorld program that you're creating doesn't need any new menus or menu items. However, as long as you're here in Interface Builder, you might as well see how menu editing works. Here I'll add a new menu that holds one menu item. I won't make use of that menu item in the HelloWorld program. However, in the next example program (the HelloWorldBeep program discussed in Chapter 3, "Events and the Carbon Event Manager"), I will give this menu item some functionality, so go ahead and follow along now.

Click the menu button in the palette window. That's the left-most button of the five buttons running along the top of the window. Then click the blue Submenu item and drag it from the palette window to the main-MainMenu window, dropping it between the Window and Help menus, as I'm doing in Figure 2.15.

Figure 2.15   Adding a new menu to a menu bar.

The result of the drag and drop is a menu titled Submenu. Interface Builder has included one menu item named Item in the menu, as shown in Figure 2.16. To give the new menu a more suitable name, double-click the Submenu name in the menu bar and then type a name for the menu. In Chapter 3, I'll add some very simple sound-playing capabilities to the HelloWorld program, so in Figure 2.17, you see that I'm in the process of naming the menu Sound. Changing a menu item name works in a similar manner: click the new menu to expose its one item, and then double-click the menu item name and type in a new name for the item. In Chapter 3, this item will cause the program to sound a single beep, so I've named this menu item Beep (see Figure 2.18).

Now that you know the trick to editing menu and menu item names, you can hone your skills by changing the name of the NewApplication menu to HelloWorld, and change the name of the About NewApplication menu item in that menu to About HelloWorld. Figure 2.19 shows how the menu bar should now look.

Figure 2.16   The newly added menu before editing the menu name.

Figure 2.17   Changing the name of a menu.

Figure 2.18   Changing the name of a menu item.

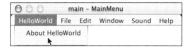

Figure 2.19   The completed menu bar.

A little later in this chapter, you'll see which menu items Project Builder automatically implements for you (such as the Quit item in the File menu). In Chapter 3, you'll reuse much of the Hello World code as a base for adding and examining other features.

Editing a Window and Its Contents

Interface Builder makes window editing as easy as menu editing. Begin by clicking the main window (the one titled Window), and then choose Show Info from the Tools menu. Doing that displays a window like the one shown on the left side of Figure 2.20. For the HelloWorld program, I'll leave these window attributes in their default settings, but feel free to take a look at the window features of which you have control. Before closing the window, click the pop-up menu located at the very top of the window. This menu lets you toggle between the display of different panes of window information. On the right side of Figure 2.20, you see the Size pane being selected. If you'd like to change the initial placement and the initial size of the program's window, go ahead and edit any or all of the four text boxes of the Size pane.

Interface Builder provides an easy and powerful means of adding items such as push buttons, checkboxes, and radio buttons to a window. Click the second-from-left button in the row of five buttons along the top of the palette window. Doing that results in a palette window that looks like the one in Figure 2.21.

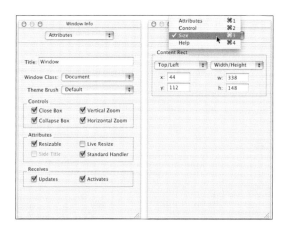

Figure 2.20   The Attributes and Size panes of the Info window.

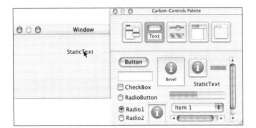

Figure 2.21   Adding a static text item to a window.

To add an item to a window, click the item in the palette window, drag it over to the window that the item is to appear in, and drop the item in place. In Figure 2.21, I clicked "StaticText" in the palette and now am about to drop that text into the window. After an item is in place, you can reposition it by clicking the item and dragging it. If an item has text accompanying it (such as the label of a button), edit that text by double-clicking the text and typing new text. I'm changing StaticText to Hello, World! in Figure 2.22.

With the window's text in place, you can save the main.nib file and return to Project Builder and the HelloWorld project. Now it's time to take a look at the source code to see how it makes use of the resources in the nib file.

Source Code and the main.c File

When a new Carbon nib-based project is created, Project Builder supplies the project with the appropriate libraries, a nib file (main.nib), and a source code file (main.c). You've just seen the nib file and how it serves as a nice, simple starting point for your project's resources. Now you'll take a look at the source code file and see how it serves as a good starting point for your project's source code. Think of this as a sort of Apple-supplied template that gives you a start on the code you'll be writing for your own program.

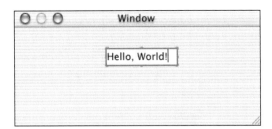

Figure 2.22   Editing a static text item in a window.

Example 2.2 shows the code. I've stripped out the error-handling lines because the code runs fine without them and because I want to emphasize how just a few lines of code can result in a program that displays a menu and opens a fully-functional window.

Example 2.2   **HelloWorld Source Code**

```
#include <Carbon/Carbon.h>


int main(int argc, char* argv[])
{
   IBNibRef    nibRef;
   WindowRef   window;
   OSStatus    err;

   err = CreateNibReference( CFSTR("main"), &nibRef );

   err = SetMenuBarFromNib( nibRef, CFSTR("MainMenu") );

   err = CreateWindowFromNib( nibRef, CFSTR("MainWindow"), &window );


   DisposeNibReference( nibRef );

   ShowWindow( window );

   RunApplicationEventLoop();

   return err;
}
```

The Source Code and Carbon API Managers

Example 2.2 has only one function—main. There are no application-defined routines (programmer-written routines), so you know that all the function calls within the example are calls to Carbon application program interfaces (API) functions. Recall from Chapter 1 that the Carbon API is conceptually divided into managers and that managers are simply an organizational scheme that helps programmers keep track of the thousands of routines that make up the Carbon API. In fact, an application doesn't care about which manager a routine "belongs" to. Instead, the managers exist to make it easier for you to determine which routines are needed to accomplish your various programming goals and to make it easier for you to find documentation concerning the Carbon API functions you use.

All the routine names that include nib (CreateNibReference, SetMenuBarFromNib, CreateWindowFromNib, and DisposeNibReference) are Nib Manager routines. The Nib

Manager is the collection of routines used to access nib files and to work with the resources within such files. ShowWindow is a Window Manager routine. Window Manager routines are used to—you guessed it—work with windows. RunApplicationEventLoop is a Carbon Event Manager function. The Carbon Event Manager holds routines that enable an application to respond to user actions.

Walking Through the Source Code

The HelloWorld example starts by including Carbon.h. You'll want to have such an #include statement in every Project Builder project you create.

```
#include <Carbon/Carbon.h>
```

The preceding statement gives a project's code access to the entire Carbon framework. The Carbon framework is a set of libraries and resources that together implement Carbon.

> *Experienced Mac Programmer*
> Your previous Mac projects might have included a number of #include statements for universal header files such as Controls.h, Dialogs.h, Menus.h, and so forth. Including <Carbon/Carbon.h> in your Mac OS X projects replaces almost all those #includes. Most programs won't need to include any other universal header files. One exception (demonstrated in Chapter 10, "Bundles and Icons") is a program that uses QuickTime. Carbon/Carbon.h doesn't cover Movie Toolbox prototypes, so a separate include of QuickTime.h is needed.

After the #include statement comes the *main* routine. This routine declares three variables. If you've never programmed the Mac, the data types of these three variables are new to you. These types aren't a part of ANSI C. Instead, they're types defined in the Carbon API.

```
IBNibRef    nibRef;
WindowRef   window;
OSStatus    err;
```

The first declaration, nibRef, is of type IBNibRef. To make use of the resources in a nib file, a program needs first to open that file. Doing that supplies the program with a nib file reference value that the program can subsequently use to access the contents of the opened file. The IBNibRef type is defined as follows:

```
typedef struct OpaqueIBNibRef *   IBNibRef;
```

Note the Opaque in the name of the OpaqueIBNibRef structure. *Opaque* means to be impenetrable or obscure. How very cryptic! Here we are on only the first line of code in the main routine and already we need to digress.

Digressing Into Opaque

The IBNibRef type is a structure. What that structure looks like can be known only by finding the definition of the OpaqueIBNibRef type—and that's something Apple discourages. Apple reserves the right to change the makeup of Carbon API data structures, so Apple wants to prevent programmers from attempting to directly access the fields of these structures. By including Opaque in the data type name, Apple is issuing a fair warning that this data type is subject to change and that your code should not rely on the organization of the fields of this data type. If your code directly accesses a Carbon data structure field, that code is dependent on an unvarying field size and order of that structure. Such code will most likely break should Apple alter the data type definition at a later date. With that said, you shouldn't in any way fear using an opaque data type. Apple will see to it that any changes to that type won't affect your code. For instance, if your code uses the IBNibRef type, and Apple changes something about the OpaqueIBNibRef type on which IBNibRef is based, you wouldn't need to update your code that uses IBNibRef. It will remain working as expected.

Experienced Mac Programmer

You might be used to examining the universal interface header files to see the fields that comprise a structure of an Apple data type. For instance, the WindowRec data structure is a window record, and an examination of the WindowRec structure type tells the order and size of window-related information (such as the window's size and position on the screen). You might have then accessed some of this information by dereferencing the pointer. As mentioned, you now need to be aware that for the most part, this kind of direct access of a data structure isn't allowed! Instead, Apple supplies you with several new accessor routines that give you access to the fields of opaque data structures. By using these accessor routines, your code is assured of working even in the event Apple changes the structures with which these accessors work. The important accessor routines are covered where applicable in this book. For instance, you'll read about window accessor routines in the windows chapter—Chapter 4, "Windows."

The window variable is used to hold a reference to a window. After a program creates a window, it will need to refer to that window often. For instance, if a program opens a window and then at a later time wants to close the window, the program needs some means of specifying the particular window to close. A variable of type windowRef serves as this window reference. The WindowRef type is of type WindowPtr, and the WindowPtr type is of type OpaqueWindowPtr. Yes, here's another example of an opaque data type—a data type whose specifics are hidden from you:

```
typedef struct OpaqueWindowPtr*    WindowPtr;
typedef WindowPtr                  WindowRef;
```

The err variable is used to hold the return value of a few of the program's calls to Carbon API routines. The OSStatus type is simply a 32-bit integer that serves to hold an error value, or code. The Carbon API makes liberal use of the OSStatus type—quite a few Carbon routines have a return value of this type. If a Carbon routine returns an OSStatus value of 0, no error occurred in the execution of the routine. If a nonzero value is returned, your application knows an error occurred and can respond accordingly. For the sake of brevity, in this first example program, the value of err is always ignored. This chapter's HelloWorldDebug and HelloWorldAlert programs provide a couple of examples of handling such errors.

After the variable declarations come calls to six Carbon API routines. Here's a line-by-line look at those calls and what they do.

```
err = CreateNibReference( CFSTR("main"), &nibRef );
```

CreateNibReference searches an application's package for the nib file named in the first parameter and then opens that file. The call specifies that the file main.nib file is the nib file to find and open. After opening the file, CreateNibReference assigns a reference value to that file and returns that value in its second parameter. When complete, CreateNibReference returns an error value to let your program know if the operation was successfully performed. Here I chose to ignore the error value. Later in this chapter, you'll see how to handle an error resulting from a call to a Carbon routine.

Two points about the first parameter to CreateNibReference bear further explanation. The first point is the reasoning for embedding the nib filename in a call to CFSTR. Many Carbon routines that require a string as a parameter don't directly accept a literal string. Instead, a routine might require a reference to a CFString, which is an object that holds a string. Passing CFSTR a literal string results in the creation of such a string object and a reference to that object. The "String Services and CFString Objects" section in this chapter provides more information about CFSTR and CFString objects.

The second point of interest regarding the first CreateNibReference parameter is the concept that CreateNibReference searches the application package for a nib file. You might have been under the impression that building an application means that all the code and resources that become that application end up merged into a single standalone file. That's the *appearance* of what occurs, but it isn't the reality.

In Mac OS X, an application is actually a *package* consisting of a folder that holds files and other folders. This situation is hidden from the user. A quick look at the desktop of your own Mac shows you that a program appears as a single application icon. Double-clicking an application icon doesn't reveal the fact that the icon actually represents a folder. Double-clicking doesn't open a folder; it launches the application.

A package is a very clever scheme that enables all sorts of interesting tricks that can be hidden from the user. For instance, a package makes it possible to store multiple versions of a program (such as an English version and a Japanese version) in what appears to be a single application. A package also enables the easy transfer from one machine to another of the several files that make up an application. The user simply copies what's thought to be a single application file and the job's done.

Examine this code:

```
err = SetMenuBarFromNib( nibRef, CFSTR("MainMenu") );
```

Creating a resource in a nib file defines the look of that resource. To have a program "bring to life" that resource requires that the program make a function call. For instance, the main.nib file in this HelloWorld example holds a menu bar resource. Back in Figure 2.19, you see what this menu resource looks like. In the main.nib window back in Figure 2.14, you see that the thumbnail image of this menu resource has the name MainMenu. To set up a menu bar based on this menu resource, a call to `SetMenuBarFromNib` is made. The first `SetMenuBarFromNib` parameter is a reference to the open nib file that holds the menu bar resource. The preceding example call to `SetMenuBarFromNib` uses the reference returned by the `CreateNibReference` call. The second `SetMenuBarFromNib` parameter is a reference to a string object. This string object holds the name of the menu bar resource to use for the menu bar.

Consider this code:

```
err = CreateWindowFromNib( nibRef, CFSTR("MainWindow"), &window );
```

The act of creating a window is similar to that of creating a menu bar. The `CreateWindowFromNib` routine sets up a window based on a window resource stored in a nib file. The first `CreateWindowFromNib` parameter is a reference to the open nib file that holds the window resource. The second parameter is a reference to the name of the window resource (as specified in the nib file). The final parameter will be filled in by `CreateWindowFromNib` and holds a reference to the window that `CreateWindowFromNib` creates.

Examine the following code:

```
DisposeNibReference( nibRef );
```

Before making use of resources in a nib file, the program needs to open that file. After a program has accessed resources in a nib file, it should close the resource file. A call to `DisposeNibReference`, with a reference to the nib file to close as the only parameter, does the job. If a program has references to nib resources, it can make use of those references even when the nib file is closed. This is possible because the references will be to resource information copied to memory (and now held in memory), not to the actual resources in the nib file.

Examine this code:

```
ShowWindow( window );
```

A call to `CreateWindowFromNib` creates a window and returns a reference to that window, but it doesn't display the window. This might seem odd, but the reasoning is simple. `CreateWindowFromNib` doesn't want to make the assumption that your program will immediately show the window, so it plays it "better safe than sorry" and leaves the window invisible. Showing a hidden window is a simple matter of calling `ShowWindow`. Pass a window reference (a `WindowRef` variable) and the invisible window becomes visible. In the previous paragraph, I mentioned that a nib resource reference can be used even after the nib file that holds the referenced resource has been closed. This call to `ShowWindow`, which follows the call to `DisposeNibReference`, provides an example of this. Consider the following code:

```
RunApplicationEventLoop();
```

A Macintosh application is event-based; that is, it watches for an event (such as a user's click of the mouse button), and then responds to that event. This watching-and-responding takes place repeatedly until the application terminates, and this process occurs within a loop that runs for the entire duration of application execution. `RunApplicationEventLoop` is the powerful Carbon routine that runs such an event loop.

A call to `RunApplicationEventLoop` actually suspends the application's execution until an event occurs. At first blush, having your program's execution suspended might sound like a bad thing, but it's not. If no events are reaching your program, your program has nothing to do. Thus, it should be a "cooperative citizen" in the machine's Mac OS X world and relinquish control of the processor so that other running applications can execute as efficiently as possible. After an event does occur (for instance, if the user clicks one of your program's windows), your program resumes execution to process (handle) the event.

Experienced Mac Programmer

`RunApplicationEventLoop` is new to Carbon. It didn't exist in the preCarbon Macintosh Toolbox API. In the past, you've used `WaitNextEvent` within a loop to obtain events. Using `RunApplicationEventLoop` is more efficient and more powerful than your using repeated calls to `WaitNextEvent` because `RunApplicationEventLoop` is better at giving up processor time and is able to automatically handle several event types. Chapter 3 provides much more information on event types, event handling, and using `RunApplicationEventLoop`.

`RunApplicationEventLoop` knows how to handle a few events on its own, including the event that generates when the user selects Quit from the File menu. When the user makes that menu selection, a quit event is generated, the application receives that event, and the `RunApplicationEventLoop` routine terminates. In general, your application will call `RunApplicationEventLoop` and have the routine run until the application quits. In other words, when `RunApplicationEventLoop` ends, the application ends.

In the HelloWorld example, the line of code that follows the call to `RunApplicationEventLoop` includes a call to `return`:

```
return( 0 );
```

The return statement causes main to end, which means the application ends. The main routine has a return type of int, so here I simply pass a value of 0 to return to fulfill the main routine's requirement of returning an integer.

Running the HelloWorld Program

To build and then run a program from within the Project Builder environment, choose Build and Run from the Build menu. Project Builder compiles main.c and builds an application from the compiled code, the main.nib resources, and the libraries that are a part of the project. Then the executable runs. For HelloWorld, that means a window with the phrase Hello, World! appears, as shown in Figure 2.23.

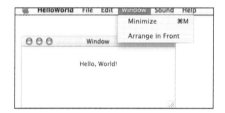

Figure 2.23   The window and menu resulting from running the HelloWorld program.

If you look at the main.c source code example for HelloWorld, you see that there is no menu-handling code. Yet the application responds to a click on a menu—the menu drops down to reveal the items in that menu. Additionally, some of the menu items are functional. For instance, in the HelloWorld menu, the functioning items include Hide HelloWorld (the HelloWorld window disappears), Hide Others (open windows from running applications other than HelloWorld disappear), Show All (open windows from all running applications appear), and Quit HelloWorld (the application quits). You have the RunApplicationEventLoop routine and the Carbon Event Manager to thank for the automatic handling of these items.

When an event occurs (such as a menu item being selected), RunApplicationEventLoop (which you'll recall is running for the duration of a program's execution) checks whether an *event handler* exists for that particular event. Carbon event handling relies on event handlers. Each event handler is a routine that holds the code that handles one type of event. When an event occurs, the Carbon Event Manager notifies RunApplicationEventLoop, and the receiving application then calls the appropriate event handler for that event. Some event handlers are prewritten for you, making the handling of some events automatic (as is the case of a quit event resulting from a selection of the Quit item from the HelloWorld menu).

Besides being able to automatically handle the Hide HelloWorld, Hide Others, Show All, and Quit HelloWorld items in the HelloWorld menu, the HelloWorld application automatically handles the Window menu Minimize item (it sends the HelloWorld window to the dock) and the Arrange in Front item (it moves the HelloWorld window to the upper-left corner of the screen). Again, the existing event handler routines make this possible. All the items in the File, Edit, and Help menus, on the other hand, aren't automatically functional. That makes sense because although items in these menus might have similar behavior from application-to-application (such as Copy in the Edit menu), they don't have an absolutely standardized behavior (one application might need the capability to copy a nontext selection, while another application might not).

Besides handling some menu items, HelloWorld automatically handles several window-related events. Note that other than the call to `CreateWindowFromNib`, main.c does not include any window-related code. Yet the application handles a user's dragging and resizing of the window. Additionally, the application handles a mouse click on the window's Close, Minimize, and Zoom buttons.

The HelloWorld project's main routine consists of less than a dozen lines of code, but from those few lines comes a program that interacts with the user in most of the ways the user has come to expect from a Macintosh application. The Carbon Event Manager is the powerful system software that makes this possible. Chapter 3 provides an in-depth examination of events.

Handling Program Errors

What happens when a user runs your program and then performs some action that your program isn't adequately set up to handle? The correct answer is this: The program informs the user of the error and then resumes execution or, if continuing execution isn't possible, it exits gracefully. With that said, you might expect this book to contain examples that are rich in error-handling code. However, it does not. There are two primary reasons for this. First, anticipating and handling errors are topics worthy of their own voluminous book. Second, if appropriate error-handling code were included in each source code example, the gist of each example would be harder to surmise. For the sake of brevity, most of this book's examples omit error handling.

Rather than fill each code snippet and example source code listing with error-handling code, I'll present one study of error-handling here. The information and techniques covered here can be applied to the code presented throughout this book. Read through this section's text and, if you're seated by your Mac, follow along as I convert the HelloWorld project to the HelloWorldDebug project.

Creating the Project

This section's example project is based on the HelloWorld project. Rather than altering the original project (you might want to refer back to it later), make a copy of it. To do that, make a copy of the entire HelloWorld folder. Go to the Finder, click the HelloWorld folder, and then choose Duplicate from the File menu. Change the name of the copied folder from HelloWorld copy to HelloWorldDebug. Open the HelloWorldDebug folder and change the name of the project file itself from HelloWorld.pbproj to HelloWorldDebug.pbproj.

Open the HelloWorldDebug project. To avoid confusing this project with the original HelloWorld project, you'll want to change the name of the executable that gets built from the project, as well as the name of the project itself.

To rename the executable, begin by clicking the Targets tab in the group of tabs that runs vertically in the project window (see Figure 2.24). Click the target name listed in the Targets list (that name is HelloWorld in this example). Now click the Build Settings tab in the group of tabs that runs horizontally in the project window. Then type `HelloWorldDebug` in the Product name text box, as shown in Figure 2.24. Each time you build an application from this project, it will have this name.

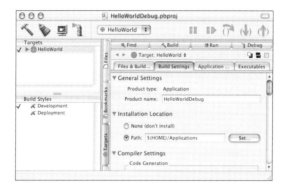

Figure 2.24   Specifying a new name for the executable that's built from the project.

The target includes specifics about the executable that gets built from the project. For instance, in Figure 2.24, you see that the executable name will be HelloWorldDebug and that the executable will be placed in the Applications folder in the home directory (the drive on which Mac OS X is installed). Project Builder lets you have more than one target in a single project. This multiple-target option can come in handy. You might want to generate different executables with, say, different names, or that have slight (or even major) code differences.

Because more than one target can exist in a single project, Project Builder supplies a name for each target. That way, as you jump between targets, you know where you are at all times. The default name for the one target Project Builder includes in a new project is the name of the project itself. As you can see in Figure 2.24, the target name is HelloWorld because this project is a copy of the HelloWorld project. The HelloWorldDebug project includes only one target, so its name isn't critical, but I still want the name to be more in line with the application I'm building. To rename the target, choose Rename from the Project menu. Project Builder highlights the target name in the Targets list and lets you type in a new name. Type `HelloWorldDebug` to rename the target.

Now you'll want to add some error-handling code to the source code in main.c and then, after a test run, alter the resources in main.nib. Let's begin with the source code.

Error-Handling Code

For any programming task, there are usually numerous solutions. You'll find that to be true for the task of adding error handling to a program. One simple method that works well is to make use of the Apple-defined routine `require_noerr`. This routine has two parameters: the error value returned by a function call and a label indicating where program execution should jump to in the event an error has occurred:

```
require_noerr(error, label)
```

Within `require_noerr`, the error value is simply tested against the Apple-defined constant `noErr`. The test looks something like this:

```
if ( (error) != noErr )
    goto label;
```

Many Apple-defined functions return an `OSStatus` value that indicates if an error occurred during the execution of the function. If the returned value is 0 (which matches the constant `noErr`), no error has occurred. If the returned value is *any* non-zero number, an error has occurred. `CreateWindowFromNib`, which was called in the HelloWorld project, is an example of a routine that returns the status of the function's execution:

```
OSStatus   err;

err = CreateWindowFromNib(nibRef, CFSTR("MainWindow"), &window);
```

To keep HelloWorld as simple as possible, I chose to ignore the error value returned by `CreateWindowFromNib`. A wiser thing to do is to pass this error value to `require_noerr`. If `require_noerr` determines that no error has taken place (the error value passed to it had a value of 0), `require_noerr` simply returns and program execution resumes at the point at which `require_noerr` was called. If instead `require_noerr` determines that an error has occurred (the error value passed to it had a value other than 0), `require_noerr` redirects program execution to the location of the label value. This snippet shows a call to require_noerr:

```
OSStatus   err;

err = CreateWindowFromNib(nibRef, CFSTR("MainWindow"), &window);
require_noerr( err, CantCreateWindow );

// ...
// other code here
// ...

CantCreateWindow:
return err;
```

In this snippet, you see that if `require_noerr` encounters an error, all the code that would be in place of the `other code here` comment would get skipped and instead execution would jump to the `return` line.

The `require_noerr` routine is simple to use. If you're going to use it, use it liberally. If an Apple-defined routine returns an error value, follow the function call with a call to `require_noerr`. You can have each call jump to a different label, or you can have all calls jump to the same label. In the HelloWorldDebug example, I include a single call to `require_noerr`. For a simple example that uses more than one call to `require_noerr`, just create a new Project Builder Carbon nib-based project and look at the main.c file included in that project. Finally, for a look at how to give the user some feedback on the error, the HelloWorldErrorAlert project supplies you with that information.

Adding the Error-Handling Code

With the HelloWorldDebug project open, display the source code by clicking the main.c file in the project window's file list. Scroll down to the call to `CreateWindowFromNib`. Immediately after that line of code, add a call to `require_noerr`. The one old line and one new line then should look like this:

```
err = CreateWindowFromNib(nibRef, CFSTR("MainWindow"), &window);
require_noerr( err, CantCreateWindow );
```

Now scroll down to the end of the `main` routine and, just above the `return` line, add a label named `CantCreateWindow`. Here's how the one new line and one old line should now look:

```
CantCreateWindow:
return err;
```

To put these changes into context, take a look at Example 2.3. This listing shows all the source code that makes up the HelloWorldDebug error-handling program.

Example 2.3   **HelloWorldDebug Error-Handling Source Code**

```
#include <Carbon/Carbon.h>

int main(int argc, char* argv[])
{
    IBNibRef    nibRef;
    WindowRef   window;
    OSStatus    err;

    err = CreateNibReference(CFSTR("main"), &nibRef);

    err = SetMenuBarFromNib(nibRef, CFSTR("MainMenu"));

    err = CreateWindowFromNib(nibRef, CFSTR("MainWindow"), &window);
    require_noerr( err, CantCreateWindow );
```

continues

Example 2.3 **Continued**

```
    DisposeNibReference(nibRef);

    ShowWindow(window);

    RunApplicationEventLoop();

    CantCreateWindow:
    return err;
}
```

The require_noerr routine determines if an error has just occurred. It does this by examining the value of the first argument. In this example, that first argument is the variable err, an error value returned by the call to CreateWindowFromNib. If CreateWindowFromNib encounters an error, it returns a code that specifies the type of error encountered. If CreateWindowFromNib executes successfully, it returns a value of noErr (the constant defined to be 0).

If after examining the first argument require_noerr determines that no error occurred, the routine returns without taking any action, and it's on to the next line of code (the call to DisposeNibReference gets called). If require_noerr instead determines that an error *has* occurred (the first argument a value *other* than the constant noErr), the routine returns, but not to the point from which require_noerr was called. Instead, program execution jumps to the location of the label that's passed as the second argument to require_noerr. In this example, that label is CantCreateWindow, so execution jumps to the return statement at the end of the main routine.

Using the Debugger to Check the Error-Handling Code

Now let's see how require_noerr works in the example program. Here I'll make use of the Project Builder debugger to verify that my error-handling code is doing what it should do. If it works, I know that I'll be able to add calls to require_noerr in other places in my source code listing.

Project Builder has a built-in debugger that's easy to use. You simply determine where in your source code listing you'd like execution to pause. You then set a breakpoint at the point. You'll typically pause at a line of code so that you can examine the current value of one or more variables to verify whether the execution of the code is proceeding as expected or whether program execution has in fact made it to a certain statement. The *breakpoint* that you set is a marker that tells the debugger where to halt program execution.

In Project Builder, you set a breakpoint at a line of code by simply clicking to the left of the line. In Figure 2.25, I've clicked to the left of the line that calls CreateWindowFromNib. The figure shows the result—a small, pointed bar appears by the designated line.

Figure 2.25   Setting a breakpoint in the HelloWorld project window.

To start a debugging session, choose Build and Debug from the Build menu. After just a moment, the executable will start running (the executable will first be rebuilt if you've made any changes to the source code). After the breakpoint is reached (which only takes a moment), execution pauses. When that happens, the breakpoint line is highlighted, and you gain control (through the debugger) of the program's execution.

In this example, the breakpoint has been set at the call to `CreateWindowFromNib`, so it's at the call to `CreateWindowFromNib` where execution pauses. To execute the current line of code, choose Step Over from the Debug menu. That has the effect of executing the call to `CreateWindowFromNib`. After that function finishes and returns, execution pauses at the next line—the line that calls `require_noerr`. Again choose Step Over from the Debug menu. The call to `require_noerr` executes. The `require_noerr` routine checks the value of the `err` argument. If `err` has a value equal to the constant `noErr` (a value of 0), it's assumed no error occurred and program execution resumes at the next line of code. If you follow these steps, no error occurs and program execution does indeed move to the line of code that calls the `DisposeNibReference` function. You can end the debugging session by choosing Stop Debugging from the Debug menu.

Your short debugging exercise has completed. We demonstrated that `require_noerr` will let a program carry on with its execution if no error occurs. However, the session didn't prove that `require_noerr` catches and handles an error, so it's time for a simple test.

Make sure the HelloWorldDebug project is open and then double-click the main.nib file to open it in Interface Builder. In the main.nib window, you see a picture of a menu and a picture of a window. As shown back in Figure 2.14, the picture of the window has the name MainWindow under it. Click the picture of the window, and then press the Delete key to remove the window. You've just removed the definition of this window resource from the nib file. Now save the main.nib file and return to the HelloWorldDebug project in Project Builder.

Now you'll repeat the debugging session that you performed before the nib file changed. Look at the source code in the main.c file and make sure the breakpoint is still set at the line of code that includes the call to `CreateWindowFromNib` (see Figure

2.25). Start the debugging session by again choosing Build and Debug from the Build menu. The executable starts running and the breakpoint is soon reached. With the program now paused, choose Step Over from the Debug menu to execute the call to `CreateWindowFromNib`. When that function executes and returns, execution pauses at the call to `require_noerr`.

Choose Step Over from the Debug menu to cause `require_noerr` to execute. Recall that `require_noerr` checks the value of the `err` argument. If `err` has any value *other than* 0, it's assumed an error *has* occurred and program execution should be sent to the label specified in the second `require_noerr` argument (`CantCreateWindow` in this example). As shown in the Variable list of Figure 2.26, `err` has a value of –10962. According to the Carbon header file IBCarbonRuntime.h, the value –10962 is a `kIBCarbonRuntimeCantFindObject` error. That makes good sense here because I removed the window resource from the nib file. This nonzero value sends program execution to the `CantCreateWindow` label. Figure 2.26 shows the break arrow now pointing to the first line of code following the label (the `return` statement). You can end the debugging session by choosing Stop Debugging from the Debug menu.

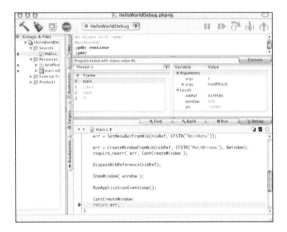

Figure 2.26   Using the debugger to step through the HelloWorld code.

As expected, the error checking worked. We learned that there was no window resource for `CreateWindowFromNib` to use, and program execution was diverted. Although skipping the code that follows the bad call to `CreateWindowFromNib` *is* a good thing, not providing the program user with a clue as to what happened *isn't* a good thing. The next section remedies that by adding an informative alert to the program.

Adding an Alert to the HelloWorldDebug Program

The HelloWorldDebug application detects an error and then exits. For your own application, you'll want to determine if the program needs to exit, or if the error can be handled in some less dramatic manner. In either case, you'll want to provide a user with some feedback as to what's taking place. In this section, you see how to do that.

In this chapter, you've already learned a little bit about menus and windows. In improving error-handling, you'll learn how your application can display another interface element—an alert. Additionally, you'll see that an interface element can be created and displayed without the use of resources.

Creating the Project

This section's example project is based on the HelloWorldDebug project. As you did for the debug project, here you'll create the new project by copying an existing project. To do that, make a copy of the entire HelloWorldDebug folder. Give the copied folder the name HelloWorldErrorAlert. Now open this HelloWorldErrorAlert folder and change the name of the project file to HelloWorldErrorAlert.pbproj.

Open the HelloWorldErrorAlert project and change the name of the executable to that which gets built from the project. You can give the executable any name, but to keep things organized, you'll want to give it a name that's the same as, or similar to, the project name. Thus, telling the project to name the executable HelloWorldErrorAlert makes sense. Recall that to do this you follow these steps:

1. Click the Targets tab.
2. Click the target name listed in the Targets list.
3. Click the Build Settings tab.
4. Type the new executable name in the Product name text box.

The project includes one target. It's currently named HelloWorldDebug. To rename the target, choose Rename from the Project menu. Project Builder highlights the target name in the Targets list and lets you type in a new name. Type `HelloWorldErrorAlert` to rename the target.

Alert Code

An alert is a type of window, which hints at the idea that an alert could be designed in Interface Builder and be included in the main.nib file that's part of a project. This is indeed true. However, there's another way to create an alert. You can let the Carbon API do the work for you. I'll tackle the task this way so that you gain more familiarity with using the Carbon API and so that you see an alternate means of creating an interface element (code versus nib resource).

The purpose of an alert is to inform the user of a situation. That's all it is intended to do. Thus, an alert is meant to be very plain. Figure 2.27 shows the alert that the HelloWorldAlert application will display should it encounter an error attempting to display the program's window.

Figure 2.27   The alert displayed by the HelloWorldAlert program.

Because an alert doesn't have a sophisticated layout (there are no controls, scroll bars, and so forth in it), it's a good candidate to be created in code. There's a second good reason to let the Carbon API create the alert. In this example, I want to display an alert in the event that a nib-based window can't be opened. Such an error could occur if the nib file is corrupt or if the window resource in the nib file is missing or corrupt. If such resource-related problems exist, there might also be an issue with the display of the alert. If the application fails to display a nib-based window, it also might fail to display a nib-based alert! That pitfall can be avoided through the use of a single Carbon API routine: CreateStandardAlert.

Creating the Alert

The CreateStandardAlert routine does just what its name implies: it creates a simple alert that contains standard alert elements. Those elements are some informative text and a button to dismiss the alert. This routine uses standard formatting rules when doing this, so, for instance, the alert will be properly sized to accommodate the items in the alert. CreateStandardAlert has five parameters:

```
CreateStandardAlert( alertType, error, explanation, param, outAlert );
```

The first parameter, alertType, specifies the type of alert to create. Here you pass in one of four Apple-defined constants: kAlertStopAlert, kAlertNoteAlert, kAlertCautionAlert, kAlertPlainAlert. The resulting alert will look similar regardless of which constant you use. The first three constants yield an alert that includes the application icon on the far left of the alert (as shown in Figure 2.27), while the last constant omits the icon.

The error parameter is where you supply the text that makes up the main message. This message appears in bold. In Figure 2.27, the string is this: Window Couldn't Be Opened.

The explanation parameter is where you supply additional text, which is the wording that supplies the user with details about the problem stated in the error parameter. In Figure 2.27, the text is this: The program can no longer run. Click the OK button to quit. This secondary text is optional. If you don't want a second line of text in the alert, pass a value of NULL for the explanation parameter.

The fourth parameter, `param`, is a record that holds additional information about the design of the alert. Although an alert is meant to be a simple interface element, it can be more involved than the one pictured in Figure 2.27. For instance, an alert might have more than one button (such as an OK button and a Cancel button). By default, `CreateStandardAlert` designs an alert that has one button—an OK button. If you want a more sophisticated alert, you'll create a record of additional alert information and use it here as the value of param. This extra information is optional, so if it's not needed in your alert, pass a value of `NULL` here.

The last parameter is `outAlert`. When `CreateStandardAlert` finishes, it will have created a new alert. The `outAlert` parameter is a reference to this alert, and it is your application's means of making use of the alert.

The following snippet includes the call to `CreateStandardAlert` that results in the alert pictured in Figure 2.27:

```
DialogRef          alert;

CreateStandardAlert(
    kAlertStopAlert,
    CFSTR("Window Couldn't Be Opened"),
    CFSTR("The program can no longer run. Click the OK button to quit."),
    NULL,
    &alert );
```

This snippet lists each argument on its own line so that you can easily match the \five example arguments to the five parameter descriptions. The first argument, `kAlertStopAlert`, simply places the application's icon in the alert (a value of `kAlertPlainAlert` omits the icon). The fourth argument, `NULL`, omits the record of additional alert information. The last argument, `alert`, tells `CreateStandardAlert` to create an alert that can be later referenced by using the `DialogRef` variable `alert`.

Earlier in this chapter, you read a description of the `WindowRef` data type. A `DialogRef` is essentially the same. A variable of this type is used to reference a window. An alert is considered a dialog, but a dialog is nothing more than a type of window. The second and third arguments are worthy of a little more discussion.

String Services and CFString Objects

Text characters and strings (groupings of text characters) are important topics in programming. An application might need to display, format, manipulate, or search through text. An application's text might need to be converted to another language. The Carbon API includes a number of routines devoted to string handling.

The Carbon API includes a number of routines categorized into what's called the *Core Foundation*. As the name implies, Core Foundation is a set of routines that are useful for core, or common, programming tasks. In Core Foundation, you won't find any functions that work with fancy interface elements or display multimedia effects. Instead, you get just the basics. Core Foundation routines exist to make OS independence (to an extent), to support data and code sharing among libraries, and to enable the internationalization of strings. The Core Foundation routines that support string internationalization (the easy translation of strings from one language to another) exist within the String Services group of routines.

String Services is in part based on the CFString data type. A program can create a CFString object to hold an array of Unicode characters. *Unicode* is an international standard that defines a uniform means of representing text characters. The Unicode standard exists to provide a way to encode *all* the characters in any written language (we're talking 39,000 characters as of this writing, with the capability to represent tens of thousands more).

When a program creates a CFString object, it can be either mutable or immutable. A *mutable* string is an object that can be manipulated by other String Services routines. Manipulation of such a string can include converting that string to a different programming format (such as a C or Pascal string), translating that string to a different written language, or appending another string to it. An *immutable* string is one that can't be altered. Such a string is usually used as a constant that gets passed to some other Carbon API routine.

One simple means of creating an immutable string is to use the CFSTR macro. A *macro* is simply a shorthand means of carrying out some programming task. In this case, the CFSTR macro calls a private Carbon API function (one that Apple restricts programmers from using directly) to create an immutable CFString object. Pass CFSTR a constant string (text surrounded in double quotes) and CFSTR returns a CFString object. That's exactly what I did in the second and third arguments of the call to CreateStandardAlert:

```
CreateStandardAlert(
    kAlertStopAlert,
    CFSTR("Window Couldn't Be Opened"),
    CFSTR("The program can no longer run. Click the OK button to quit."),
    NULL,
    &alert );
```

Using the CFSTR macro as part of the argument generates a reference to a CFString, and that reference is passed to CreateStandardAlert. Using CFSTR in this manner does the trick, but it doesn't allow for any future reference of this particular string. If I wanted to make use of a string (such as Window Couldn't Be Opened) more than once, I could instead do something like this:

```
CFStringRef cantOpenWindowStr = CFSTR("Window Couldn't Be Opened");
```

The preceding declaration creates a CFString object and assigns that object a value of Window Couldn't Be Opened. I then could pass cantOpenWindowStr as the second argument to CreateStandardAlert:

```
CreateStandardAlert(
    kAlertStopAlert,
    cantOpenWindowStr,
    CFSTR("The program can no longer run. Click the OK button to quit."),
    NULL,
    &alert );
```

Make sure you understand how the CFSTR macro is used. You'll see CFSTR used throughout this book, and throughout Apple sample source code as well.

Displaying and Controlling the Alert

A call to `CreateStandardAlert` creates an alert, but it doesn't do anything with that alert. Your program now needs to display the alert and then go into a loop that awaits the user's dismissal of the alert. That's easily accomplished with a call to just one more Carbon API routine—`RunStandardAlert`. A call to `RunStandardAlert` makes the previously hidden alert visible. It also runs a modal dialog loop that processes alert-related events.

`RunStandardAlert` posts (displays) the specified alert as modal. A *modal* dialog is one that is in one particular mode. That mode is fixed; a modal dialog can't be moved, and its presence takes control of the application to which it belongs. A dialog that can be moved, and that enables other operations to take place in an application, is referred to as a *modeless* dialog (it has no single mode).

`RunStandardAlert` processes events that occur in the specified alert. For a simple one-button alert like the one shown in Figure 2.27, the only event that needs processing is a mouse button clicking the OK button. When the user does that, `RunStandardAlert` dismisses the alert and enables program execution to resume. `RunStandardAlert` has three parameters:

```
RunStandardAlert( inAlert, filterProc, outItemHit );
```

The first parameter, `inAlert`, is a DialogRef variable that references the alert created in a prior call to `CreateStandardAlert`. In short, you're using the output of `CreateStandardAlert` as the input to `RunStandardAlert`.

The `filterProc` parameter is an *event filter function*, which is an application-defined routine (a function you write) that handles events that don't apply to the alert. This parameter usually can be safely ignored. You can do that by passing a value of `NULL` in its place.

When the user clicks a button in the alert to dismiss the alert, `RunStandardAlert` terminates its modal dialog loop and returns to the program an item index for the button the user clicked. For a simple one-button alert, this value isn't of importance, but for a multiple-button alert (such as one that has both a Cancel and OK button), it is of value. Your program will want to react in different ways depending on which button the user clicked.

The following code snippet includes a call to `RunStandardAlert`. The first argument is the DialogRef variable that was returned by the recent example call to `CreateStandardAlert`. The value of `NULL` passed as the second argument indicates that there are no events outside the modal dialog loop that are of concern. The final value—the address of a `DialogItemIndex` variable—will hold the item index for the button used to dismiss the alert.

```
DialogItemIndex     outItemHit;

RunStandardAlert( alert, NULL, &outItemHit );
```

Adding the Alert Code

Calling `CreateStandardAlert` creates an alert. Calling `RunStandardAlert` posts that alert and retains application control until the user dismisses the alert. After `RunStandardAlert` completes its execution, your application should either handle the situation that brought about the alert, or it should quit (if there is no way to recover from the problem). Before looking at the new error-handling code, let's take another look at how the previous example project, HelloWorldDebug, took care of a window-related error:

```
CantCreateWindow:
return err;
```

HelloWorldDebug took the easy way out: the `require_noerr` label `CantCreateWindow` is placed at the end of `main` so that all the code after the call to `CreateWindowFromNib` gets skipped, and execution resumes at the `return` statement (thus ending the program). Such a simplistic solution might not always be possible.

One problem with the preceding code is that the call to `DisposeNibReference` gets skipped. `DisposeNibReference` closes the nib file that was previously opened by the call to `CreateNibReference`. A safer exit would include another call to `DisposeNibReference`, which is a call that doesn't get skipped. In addition, while we're on the subject of safety, it's best to exit the application by way of a call to the Carbon API function `ExitToShell`. Although the `return` call does the job of bringing about a clean exit, it's best to get used to the idea that error-handling code might not always end up being placed immediately preceding the `return` statement in `main`.

Here's what the error-handling code looks like:

```
CantCreateWindow:
CreateStandardAlert( kAlertStopAlert,
   CFSTR("Window Couldn't Be Opened"),
   CFSTR("The program can no longer run. Click the OK button to quit."),
   NULL, &alert );
RunStandardAlert( alert, NULL, &outItemHit );
DisposeNibReference(nibRef);
ExitToShell();
return err;
```

The code that follows the `CantCreateWindow` label gets executed if the application jump to the label. However, it also gets executed when the application flow of control reaches the label naturally. That is, even if there is no window-related error, the code following the label eventually is reached. When the only code following the label was a `return` statement, this fact wasn't an issue. Now that the error-handling code has been expanded upon, this becomes an issue. I don't want an alert posted (or calls made to `DisposeNibReference` and `ExitToShell`) if there is no error. To specify that the error-handling code execute only in the event of an error, I can test the `err` variable (which obtained its value from the call to `CreateWindowFromNib`) against the constant `noErr` and execute the error-handling code only if an error did in fact occur:

```
CantCreateWindow:
if ( err != noErr )
```

```
    {
      CreateStandardAlert( kAlertStopAlert,
        CFSTR("Window Couldn't Be Opened"),
        CFSTR("The program can no longer run. Click the OK button to quit."),
        NULL, &alert );
      RunStandardAlert( alert, NULL, &outItemHit );
      DisposeNibReference(nibRef);
      ExitToShell();
      }
   return err;
```

Take a look at Example 2.4 to see how the error-handling code fits in with the rest of the application code. It shows all the code in the main.c file from the HelloWorldErrorAlert project.

Example 2.4   **HelloWorldErrorAlert Error–Handling Source Code**

```
#include <Carbon/Carbon.h>


int main(int argc, char* argv[])
{
   IBNibRef          nibRef;
   WindowRef         window;
   OSStatus          err;
   DialogRef             alert;
   DialogItemIndex      outItemHit;

   err = CreateNibReference( CFSTR("main"), &nibRef );

   err = SetMenuBarFromNib( nibRef, CFSTR("MainMenu") );

   err = CreateWindowFromNib( nibRef, CFSTR("MainWindow"), &window );
   require_noerr( err, CantCreateWindow );

   DisposeNibReference( nibRef );

   ShowWindow(window);

   RunApplicationEventLoop();

CantCreateWindow:
   if ( err != noErr )
   {
      CreateStandardAlert( kAlertStopAlert,
        CFSTR("Window Couldn't Be Opened"),
        CFSTR("The program can no longer run. Click the OK button to quit."),
        NULL, &alert );
      RunStandardAlert( alert, NULL, &outItemHit );
```

continues

Example 2.4   **Continued**

```
 DisposeNibReference( nibRef );
     ExitToShell();
        }
   return err;
}
```

Running the HelloWorldErrorAlert Program

If you created the HelloWorldErrorAlert project from the HelloWorldDebug project, building and running the executable should result in the display of the alert pictured in Figure 2.27. That's because the HelloWorldDebug project included a main.nib file that didn't have a window resource. If, at some point, you edit the main.nib file and add a window resource named MainWindow, you won't see the alert.

If the project's main.nib file is without a window resource, you can go ahead and add that object now. Again, build and run the application to verify that the error-handling code now gets skipped. If you'd like to perform another very simple test, change the second argument to CreateWindowFromNib. That function call looks like this:

```
   err = CreateWindowFromNib( nibRef, CFSTR("MainWindow"), &window );
```

If you change the string that's used to create the CFString object, the call to CreateWindowFromNib will fail. It will fail because this string represents the name of a window resource in the main.nib file. If the string doesn't match the name of an existing window resource, a window can't be created. To see the error-handling code execute even when main.nib file includes a window resource, change the CreateWindowFromNib call to look something like this:

```
   err = CreateWindowFromNib( nibRef, CFSTR("Testing123"), &window );
```

Adding a Picture to the HelloWorld Program

The HelloWorld project is about as simple a project as can be created, yet it's a valuable learning tool. From examining and editing the code and resources in this project, you've seen how to work with nib menu resources and window resources, add error-handling capabilities to source code, work with the debugger, create string objects, and create and control an alert without the use of resources.

HelloWorld has brought us pretty far, so we might as well make use of it one more time before the end of the chapter. In this part of the chapter, you'll see how to add an image to a project's nib file and have that image displayed in a window resource in the same nib file. When you build and run an executable from the project, that program will open a window and display the picture. Adding the picture to the window resource tells the program to treat the picture as it would any other resource item in a window: the program draws and properly updates the picture without your adding any supporting source code.

Creating the Project

You can start with any one of this chapter's projects, but you might want to select the original HelloWorld project as your starting point. The other projects in this chapter had you remove the window resource, so if you start with one of those projects, you'll need to re-add the window resource. If you want your name to match the ones used here, call this latest effort HelloWorldPict.

By now you know the drill: copy an existing project folder, rename the folder and project file, and then, from within the project, change the target name and executable name. Look back at either of the previous two projects (HelloWorldDebug or HelloWorldErrorAlert) if you need help with these steps.

Creating a Picture Resource

You can use any type of image as the source of a picture that gets displayed in a window. The image can start out as a scanned image, a piece of clipart, a downloaded graphics file, or something you've drawn in a graphics program. Whatever type of image you start with is unimportant, but you'll need to convert that image to a resource to make use of it.

Regardless of the source of your image, you'll want to select and copy the image in preparation for saving it as a resource. To find a nice little image of the world (to match this chapter's Hello, World! theme), I had to look no further than my Mac's desktop. Opening a new Finder window results in the display of a small globe (see Figure 2.28). To get the image, I captured the screen using the Grab utility (located in the Utilities folder of the Applications folder). The resulting .tif document was saved, closed, and then opened in a graphics program where everything except the image of the world was cropped.

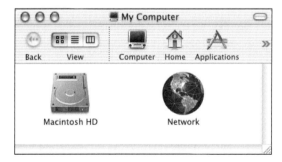

Figure 2.28   The Finder window displays an image of the world.

After you have the desired image, you need to save it as a resource. Several Macintosh graphics programs are capable of saving a document as a resource. One such Macintosh program is GraphicConverter—the same one I used to open the screen dump .tif file and crop the world image. GraphicConverter is a very popular shareware program available for downloading from Lemke Software (`http://www.lemkesoft.com`). GraphicConverter itself is also an excellent example of a Mac OS X program written using Carbon. Regardless of the graphics program you use, you'll open a new document and paste the image to that document. Minimize the document's size to eliminate surrounding white space (if you use GraphicConverter make use of the Smart Trim item from the Edit menu).

Your next step is to save that document as a file of type resource. Figure 2.29 shows the Resource(★.RSRC) format being selected in GraphicConverter. Your graphics program might call this type resource or rsrc. You can give the file any name, but make sure to end the name with an extension of .rsrc. If you'd like your file's name to match the name used in this example, call the file world.rsrc. Save this file to the HelloWorldPict folder. If you inadvertently save it to a different location, make sure to return to the Finder and move the file to the project folder.

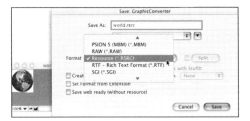

Figure 2.29 Saving a GraphicConverter graphic document as a resource.

If your graphics editor of choice doesn't support saving a document as a resource file, don't despair. If you're familiar with Apple's ResEdit program, you can use that programming tool in conjunction with your graphics editor of choice. Use your graphics program to first select and copy the image you want saved as a resource. Then launch ResEdit and create a new resource file, saving that file in your project's folder. Now, with the graphic image copied to the Clipboard, choose Paste from the Edit menu of ResEdit. That pastes the image to the new resource file and stores it there as a PICT resource. Save the resource file, giving it a name of your choosing with a .rsrc extension. Now close the file.

Adding the Picture Resource to the Project

Now that you have a resource file that holds a picture, you need to include that file in the project that will use it. If the HelloWorldPict project isn't open, open it now. Choose Add Files from the Project menu and select the image file. If faced with a window that asks you to tell Project Builder to which targets to add the file, click the Add button. The file's name will appear in the Groups & Files list, as shown in Figure 2.30. In that figure, you see that the world.rsrc file appears under the Resources folder.

If your newly added file appears elsewhere in the list, simply drag and drop it in the Resources folder.

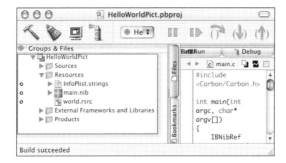

Figure 2.30   The HelloWorldPict project with the world.rsrc file added.

The picture resource file is now a part of the project. Interestingly enough, the main.nib file now knows about the contents of this file. To see that, double-click the main.nib name in the project window to open the nib file in Interface Builder. In Interface Builder, click the Images tab in the main.nib window.

As shown in Figure 2.31, the world image that's stored in the world.rsrc file appears along with a few other images. Three of the images (caut, note, and stop) are a part of every main.nib file—they're images that are sometimes used in alerts. The other three images all come from the world.rsrc file. When a graphics program saves a picture as a resource, it might save the image in a few different formats. You'll want to use one of the PICT images.

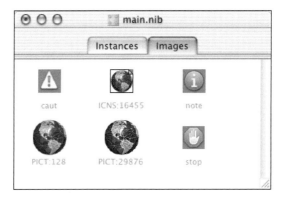

Figure 2.31   The image of the world appears in the main.nib file.

The image now is ready to use in any window resource. You can easily add it to the one window resource currently in the main.nib file. Begin by clicking the window. If it's not already open, click the Instances tab in the main.nib window and then double-click the MainWindow. Now click the middle of the five buttons that run across the top of the palette. As shown in Figure 2.32, you will see a number of controls. Click the blue PICT control and drag and drop it on the window. You can resize the PICT by clicking its edge and dragging. In Figure 2.32, you see that I've placed the PICT to the left of the Hello, World! text and resized the PICT to become a small square.

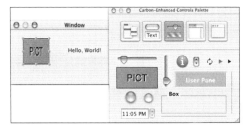

Figure 2.32   Adding a picture item to a window in the HelloWorld nib file.

The PICT item needs to be told what image it's to display. There are a couple of ways you can do this. One way is to click the PICT item that you've just created (the PICT you've just placed in the window) and choose Show Info from the Tools menu. Make sure the Attributes pane is displayed, and then enter the resource ID of the image. In Figure 2.33, I've entered an ID of 128, which matches the ID Interface Builder assigned to the world image (refer back to Figure 2.31). A second, easier way to specify the image to use is to click the Instances tab in the main.nib window, click the image to use, and then drag and drop it on the PICT item in the window.

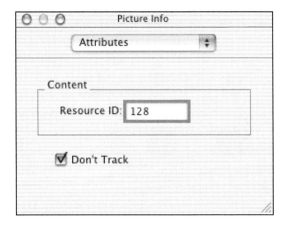

Figure 2.33   Specifying the ID of the image that's to be displayed in the picture item.

After entering a resource ID in the PICT item's Info window (or after directly dragging the image to the PICT item), the PICT item takes on the look of the selected
image, as shown in Figure 2.34. If you'd like to change the size or location of the picture in the window, just click it and drag it.

Figure 2.34   The picture displayed in the window in the nib file.

Running the HelloWorldPict Program

To see the results of your efforts, build and run an executable from within the
HelloWorldPict project. As mentioned, you don't need to alter any of the project's
source code. As long as the code includes a call to CreateWindowFromNib, the program will know how to display all the resource items in the window it creates.

For More Information

For more information about Apple's Project Builder and Interface Builder tools, or to
find references to other major topics from this chapter, visit the following web sites:

- **Project Builder:** http://developer.apple.com/tools/projectbuilder/
- **Interface Builder:** http://developer.apple.com/tools/interfacebuilder/
- **Metrowerks CodeWarrior:** http:// www.metrowerks.com/desktop/
- **Resources:** http://www.MacKiDo.com/Software/NewResources.html

3

Events and the Carbon Event Manager

MACINTOSH PROGRAMS ALWAYS HAVE BEEN EVENT-BASED. An event is an action of some kind, such as a click of the mouse button or the press of a key. When it occurs, the program responds. The Event Manager always has been the part of the application program interface (API) that defined event-handling routines and the component of the system software that worked with events. Now, with the new Carbon API and the new Mac OS X system software, you have the new Carbon Event Manager.

If you've programmed the Mac before, you'll appreciate how the Carbon Event Manager takes over and handles many of the event-related tasks for which your own code was normally responsible. If you're new to Mac programming, you'll be pleased to know that your mastery of this important part of writing a Macintosh program will take a lot less time than it would have if you started programming the Mac just a little while ago!

In this chapter, you'll read about the important routines that make up the Carbon Event Manager. You'll see how an event is defined, how you specify the events in which your program is interested, and how the Carbon Event Manager plays middle-man in passing events to your application and in helping your application handle events. This is an important chapter for any Mac OS X programmer. After you know the basics of event handling, you're well on your way to creating powerful programs with functional menus and operational controls.

Events and Event Handlers

The number of different types of events that can occur is vast. A mouse button click on a control, a mouse button click on a menu, a window collapsing, expanding, zooming, or closing, a disc inserted into the computer, and many, many other actions cause the generation of an event.

Your program won't need to watch for, or respond to, every type of event. Instead, you'll define the event types for which your program should watch. You'll relay this information, along with information about an application-defined routine that handles the event, to the Carbon Event Manager. The routine is one that you write for the purpose of handling a particular event. It specifies what your program should do in response to the occurrence of an event of interest. Such a routine is called an *event handler*. After these steps are completed, you don't have to write any additional event-handling code because now the responsibility of watching for and handling particular events falls on the Carbon Event Manager.

Event Types

To distinguish one event from another, each Carbon event has an event class and an event kind associated with it. The *event class* specifies the broad category, such as a mouse event, to which the event belongs. The *event kind* further hones in on the particular nature of the event by specifying the kind of event, such as a mouse-down event, within the class. Together, the event class and event kind are referred to as an *event type*.

A commonly occurring event is the mouse-down event. Such an event is generated in response to a user clicking the mouse button. A click of the mouse button results in an event that has an event class of mouse event and an event kind of mouse-down. That wording might be understandable to you, but of course, the operating system needs that information in a more "code-like" manner. Apple defines a wealth of event class and event kind constants for this purpose. For a mouse click, the pertinent constants are as follows:

```
KEventClassMouse = FOUR_CHAR_CODE('mous');
KEventMouseDown  = 1;
```

Both the event class constant and the event kind constant are integers, although the event class constant is specified by a four-character value that gets translated to a 32-bit integer (by way of the FOUR_CHAR_CODE macro).

In all cases, you'll be pleased to know that you aren't responsible for knowing any of the actual four-character or integer values. You need only become familiar with some of the constants with which you'll be working. The CarbonEvents.h header file lists them all, but you might want to read through this chapter before tackling the hundreds of constants found there. In this chapter, you'll find explanations and examples that use the most common event constants. Tables 3.1 and 3.2 introduce you to two important event classes: the mouse event class (kEventClassMouse) and the window event class (kEventClassWindow). These tables list a few (but not all) of the event kinds in those two classes.

3.1   **The Mouse Event Class** *(kEventClassMouse)* **and Some of Its Event Kinds**

Event Kind		Cause of Event Kind
kEventMouseDown	Mouse	Mouse button clicked
kEventMouseUp		Mouse button released
kEventMouseMoved		Mouse position changed
kEventMouseDragged		Mouse dragged

3.2   **The Window Event Class** *(kEventClassWindow)* **and Some of Its Event Kinds**

Event Kind	Cause of Event Kind
kEventWindowActivated	Window brought to front
kEventWindowDeactivated	Window sent behind
kEventWindowDrawContent	Draw (update) window's contents
kEventWindowShown	Window became visible
kEventWindowHidden	Window became invisible
kEventWindowCollapsed	Window collapsed (minimized to Dock)
kEventWindowExpanded	Window expanded (enlarged from Dock)
kEventWindowZoomed	Window zoomed

When an event class and an event type are paired, the result specifies one and only one type of event. Such a pairing is called an *event type specifier*. The EventTypeSpec is a structure that represents an event type specifier:

```
struct EventTypeSpec
{
    UInt32 eventClass;
    UInt32 eventKind;
};
```

Each event type has an event class and an event kind. Some event types also have event parameters (also called *event attributes*). The number, and purpose, of an event's parameters depends on the event type in question. For instance, the already-discussed mouse-down event type, which has an event class of kEventClassMouse and an event kind of kEventMouseDown, has four parameters that hold further information about the mouse-down event. Table 3.3 lists these event parameters and their purposes.

3.3   **The Mouse-Down Event Parameters**

Parameter	Represents
kEventParamMouseLocation	Location of cursor at time of mouse click
kEventParamKeyModifiers	Modifier keys pressed at time of mouse click
kEventParamMouseButton	Mouse button clicked (for the instance of a multiple-button mouse)
kEventParamClickCount	Number of mouse clicks (such as a double-click)

The `EventTypeSpec` keeps track of just two pieces of information—the event class and event kind—to define an event type. A different data type, the `EventRef`, keeps track of this same information *and* event parameter information. As shown in the `struct` definition, the composition of an `EventTypeSpec` structure is documented. The same isn't true of the `EventRef` data type.

The `EventRef` is an opaque type. Apple would prefer that a programmer not know its exact makeup. As described in the source code walkthrough of the HelloWorld program in Chapter 2, "Overview of Mac OS X Programming," making a data type opaque assures Apple that they can alter the internals of the data type at a future date without being concerned that programmers have written code that directly accesses fields of the data type.

When working with events, you'll declare a variable of type `EventTypeSpec` and then fill in the two fields of that structure. You'll also make use of an `EventRef` variable, but you'll often enable the system to fill in that structure's fields. Examples of both of these situations appear in the description of event handlers later in this chapter.

Your first step in handling an event is defining the event type in which your program is interested. To do this, declare an event type specifier for the event type of interest. For the upcoming discussion of installing an event handler, consider a program that's waiting for a click a button in a window. The class of such an event is considered a command, and the event kind is the processing of that command. For this situation, the event type specifier might look like this:

```
EventTypeSpec    eventType;

eventType.eventClass = kEventClassCommand;
eventType.eventKind  = kEventProcessCommand;
```

An alternate way of declaring the event specifier and assigning values to its fields would be to do the work at the time of the declaration:

```
EventTypeSpec    eventType = { kEventClassCommand, kEventProcessCommand };
```

Command events, as well as several other classes of events, are covered throughout this chapter. As you read this chapter, and as you study its numerous example programs, you'll come to understand how to set up event specifiers for the circumstances your program will encounter.

Installing an Event Handler

One of the primary jobs of the Carbon Event Manager system software is to watch for events. When this system software encounters an event about which your program is to be notified, it passes that event on to your program. In particular, it sends the event to a routine that you've written specifically to handle this type of event. Such a routine is an event handler. You'll need to write this routine (that task is covered next), and you'll need to install this routine.

To *install* the event handler means to provide the Carbon Event Manager system software with an association between the event type specifier (the type of event to be handled) and the event handler (the application-defined routine that should be executed at the occurrence of an event of the specified type). Pairing an event type with an event handler routine and making the Carbon Event Manager aware of this pairing requires a call to the Carbon API routine `InstallEventHandler`. Here's the prototype for that function:

```
OSStatus InstallEventHandler( EventTargetRef        target,
                              EventHandlerUPP       handlerProc,
                              UInt32                numTypes,
                              const EventTypeSpec*  typeList,
                              void*                 userData,
                              EventHandlerRef*      handlerRef );
```

The `InstallEventHandler` parameter list might look a little daunting, so I'll cover this routine in detail here. After looking over this chapter's example programs, and after you've used this routine a few times yourself, you'll see that the arguments you pass to the function are easy to discern.

A program specifies an event type to watch for, and it defines an event handler routine to handle an occurrence of such an event. When the Carbon Event Manager encounters an event of the specified type and invokes the appropriate event handler routine, it needs to know upon what object the handler should act. In other words, you need to specify the *target* of the event. A target is a window, menu, control, or even the application itself. The target you specify should be the object "closest" to the event. For instance, if a program is watching for events that occur in a window, the window can be considered the target. Simply telling the Carbon Event Manager that a window is to be the target is not enough, though. You need to tell the Carbon Event Manager which window is the target. In addition, you need to supply this information as an `EventTargetRef` variable rather than as the window reference itself.

This target information is sent to the Carbon Event Manager by way of the first `InstallEventHandler` parameter, which is the target. You can create an `EventTargetRef` value by passing the intended target to the proper target routines: `GetWindowEventTarget`, `GetMenuEventTarget`, `GetControlEventTarget`, or `GetApplicationEventTarget`. Each routine takes the one argument passed to it and generates an `EventTargetRef` from that argument. In the following code snippet, the target of an event handler routine is to be a window that's referenced by the `WindowRef` variable window, and it's assumed that this window has already been created

by a call to CreateWindowFromNib. The following code would generate an
EventTargetRef that then could be used as the first argument to
InstallEventHandler:

```
WindowRef        window;
EventTargetRef  target;

target = GetWindowEventTarget( window );
```

The second InstallEventHandler parameter is handlerProc, an EventHandlerUPP. The
UPP in EventHandlerUPP stands for universal procedure pointer. In short, any time you
see UPP in a variable or type name, you can expect that a pointer to a routine is
involved. If the Carbon Event Manager is to invoke the event handler function, it
needs to know where that function's code is in memory. The handlerProc variable
holds a pointer to the event handler routine. You can generate such a pointer by calling the NewEventHandlerUPP function. Simply pass the name of the event handler routine to NewEventHandlerUPP and the function returns a pointer to that function.
Assuming that the as-yet unwritten event handler routine will be called
MyEventHandler, the call to NewEventHandlerUPP appears as shown in the following
code. The resulting EventHandlerUPP then could be passed as the second argument to
InstallEventHandler.

```
EventHandlerUPP      handlerUPP;

handlerUPP = NewEventHandlerUPP( MyEventHandler );
```

The third InstallEventHandler parameter, which is numTypes, is the number of event
types to which this one event handler can respond. Although so far the focus has been
on one event type and one event handler routine, it is possible to have a single event
handler that's capable of handling more than one type of event. In Chapter 4,
"Windows," you'll see a program that provides an example of such a situation.

The next parameter is typeList—a pointer to the event type or event types that
this event handler routine handles. As mentioned, an event handler can serve more
than one event type. Here's where the Carbon Event Manager gets the EventTypeSpec
for each event type. The typeList variable is a pointer that points to either one
EventTypeSpec or to an array of EventTypeSpecs.

The userData parameter is used to pass a pointer to any information that might be
of use to the event handler. The pointer is passed to the Carbon Event Manager, which
in turn passes the pointer to the event handler routine each time it's called. One common use for this pointer is to use it to pass a pointer to the window in which the event
took place. For the handling of some event types, it might not make sense to pass supplemental information, and in such a case, you can use a value of NULL here.

The last InstallEventHandler parameter is a pointer to an event handler reference.
This is a value that the Carbon Event Manager fills in for use by your program. Your
program will need to use this value only if your program will be dynamically changing the event types that make use of the event handler routine. This is a situation you
won't encounter often, so expect to simply pass a value of NULL here.

Now let's gather things together and take a look at a snippet that defines one type of event and installs an event handler that's to handle events of that type. The event type is used to watch for a command (such as a mouse click on a button in a window), and the event handler routine that will handle such an event is named MyEventHandler. We develop and discuss this routine later in the chapter.

```
WindowRef        window;
EventTypeSpec    eventType;
EventTargetRef   target;
EventHandlerUPP     handlerUPP;

eventType.eventClass = kEventClassCommand;
eventType.eventKind  = kEventProcessCommand;

target = GetWindowEventTarget( window );
handlerUPP = NewEventHandlerUPP( MyEventHandler );

InstallEventHandler( target,
                     handlerUPP ),
                     1,
                     &eventType,
                     (void *)window,
                     NULL );
```

Writing an Event Handler

When the Carbon Event Manager encounters an event, it checks whether your program has installed an event handler for that particular type of event. If it has, the Carbon Event Manager calls that routine. This *callback* system (in which you install an event handler in the Carbon Event Manager, and the Carbon Event Manager calls back that routine when appropriate) is a powerful feature of the new Carbon Event Manager. You tell the Carbon Event Manager which routine to call under what circumstances, and the Carbon Event Manager takes over.

Event Handler Routine Format

To make this system work, you need to write your program's event handler routine in a way that makes it easy for the Carbon Event Manager to invoke. That simply means that your event handler routine always has the following prototype:

```
pascal OSStatus routineName( EventHandlerCallRef  nextHandler,
                             EventRef             theEvent,
                             void*                userData );
```

In the preceding prototype, routineName is a placeholder of sorts. Your event handler can have any name (I've been using MyEventHandler in previous snippets).

The event handler has a return type of OSStatus. When the event handler function is finished executing, it should return one of two values: noErr if it has successfully handled the event or eventNotHandledErr if for some reason the event couldn't be properly dealt with. This returned value makes it back to the Carbon Event Manager and, if the value is eventNotaHandledErr, the Carbon Event Manager passes the event to another event handler routine. This other routine might be one that your program defined, or it could be a standard default event handler routine that the Carbon Event Manager has defined. Default handlers are discussed later in this chapter.

It's possible to have your event handler routine pass an event by calling `CallNextEventHandler`. It would pass this routine the value submitted by the Carbon Event Manager in the `nextHandler` parameter. Keep in mind that while you will be writing the code for the event handler routine, it is the Carbon Event Manager that always will be calling it.

The `EventRef` parameter `theEvent` is an event reference that describes the event that's to be handled. Recall that an `EventRef` includes the same event class and kind information as an `EventTypeSpec`, but that it also includes extra parameter information about an event. The `userData` parameter is a pointer to the supplemental information that you included when installing the event handler.

The code in Example 3.1 shows the *format* of a typical event handler routine. I've emphasized the word "format" because this example doesn't provide a complete source code listing for an event handler. Instead, it's intended to show the setup of such a routine. Notice that there are three parameters to this `MyEventHandler` function and that the data type of each parameter matches the type defined in the prototype of the event handler routine. Regardless of the name you give your event handler, and regardless of the type of event it's to handle, you'll always have these same three parameters. Carbon Event Manager will be looking for them when it invokes this routine.

Example 3.1   **Partial Listing of an Event Handler Routine**

```
pascal OSStatus MyEventHandler( EventHandlerCallRef  handlerRef,
                                EventRef             event,
                                void *               userData )
{
   OSStatus    result = eventNotHandledErr;

   if [ based on the event parameter this is an event to be handled... ]
   {
      [ handle the event ]
      result = noErr;
   }
   return result;
}
```

`MyEventHandler` starts by setting `result` to a constant that obviously implies that the event handler *hasn't* taken care of the passed-in event. A test then is made to verify whether the event can be handled. If the event is the one `MyEventHandler` was created to handle, the code in the body of the `if` statement is executed. The `result` variable then is set to `noErr` to tell the Carbon Event Manager that the handler did indeed handle the event. If the event *isn't* the one for which `MyEventHandler` is responsible, the `if` statement is skipped and the event handler routine ends by returning the `eventNotHandledErr` constant back to the Carbon Event Manager so that the manager can attempt to handle the event.

When the Carbon Event Manager invokes `MyEventHandler`, it passes the routine three values. The event handler routine should look at the `event` value to determine if the event is one that it should handle. Recall that the Carbon Event Manager invokes the event handler routine based on a match; the event type of the event that it encountered must match the event type specified when the event handler was installed. Thus, if the Carbon Event Manager invokes an event handler, how could the event handler *not* need to handle the event? The `eventClass` and `eventKind` fields of the `EventRef` variable `event` will both match the event class and event kind values of the event type specified during the installation of the event handler. However, the Carbon Event Manager passes an `EventRef` to the event handler routine, and an `EventRef` contains event parameter information in addition to the event class and event kind information that make up the `EventTypeSpec` used in the event handler installation. This is implied in the code for the MyEventHandler. In addition, it is illustrated in Figure 3.1.

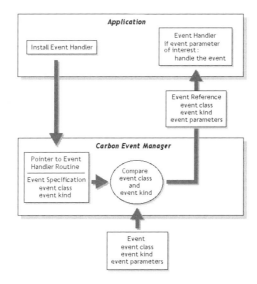

Figure 3.1   Installing and executing an event handler.

Figure 3.1 shows an application installing an event handler in the Carbon Event Manager. When the Carbon Event Manager becomes aware of an event, it compares that event type to the event type of the installed handler. If there's a match, an event reference is sent to the event handler routine in the application. There the handler routine looks at the event parameter information to verify whether this event is truly one that it is set up to handle.

Getting an Event Parameter in the Event Handler Routine

Example 3.1 provides an overview of how an event handler routine is written, but it doesn't go into much detail. In particular, it doesn't explain how the routine makes the final determination as to whether it can handle the event that's been passed to it, and it doesn't provide an example of how the event handler routine might actually handle an event. It's time to clear up the cryptic nature of Example 3.1.

When the Carbon Event Manager sends an event to an application's event handler routine, it includes the event's parameter information. Recall that an event can have information other than its class and kind associated with it. This extra information is held in the event's *parameters*, and this information varies depending on the type of the event.

A parameter always has an *event parameter name* and an *event parameter type*. In this chapter, I've mentioned the mouse-down event, which is an event that has an event class of kEventClassMouse and an event kind of kEventMouseDown. This particular event type has four event parameters. Table 3.4 shows the name and type of each.

3.4   **The Mouse-Down Event Parameters**

Name	Type	Information
kEventParamMouseLocation	typeQDPoint	Screen coordinates of mouse button click
kEventParamMouseButton	typeMouseButton	Pressed mouse button
kEventParamKeyModifiers	typeUInt32	Pressed modifier keys at time of click
kEventParamClickCount	typeUInt32	Number of clicks

To extract the parameter information from an event, make use of the GetEventParameter routine. Here's a look at the function's prototype:

```
OSStatus GetEventParameter( EventRef          inEvent,
                            EventParamName    inName,
                            EventParamType    inDesiredType,
                            EventParamType *  outActualType,
                            UInt32            inBufferSize,
                            UInt32 *          outActualSize,
                            void *            outData);
```

Wow! Yet another daunting function prototype! Fortunately, a look at the arguments, along with an example call to the function, reveals that using GetEventParameter isn't as difficult as might be expected.

The first argument, inEvent, is the event from which the parameter data is to be extracted. When GetEventParameter is called from within an event handler, the EventRef argument event that the Carbon Event Manager passes can be used. Here's another look at the event handler declaration:

```
pascal OSStatus MyEventHandler( EventHandlerCallRef  handlerRef,
                                EventRef             event,
                                void *               userData )
```

From within `MyEventHandler`, a call to `GetEventParameter` would start out like this:

```
GetEventParameter( event, ...
```

The second and third arguments, `inName` and `inDesiredType`, are the name and type of the parameter for which you're looking. If your event handler is calling `GetEventParameter`, it's doing so to verify whether the Carbon Event Manager passed in an event that has a particular parameter. This is done so that you'll know the parameter name and type for which you're checking. You can find the parameter constants in the CarbonEvents.h header file.

Consider this example: You want your event handler to know the screen coordinates at the time the mouse button was pressed. You've previously set up your program so that it looks for a mouse-down event. You did this by defining an `EventTypeSpec` variable that had an event type of `kEventClassMouse` and an event kind of `kEventMouseDown`. You determined that those were the correct values either by reading this chapter or by perusing the CarbonEvents.h header file. Next, you used this `EventTypeSpec` in a call to `InstallEventHandler`. You now know that an event that comes into your event handler routine will be a mouse-down event. If an event *wasn't* of that type, your event handler wouldn't have been invoked by the Carbon Event Manager. Now you want to further examine the event to find out the point that defines the screen coordinates at which the mouse button was pressed. Browsing the CarbonEvents.h header file shows you that the parameter of interest is `kEventParamMouseLocation`:

```
        Parameters for mouse events:
        kEventMouseDown
            -->     kEventParamMouseLocation     typeQDPoint
            -->     kEventParamKeyModifiers      typeUInt32
            -->     kEventParamMouseButton       typeMouseButton
            -->     kEventParamClickCount        typeUInt32
```

The values `kEventParamMouseLocation` and `typeQDPoint` become the second and third arguments to `GetEventParameter`.

The fourth `GetEventParameter` argument, `outActualType`, is filled in by the Carbon Event Manager. This type should match the type you specify in the third argument. It's unlikely that this information will be of value to your event handler, so you can pass a value of `NULL` here.

The next argument is `inBufferSize`, which is the size of the buffer that is to hold the parameter value that `GetEventParameter` returns. Use `sizeof` with the data type of the expected return value. The `outActualSize` argument will be filled in with the actual size of the returned data. Pass a value of `NULL` here if this information isn't needed.

The last `GetEventParameter` is `outData`. This is a pointer to the memory that will receive the parameter data.

An Event Handler to Handle a Command Event

The most common event you'll want any of your Macintosh programs to handle is probably the command event. A *command event* is generated when a menu item is selected or when a control is chosen. Every program has a menu bar, and almost any program includes at least one button in a window. Thus, if you understand how a command event is handled, you're on your way to adding a great deal of functionality to your Macintosh application.

As is typically the case when working with an interface element, you need to coordinate the work that goes into your project's nib resource file and source code file. For instance, in creating a window, you define a window nib resource, take note of its name (such as `MainWind`), and then make a call to `CreateWindowFromNib` using that resource's name. To handle a command, you'll do similar work.

Associating a Command With a Resource

A control, such as a button, can have a command associated with it. A command consists of four characters, and it should be unique for your resources. That is, if you have ten buttons in various window resources in your main.nib resource file, you'll want to think of ten different commands so that you can give each a unique four-character command. The characters you choose to use to compose a command aren't critical, as long as each command is unique. In Figure 3.2, I clicked the Do This button, selected Show Info from the Tools menu, selected the Control pane in the Info window, and typed the characters `this` in the Command field.

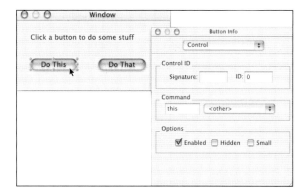

Figure 3.2   Setting a button's command in Interface Builder.

To associate a command with the other button in the window, I follow the same steps, making sure, however, to enter a different command. For instance, the command for the Do That button could be the four characters of *that*. Note that I've intentionally used the vague-sounding button names Do This and Do That because the emphasis here isn't on what particular actions I want the buttons to perform. That doesn't matter when assigning a command to a control. What occurs when a button is clicked will be established in the source code. Here, the point is simply to assign a value to a control so that the program knows which control has been selected.

When choosing a four-character command, avoid the several commands that Apple already has defined. If you do use one of those commands, and then try to give the command some type of action in your code, your program might not behave as expected. The commands to avoid (unless you're trying to implement the command's behavior), are listed in CarbonEvents.h, and are repeated in the following code:

```
kHICommandOK               = FOUR_CHAR_CODE('ok  '),
kHICommandCancel           = FOUR_CHAR_CODE('not!'),
kHICommandQuit             = FOUR_CHAR_CODE('quit'),
kHICommandUndo             = FOUR_CHAR_CODE('undo'),
kHICommandRedo             = FOUR_CHAR_CODE('redo'),
kHICommandCut              = FOUR_CHAR_CODE('cut '),
kHICommandCopy             = FOUR_CHAR_CODE('copy'),
kHICommandPaste            = FOUR_CHAR_CODE('past'),
kHICommandClear            = FOUR_CHAR_CODE('clea'),
kHICommandSelectAll        = FOUR_CHAR_CODE('sall'),
kHICommandHide             = FOUR_CHAR_CODE('hide'),
kHICommandPreferences      = FOUR_CHAR_CODE('pref'),
kHICommandZoomWindow       = FOUR_CHAR_CODE('zoom'),
kHICommandMinimizeWindow   = FOUR_CHAR_CODE('mini'),
kHICommandArrangeInFront   = FOUR_CHAR_CODE('frnt'),
kHICommandAbout            = FOUR_CHAR_CODE('abou')
```

A menu resource also enables a command to be associated with it. In fact, as you'll see when writing the event handling code, your program will not need to distinguish between a control command and a menu command. Your program will view each as simply a command to be carried out, and it won't care about the source of the command. To demonstrate that, Figure 3.3 illustrates that a menu item can be given the same command as a button by selecting the menu item, choosing Show Info from the Tools menu, and typing the command in the Command field. Note that in Figure 3.3, the This menu item now has the same command (this) associated with it as the This button in the window pictured in Figure 3.2.

I said that each command should be unique, but here I've given two resources the same command. That means that both resources will be bound to the same action. Whether the user clicks the Do This button or chooses the This menu item, the event handler that handles the command event will respond in the same manner. Let's move on to the source code now to see just how the event handler does in fact handle a command event.

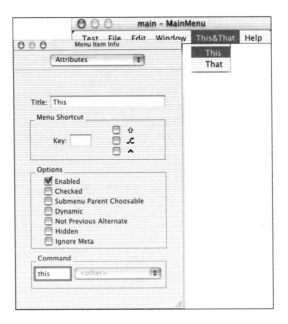

Figure 3.3 Setting a menu's command in Interface Builder.

Handling a Command Event

Back near the end of the "Event Types" section in this chapter, you saw the code for creating an `EventTypeSpec` for a command event:

```
EventTypeSpec    eventType;
eventType.eventClass = kEventClassCommand;
eventType.eventKind  = kEventProcessCommand;
```

The "Installing an Event Handler" section illustrated how an event handler is installed:

```
WindowRef        window;
EventTargetRef   target;
EventHandlerUPP     handlerUPP;

target = GetWindowEventTarget( window );
handlerUPP = NewEventHandlerUPP( MyEventHandler );

InstallEventHandler( target,
                     handlerUPP ),
                     1,
                     &eventType,
                     (void *)window,
                     NULL );
```

Now let's write the event handler routine. The `MyEventHandler` routine in Example 3.2 is an event handler routine that handles a command event. It also fills in some of the missing code from Example 3.1.

Example 3.2   **An Event Handler Routine**

```
#define  kThisCommand  'this'
#define  kThatCommand  'that'

pascal OSStatus MyEventHandler( EventHandlerCallRef  handlerRef,
                                EventRef             event,
                                void *               userData )
{
   OSStatus      result = eventNotHandledErr;
   HICommand     command;

   GetEventParameter( event,
                      kEventParamDirectObject,
                      typeHICommand, NULL,
                      sizeof (HICommand), NULL,
                      &command );

   switch ( command.commandID )
   {
     case kThisCommand:
        MyThisCommandHandler( (WindowRef)userData );
        result = noErr;
        break;
     case kThatCommand:
        MyThatCommandHandler( (WindowRef)userData );
        result = noErr;
        break;
   }
   return result;
}
```

Example 3.2 starts with the definitions of two constants, each matching one of the two unique commands in the resources. You need to make your source code aware of each unique command that's associated with a resource, and using a #define for each is one way to do that.

In Example 3.2, you see how `GetEventParameter` is used to get the parameter held in the argument `event` and store it in the variable `command`. `MyEventHandler` calls `GetEventParameter` to get parameter data from an event with a class of `kEventClassCommand` and a kind of `kEventProcessCommand`. From the CarbonEvents.h header file, you see that an event with a kind of `kEventProcessCommand` has two parameters:

```
Parameters for command events:

kEventCommandProcess
```

```
                    kEventParamDirectObject      typeHICommand
                    kEventParamKeyModifiers      typeUInt32 (optional)


            kEventCommandUpdateStatus
                    kEventParamDirectObject      typeHICommand
```

The kEventParamDirectObject parameter has a type of HICommand. Looking again at
the CarbonEvents.h header file reveals the definition of this data type:

```
struct HICommand {
    UInt32              attributes;
    UInt32              commandID;
    struct {
        MenuRef         menuRef;
        MenuItemIndex   menuItemIndex;
    }                   menu;
};


typedef struct HICommand    HICommand;
```

By now, you should be repeating this mantra often: "The CarbonEvents.h header file is
my friend. The CarbonEvents.h header file is my friend." It is this header file that
holds a wealth of information about event types; you should be searching and browsing through it early and often.

If GetEventParameter is called and the call specifies that the parameter of interest is
the kEventParamDirectObject parameter, an HICommand structure ends up being placed
in the last GetEventParameter argument. This happens because the parameter type is
HICommand. Take another look at the call to GetEventParameter to verify that the second and third arguments specify the parameter's name and type and that the last argument is of the data type that enables it to hold the parameter that GetEventParameter
will place here:

```
GetEventParameter( event,
                   kEventParamDirectObject,
                   typeHICommand, NULL,
                   sizeof (HICommand), NULL,
                   &command );
```

Now the command variable holds an HICommand structure. An event handler routine
that's handling a command needs this parameter data. In particular, the event handler
will want to look at the commandID field of the HICommand structure:

```
switch ( command.commandID )
{
   case kThisCommand:
      MyThisCommandHandler();
      result = noErr;
      break;
   case kThatCommand:
       MyThatCommandHandler();
      result = noErr;
      break;
}
```

When the user clicks the Do This button or chooses the This menu item, an event occurs. Your program doesn't create this event; it's a system action. In creating the event, the system assigns it a class (`kEventClassCommand`) and a kind (`kEventProcessCommand`). It also supplies the values to the parameters that are part of this event's kind (`kEventParamDirectObject` and `kEventParamKeyModifiers`). The system places the command (in this example, the characters *this*) in the `commandID` field of the `HICommand` structure that is the `kEventParamDirectObject` parameter. The system then sends the event to the Carbon Event Manager (see the bottom of Figure 3.1). The Carbon Event Manager compares this event to any event handlers your program has installed. If there's a class and kind match, the Carbon Event Manager invokes the corresponding event handler in your program, passing along the event as it does so (see the right side of Figure 3.1).

This event handler's main task is to get the command from the event. The call to `GetEventParameter` extracts the `HICommand` structure, enabling the `commandID` field of that structure to be examined in a `switch` statement. Herein lies the power of the event handler. A single event handler can handle any number of commands. This example handles two commands (`kThisCommand` and `kThatCommand`), so there are two `case` labels in the body of the `switch` statement. If I modify the nib resource file to give commands to other controls and other menu items, I don't need to write any new event handler routines. Instead, I define more constants and add more `case` labels to the `switch` statement in the `MyEventHandler` routine.

Under each `case` label is a call to an application-defined routine that includes the code to handle one command. You *could* place the command-handling code right here under the `case` label, but moving that code to its own routine and placing a call to that routine in the case section makes things easy on the eye. We certainly do want tidy code, right?

There's no naming or calling convention that a command-handling routine needs to follow. In Example 3.2, I call the routines `MyThisCommandHandler` and `MyThatCommandHandler`, and neither gets passed any values. Here's a look at `MyThisCommandHandler`:

```
pascal void MyThisCommandHandler( void )
{
   // perform 'this' action here
}
```

Not too interesting, I agree, but in this discussion, the action that the command performs isn't important. Instead, how program execution gets to the point where the command is handled is what matters. What a command-handling routine does is application-specific. The body of the routine looks different for every command and every program. If, for the sake of thoroughness, you must see a complete, fully operational command-handling routine, check out this new version of `MyThisCommandHandler`:

```
pascal void MyThisCommandHandler( void )
{
   SysBeep( 1 );
}
```

`SysBeep` is a Carbon API routine that simply plays the alert sound on the Mac. You'll have a chance to see `SysBeep` in action in this chapter's first complete example program: BeepWorld.

My oh-so-simple command-handling routine doesn't have any reason to work with the window that holds the Do This button, but if it did, it would be an easy task to get that information to the routine. Recall that the second-to-last `InstallEventHandler` argument is a pointer to `userData`. This `userData` variable can hold any supplemental data that you want your event handler routine to receive each time the Carbon Event Manager invokes it. Earlier in this section, the event handler was installed and when that installation took place, the window that serves as the target also was used as the `userData` variable. The following snippet illustrates this. The fifth argument to `InstallEventHandler` is the pointer to the `userData` parameter, and here you see that a pointer to the `WindowRef` variable `window` is used:

```
WindowRef      window;

target = GetWindowEventTarget( window );
handlerUPP = NewEventHandlerUPP( MyEventHandler );

InstallEventHandler( target,
                     handlerUPP ),
                     1,
                     &eventType,
                     (void *)window,
                     NULL );
```

Now take a look at the `MyEventHandler` routine's parameters. The third parameter holds the pointer to the window:

```
pascal OSStatus MyEventHandler( EventHandlerCallRef  handlerRef,
                                EventRef             event,
                                void *               userData )
```

`MyEventHandler` now almost has access to the target window. I say "almost" because `userData` is simply a generic pointer. By the way I invoked `InstallEventHandler`, I know that this pointer points to memory that holds a window reference, so casting the pointer to that type provides the sought-after window reference:

```
WindowRef      window;

window = ( WindowRef )userData;
```

After that, the window could be passed to a command handler, if necessary:

```
case kThisCommand:
   MyThisCommandHandler( window );
   result = noErr;
   break;
```

On the receiving end, `MyThisCommandHandler` would accept the passed window in the following manner:

```
pascal void MyThisCommandHandler ( WindowRef window )
{
    // use the window reference variable window here as you
    // would anywhere else in your program, as in:
    // ShowWindow( window )
}
```

Example Programs

Collectively, events, event handlers, and the Carbon Event Manager provide you with the means to accomplish an amazing number of programming tasks. When you know how to work with events, you're well on your way to knowing how to program the Mac. The first part of this chapter gave you a sound understanding of how to use events. The best way to continue to learn about events is to start writing programs that use them. In this section, you'll find a number of short, simple example programs. Each offers a different event-handling technique.

By now, you're well versed in the steps to creating a project, so none of this chapter's examples will go into the details of creating a new project or copying an existing one. Instead, if an example is based on a previously created project, I'll just mention that fact so that you can use the already-created project as your starting point. If you do need tips on projects, refer back to the example programs in Chapter 2.

BeepWorld: Implementing a Button

The purpose of BeepWorld is to demonstrate command event handling for a single button in a window.

This chapter's "An Event Handler to Handle a Command Event" section spelled out the details of how a program can handle an event that arises from the click of a button or the choosing of a menu item. The BeepWorld program displays a window with one button. Clicking the button initiates a command event, and the program handles it by beeping the speakers of the user's computer.

The BeepWorld program modifies the last chapter's HelloWorld program to provide an example of command handling. You can make a copy of the Chapter 2 HelloWorld project to serve as the starting point of the BeepWorld project.

Creating the Button and Command in the Nib File

Supplying the program's window with a button is taken care of by editing the window resource. Start by opening the main.nib resource file. If you created the BeepWorld project from the HelloWorld project, the window resource will already include a static text item displaying *Hello, World!* as its text. Add a button to the existing window, change its name to Beep, and give it a command of `beep`. You can use these steps to accomplish the tasks:

1. Add the button by clicking the Button item in the palette window, and then dragging and dropping the item onto the window.

2. Change the button's title from Button to Beep by double-clicking the button and typing the new title.

3. Click the button item in the window to make it active, and then choose Show Info from the Tools menu to display the Button Info window.

4. Make the button the default button by selecting the Attributes pane in the Button Info window's pop-up menu, and then clicking the Default option button under the Button Type heading.

5. Give the button the command of `beep` by selecting the Control pane in the Button Info window's pop-up menu, and then typing beep in the Command field.

Figure 3.4 shows the results of following the preceding list of steps. It isn't critical to make the Beep button the default button, but because this is the book's first example program that uses a button, it's as good a time as any to see how this is done! Making the button the default button gives it an undulating appearance and enables a press of the Return key to be the same as clicking the button.

Now save the main.nib file and return to the Project Builder project window.

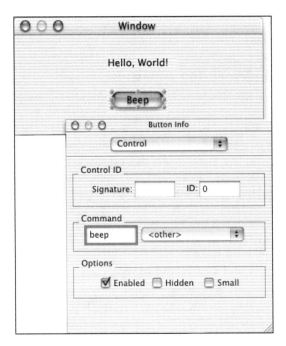

Figure 3.4   Giving the Beep button a command.

Writing the Source Code

The code for the BeepWorld program doesn't need much explanation. This chapter's
"Handling a Command Event" section includes detailed descriptions of all the
programming concepts presented here. BeepWorld sums all the command event
information from earlier in this chapter; Example 3.3 provides the complete listing
for this program.

Example 3.3   **Source Code for the BeepWorld Program**

```
#include <Carbon/Carbon.h>


#define      kBeepCommand      'beep'

pascal OSStatus CommandEventHandler( EventHandlerCallRef handlerRef,
                                     EventRef event, void *userData );
pascal void    BeepCommandHandler( void );


int main( int argc, char* argv[] )
{
   IBNibRef        nibRef;
   WindowRef       window;
   OSStatus        err;
   EventTargetRef  target;
   EventHandlerUPP handlerUPP;
   EventTypeSpec   cmdEvent;


   cmdEvent.eventClass = kEventClassCommand;
   cmdEvent.eventKind  = kEventProcessCommand;

   err = CreateNibReference( CFSTR("main"), &nibRef );

   err = SetMenuBarFromNib( nibRef, CFSTR("MainMenu") );

   err = CreateWindowFromNib( nibRef, CFSTR("MainWindow"), &window );

   DisposeNibReference( nibRef );

   target = GetWindowEventTarget( window );
   handlerUPP = NewEventHandlerUPP( CommandEventHandler );

   InstallEventHandler( target, handlerUPP, 1, &cmdEvent,
                        (void *)window, NULL );

   ShowWindow( window );
```

continues

Example 3.3 **Continued**

```
RunApplicationEventLoop();

   return( 0 );
}




pascal OSStatus CommandEventHandler( EventHandlerCallRef handlerRef,
                                     EventRef event, void *userData)
{
   OSStatus    result = eventNotHandledErr;
   HICommand   command;

   GetEventParameter( event, kEventParamDirectObject, typeHICommand,
                 NULL, sizeof (HICommand), NULL, &command);

   switch ( command.commandID )
   {
      case kBeepCommand:
         BeepCommandHandler();
         result = noErr;
         break;
   }
   return result;
}


pascal void BeepCommandHandler ( void )
{
   SysBeep( 1 );
}
```

Running the Program

Build and run BeepWorld and you'll see a window that displays the *Hello, World!* string and the Beep button. Click the button to hear the beep sound. If you made the Beep button the default button, you can press the Return key in place of clicking the mouse on the button.

BeepWorld 2.0: Implementing a Menu Item

The purpose of BeepWorld 2.0 is to demonstrate command event handling for a single button and for a menu item, with both providing the same action.

We're running a little low in liquid assets, so it's time to do what any good software firm would do in such circumstances—put out an upgrade of BeepWorld and get some much-needed revenue from our installed base of users! Clicking the Beep button to generate a simple noise works great, but customers are demanding an alternate means of hearing that sound. Our revision of BeepWorld provides that feature by implementing the Beep menu item in the Sound menu.

The work involved in changing the original BeepWorld program to BeepWorld 2.0 is so minimal that you might not want to bother creating a new project. Instead, use the original BeepWorld project and make just one small change to its main.nib resource file. You won't have to edit or add to the main.c source code file.

If you created the BeepWorld project from the Chapter 2 HelloWorld project, the main.nib file already has a Sound menu in its menu bar, and that menu has a Beep menu item in it. If your project is lacking that menu, refer back to Figures 2.15 through 2.18 in Chapter 2 to see the steps involved in adding a new menu to a menu bar resource.

To get the Beep menu item to do something, you need to assign a command to it, just as you assigned a command to the Beep button in the original BeepWorld program. If you assign the menu item the command beep, choosing this item has the exact same effect as clicking the Beep button. An event will be generated, and the beep command will end up in the commandID field of the HICommand structure of the kEventParamDirectObject parameter of that event. Go ahead and give the Beep menu item a command of beep. For help in doing that, refer back to Figure 3.3.

Because the BeepWorld source code already is set up to handle a beep command (the event handler CommandEventHandler handles that command regardless of what action creates it), you don't have to make any changes to the BeepWorld source code to get the Beep menu item to work. This is the power of the Carbon Event Manager way of doing things. After your code is written to handle one command, it's simple to add the handling of other commands.

Build and run the program. Click the Beep button to verify that it still works. Then choose the Beep menu item from the Sound menu to witness that it acts in the same manner as clicking the Beep button.

BeepWorld 3.0: Implementing Buttons and Menu Items

The purpose of BeepWorld 3.0 is to demonstrate command event handling for a single button and for a menu item, with each providing a different result.

In BeepWorld 2.0, clicking the Beep button and choosing the Beep menu item had the same effect—a single playing of the system alert sound. That demonstrated that to the system, "a command is a command." That is, the system doesn't care about the source of the command; it simply views it as a signal that some action needs to take place. Although your own program might have a menu item and a button that perform the same action, it's more likely that you'll have buttons and menu items that all perform individual, unique acts. In BeepWorld 3.0, that's the case.

For demonstration purposes, the action that takes place in response to a click of a button or a selection from a menu is unimportant, as long as the actions are different.

Because you're now familiar with the SysBeep function, I'll again use a call to that routine here. If the user clicks the Beep button, the system sound plays once. If the user instead chooses the Beep menu item, the system sound will be heard twice.

Start with either the original BeepWorld or the BeepWorld 2.0 project and open the main.nib resource file. To get the Beep menu item to do something other than the Beep button, you need to assign a unique command to it. This command must differ from the command assigned to the button. The button has a command of beep. Give the Beep menu item a command of bep2. If you're working from the BeepWord 2.0 project, that menu item already has a command of beep. Simply edit the command in the menu item's Info window. Figure 3.3 illustrated how to give a menu item a command.

To give the menu item functionality, you need to edit the source code. As it stands now, the source code knows how to handle a beep command, but the bep2 command holds no meaning to it. Open the main.c file and add a new constant beneath the existing kBeepCommand constant:

```
#define      kBeepCommand      'beep'
#define      kBeep2Command     'bep2'
```

The event handler calls the application-defined routine BeepCommandHandler to perform the action associated with the beep command. You'll write another routine to perform the action associated with the new bep2 command. Add a prototype for the function to help the compiler know the format of this routine. Again, the name of this routine can be any name of your choosing.

```
pascal void    BeepCommandHandler( void );
pascal void    Beep2CommandHandler( void );
```

The original CommandEventHandler routine uses GetEventParameter to determine what command occurred. It then uses a switch statement to call the correct routine to handle that command. The original BeepWorld program watched for one command only, so there's only one case label in the switch statement:

```
pascal OSStatus CommandEventHandler( EventHandlerCallRef handlerRef,
                                     EventRef event, void *userData)
{
    OSStatus    result = eventNotHandledErr;
    HICommand   command;

    GetEventParameter( event, kEventParamDirectObject, typeHICommand, NULL,
                   sizeof (HICommand), NULL, &command);

    switch ( command.commandID )
    {
      case kBeepCommand:
          BeepCommandHandler();
          result = noErr;
          break;
    }
    return result;
}
```

For each new command your program is to watch for, you need a new `case` label in the event handler routine. Add a section that handles a `bep2` command. This section responds to that command (using the `kBeep2Command` constant) by calling the new routine `Beep2CommandHandler`. Here's how the `switch` statement looks now:

```
switch ( command.commandID )
{
    case kBeepCommand:
        BeepCommandHandler();
        result = noErr;
        break;

    case kBeep2Command:
        Beep2CommandHandler();
        result = noErr;
        break;
}
```

Now you need to write the new command handler routine. Recall that the command handler routine for the beep command looks like this:

```
pascal void BeepCommandHandler ( void )
{
    SysBeep( 1 );
}
```

To keep things simple, write the new command handler by copying the original routine and then adding a second call to `SysBeep`:

```
pascal void Beep2CommandHandler ( void )
{
    SysBeep( 1 );
    SysBeep( 1 );
}
```

That's it. The project now is set up to create a program that responds depending on whether the Beep button or the Beep menu item is selected. Build and run the program. Click the button to hear a single beep, and then choose the menu item to hear two beeps.

Now that the project is set up to handle both a button click and a menu selection, it's easy to change the functionality of either interface element. To change what happens when the button is clicked, edit the `BeepCommandHandler` function. To change the effect of choosing the menu item, edit the `Beep2CommandHandler` function. If you don't have a Mac programming background, easily achieving some noticeable action might not be possible. `SysBeep` might be the only routine you know about! If that's the case, move on to BeepWorld 4.0 to see how to give a program the capability to draw to a window in response to a menu item selection.

BeepWorld 4.0: Drawing to a Window

The purpose of BeepWorld 4.0 is to demonstrate how to draw some text to a window in response to a menu item selection. A command event can be interpreted by a program in whatever way a programmer wants. If a selection of a menu item is to initiate the drawing of words or graphics to a window, the programmer sets up the program to do so. BeepWorld 4.0 demonstrates how to do this.

When a user of BeepWorld 4.0 chooses the Beep menu item, the system sound plays twice, and *Beep!* is drawn twice to the window as well. Figure 3.5 shows what the BeepWorld 4.0 window looks like. Here the command is issued from a menu selection, but it just as easily could have come from a click on a button.

Figure 3.5   The BeepWorld 4.0 window with text drawn in it.

Start with the BeepWorld 3.0 project. The main.nib resource file remains the same, so you need not open that file. Instead, open main.c to edit the source code. To enable the `Beep2CommandHandler` to draw to the program's window, you need to make the routine aware of that window. If you don't, the drawing could (and very likely would) take place directly on the screen. Passing a reference to the program's window is how you'll let `Beep2CommandHandler` know where to draw. Start the code changes by modifying the `Beep2CommandHandler` prototype. It looked like this before:

```
pascal void    Beep2CommandHandler( void );
```

Now let the compiler know that this routine will be receiving an argument. In particular, it will receive an argument of the type `WindowRef`:

```
pascal void    Beep2CommandHandler( WindowRef window );
```

The `CommandEventHandler` routine invokes `Beep2CommandHandler`. `CommandEventHandler` gets the reference to the affected window directly from the Carbon Event Manager. Recall that when the event handler routine was installed, some user data accompanied the call to `InstallEventHandler`. This could be any data, but I chose to pass a pointer to the program's window. It's the second-from-last argument in the call to `InstallEventHandler`:

```
InstallEventHandler( target, handlerUPP, 1, &cmdEvent,
                     (void *)window, NULL );
```

When the Carbon Event Manager invokes `CommandEventHandler` in response to a command event, it passes the routine three arguments. The last argument is the pointer to the data that was installed:

```
pascal OSStatus CommandEventHandler( EventHandlerCallRef handlerRef,
                                     EventRef event, void *userData)
```

Here `userData` is a generic pointer, so it has to be typecast to the more specific reference to a window:

```
WindowRef     window;

window = ( WindowRef )userData;
```

Now the variable `window` can be used as a `WindowRef` argument in the call to `Beep2CommandHandler`:

```
Beep2CommandHandler( window );
```

Here's the new version of `CommandEventHandler` with the new window-referencing code added to it:

```
pascal OSStatus CommandEventHandler( EventHandlerCallRef handlerRef,
                                     EventRef event, void *userData)
{
   OSStatus     result = eventNotHandledErr;
   HICommand    command;
   WindowRef    window;

   window = ( WindowRef )userData;

   GetEventParameter( event, kEventParamDirectObject, typeHICommand, NULL,
                      sizeof (HICommand), NULL, &command);

   switch ( command.commandID )
   {
      case kBeepCommand:
         BeepCommandHandler();
         result = noErr;
         break;

   case kBeep2Command:
      Beep2CommandHandler( window );
      result = noErr;
      break;
   }
   return result;
}
```

You now need to edit `Beep2CommandHander` so that it draws to the window. The following version of `Beep2CommandHandler` includes calls to three routines with which you might not be familiar. `SetPortWindowPort` ensures that subsequent drawing takes place in the specified window. This routine is described in Chapter 4 and Chapter 7

The `MoveTo` routine specifies a pixel coordinate at which subsequent drawing actions should take place. The first call to `MoveTo` marks 40 pixels from the left edge of the window and 50 pixels down from the top of the window as the place to position the start of the drawing. The `DrawString` routine does just what it says; it draws a string. The `\p` that precedes the text of the string is necessary for `DrawString` to accept the string in Pascal format. Both the `MoveTo` and `DrawString` routines are covered in Chapter 7, "QuickDraw Graphics."

```
pascal void Beep2CommandHandler ( WindowRef window )
{
    SysBeep( 1 );
    SysBeep( 1 );

    SetPortWindowPort( window );
    MoveTo(40,50);
    DrawString("\pBeep!");
    MoveTo(40,80);
    DrawString("\pBeep!");
}
```

Now you're ready to build and run the application. Running BeepWorld 4.0 results in the window shown back in Figure 3.5, less the two lines of text that say *Beep!*. To draw that text to the window, choose the Beep item from the Sound menu.

Experienced Mac Programmer

You probably are familiar with `SetPort`, which is the port-setting routine that's part of the original Macintosh Toolbox. That function accepts a `WindowPtr` as its argument. In Carbon, the `WindowPtr` is out and the `WindowRef` is in. The new `SetPortWindowPort` exists to take the place of `SetPort`. After the port is set, drawing proceeds as it has for Mac OS 8/9, for the most part. Use QuickDraw routines such as `MoveTo` and `DrawString` to achieve the graphics results you want. As shown in the preceding code snippet, those two routines—and most other original QuickDraw routines—remain a part of the API.

MyCloseWindow: Handling a Window-Related Event

The purpose of MyCloseWindow is to demonstrate how to handle a window-related event in a manner different from that governed by the window's standard behavior. In particular, the program responds to a click on the Close button of the program's only window. Instead of just closing the window, the program sounds a beep and then closes the window.

Normally, the Carbon Event Manager's default window event handler handles most window-related events (dragging, resizing, closing, and so forth). It's possible, though, to override the standard behavior the system takes to implement a new behavior. Using this example's technique, you can intervene on any window-related event and then either completely handle the event or handle the event as your program sees fit and then enable the standard behavior to occur.

You can base the MyCloseWindow project on any of the example projects from this chapter. I started with the last version of BeepWorld and made a couple of changes to its resource file and then edited the source code file.

Editing the Nib File

The MyCloseWindow program requires only the standard window and menu bar that are part of any main.nib file created by Project Builder. The window doesn't need to have any buttons; in fact, it doesn't need any items in it at all. In Figure 3.6, you see that I did include one static text item in the window, but that's optional.

Figure 3.6   The MyCloseWindow window and the menu bar nib resources.

If you're working with a copy of a main.nib file that was used with one of the BeepWorld projects, that file's menu bar will include a Sound menu. That menu isn't needed in this MyCloseWindow project. You can leave it in the menu bar, or you can click the Sound menu and press the Delete key to remove it. That's what I did in Figure 3.6. I also edited the name of the application menu so that it now is named MyCloseWindow. Again, that step isn't critical either because this menu won't be used in this example.

Writing the Source Code

Before proceeding, make sure you have a handle on this business of event types. An event type consists of an event class. Direct from our favorite header file, CarbonEvents.h, here are the event class choices from which you can pick:

```
enum {
    kEventClassMouse          = 'mous',
    kEventClassKeyboard       = 'keyb',
    kEventClassTextInput      = 'text',
    kEventClassApplication    = 'appl',
    kEventClassAppleEvent     = 'eppc',
    kEventClassMenu           = 'menu',
    kEventClassWindow         = 'wind',
```

```
            kEventClassControl          = 'cntl',
            kEventClassCommand          = 'cmds',
            kEventClassTablet           = 'tblt',
            kEventClassVolume           = 'vol '
      };
```

All this chapter's previous examples watched for command events, so each example was interested in an event that had a class of `kEventClassCommand`. If you want your program to watch for a particular event that occurs in a window (such as a mouse button click on a window's Close button), the event class you're interested in is `kEventClassWindow`. Now you need to narrow it down to the particular window-related action for which your program is set to watch. For command events, the command kind was `kEventProcessCommand`. I just mentioned a click on the window's Close button, so let's look through the CarbonEvents.h header file to see which window-related kind constant would apply to that type of event:

```
      enum {
            kEventWindowCollapse        = 66,
            kEventWindowCollapsed       = 67,
            kEventWindowCollapseAll     = 68,
            kEventWindowExpand          = 69,
            kEventWindowExpanded        = 70,
            kEventWindowExpandAll       = 71,
            kEventWindowClose           = 72,
```

At the bottom of the list is the event kind of interest—`kEventWindowClose`. If you think that it's odd that this group of constants starts with the value 66, and if you think that it's even more odd that the list holds just seven window-related event kinds (all having to do with a window's size), you're right on with your observations. There are actually *dozens* of window-related event kind constants. They cover just about every conceivable window action. To find out if a window needs updating (that is, if it needs to be redrawn or refreshed), there's `kEventWindowUpdate`. Want to do something special if one of your program's windows is activated (clicked when another window is in front of it)? Make use of the `kEventWindowActivated` event kind constant.

The list goes on and on. For brevity, I've elected to show just a few of the window-related event kind constants. Plenty more are shown, and covered, in Chapter 4. If you want to see *all* the sixty-or-so window-related events covered in a detailed, tutorial fashion, you'll need to make a request to my publisher to put out Volume II–X of this book!

The event type to watch for has a class of `kEventClassWindow` and a type of `kEventWindowClose`. I've changed the name of the `EventTypeSpec` variable from `cmdEvent` to `windowEvt` just to make it clear that this event is window-related rather than command-related:

```
      EventTypeSpec       windowEvent;

      windowEvent.eventClass = kEventClassWindow;
      windowEvent.eventKind  = kEventWindowClose;
```

Most of the `main` function looks the same as other versions of this routine. The few changes are cosmetic rather than functional. In addition to the `EventTypeSpec` name change, I've changed the name of the event handler routine from `CommandEventHandler` to `WindowEventHandler` to reflect the fact that the program now is watching for window-related events rather than command-related events. Here's the affected code:

```
handlerUPP = NewEventHandlerUPP( WindowEventHandler );

InstallEventHandler( target, handlerUPP, 1, &windowEvent,
                     (void *)window, NULL );
```

The event handler routine has the same prototype as before. Recall that it *must* have the same three parameters so that the Carbon Event Manager knows how to invoke it. The body of the routine, however, has changed significantly:

```
pascal OSStatus WindowEventHandler( EventHandlerCallRef handlerRef,
                                    EventRef event, void *userData)
{
    OSStatus    result = eventNotHandledErr;
    UInt32      eventKind;

    eventKind = GetEventKind( event );

    if ( eventKind == kEventWindowClose )
    {
        SysBeep( 1 );
//      result = noErr;   * comment out to force default handler to close window
    }
    return result;
}
```

For command events, I was interested in more than just the event class and kind. I wanted to know the value of the event parameter. Calling `GetEventParameter` tested the parameter to verify whether it was the desired one (kEventParamDirectObject) and, if it was, to return the `HICommand` structure so that the command ID could be extracted. That approach isn't needed in this new event handler. Here, the program isn't interested in the occurrence of a command. It's interested in a click on the window's Close button. That information is held in the event's kind, so the event's parameter value is unimportant now. Just as the `GetEventParameter` returns the value held in one of the parameters of an event, so too does the `GetEventKind` return the value held in the event kind of an event. Pass `GetEventKind` an event and the routine returns the event's kind. An event kind is always of type UInt32 (an unsigned 32-bit integer), so that's the data type of the value that `GetEventKind` returns.

```
UInt32      eventKind;

eventKind = GetEventKind( event );
```

Now test the event kind to see if it corresponds with the event being watched for, which is a close window event. If it is, handle the event. Again, for simplicity, a beeping of the speakers provides the feedback that demonstrates that the code is working.

One very interesting change to the event handler is the removal of the assignment of noErr to the result variable. I've commented out this line of code so that I could leave it in place as a reminder of how this chapter's previous examples worked. The other examples set result to noErr to signal that the event had been handled by the event handler. It was done also to let the Carbon Event Manager know that no further processing of the event was needed. Here in MyCloseWindow, I don't make the assignment, so the event handler ends and returns the initial value of result, which is eventNotHandledErr, to the Carbon Event Manager.

You might wonder what this eventNotHandledErr tells the Carbon Event Manager. It implies that the event wasn't handled and that the Carbon Event Manager needs to perform its standard, default action for an event of this type. Of course, the event handler *did* handle the event as planned, but in using this technique, you also forced the Carbon Event Manager to carry out its normal handling of the event. That normal handling of a window close event would be...yes, to close the window. I want the clicking of the window's Close button to close the window as the user expects. However, I also want another action to take place. That action is the playing of the system sound. Now I've achieved both tasks.

You've seen bits and pieces of the MyCloseWindow code. Take a look at Example 3.4 to see the complete source code listing. Note that because the program doesn't watch for command events, there are no command constants (such as the #define of kBeepCommand) and there is no command-handling routine (such as BeepCommandHandler).

Example 3.4   **Source Code for the MyCloseWindow Program**

```
#include <Carbon/Carbon.h>


pascal OSStatus WindowEventHandler( EventHandlerCallRef handlerRef,
                                    EventRef event, void *userData );

int main( int argc, char* argv[] )
{
   IBNibRef          nibRef;
   WindowRef         window;
   OSStatus          err;
   EventTargetRef    target;
   EventHandlerUPP   handlerUPP;
   EventTypeSpec     windowEvent;

   windowEvent.eventClass = kEventClassWindow;
   windowEvent.eventKind  = kEventWindowClose;
```

```
    err = CreateNibReference( CFSTR("main"), &nibRef );

    err = SetMenuBarFromNib( nibRef, CFSTR("MainMenu") );

    err = CreateWindowFromNib( nibRef, CFSTR("MainWindow"), &window );

    DisposeNibReference( nibRef );

    target = GetWindowEventTarget( window );

    handlerUPP = NewEventHandlerUPP( WindowEventHandler );

    InstallEventHandler( target, handlerUPP, 1, &windowEvent,
                         (void *)window, NULL );

    ShowWindow( window );

    RunApplicationEventLoop();

    return( 0 );
}


pascal OSStatus WindowEventHandler( EventHandlerCallRef handlerRef,
                                    EventRef event, void *userData)
{
   OSStatus   result = eventNotHandledErr;
   UInt32     eventKind;

   eventKind = GetEventKind( event );

   if ( eventKind == kEventWindowClose )
   {
      SysBeep( 1 );
//    result = noErr;  * comment out to force default handler to close window
   }
   return result;
}
```

Do you want your program to sound a beep whenever a user closes a window? Probably not. However, you now know the technique for intercepting a window-related event and adding you own actions to the normal handling of that event. In Chapter 4, you'll see more practical reasons for doing this.

For More Information

For more information about events and the Carbon Event Manager, visit the following web site:

- **Carbon Event Manager API:** `http://`
  `developer.apple.com/techpubs/macosx/Carbon/oss/CarbonEventManager/`
  `Carbon_Event_Manager/index.html`

4

Windows

To display information, a program needs to open at least one window. Most programs, however, enable more than one window to be open at any given time. In this chapter, you'll see how to implement the New item in the File menu so that selecting that menu item opens a new window. You'll also see how to add a second New item to give a user the ability to open a second type of window.

When there are two or more windows on the screen, the task of tracking the windows becomes important. When it comes time to redraw the contents of its windows, you'll want to make sure your program draws the proper content to each window. Thus, window-updating techniques make up an important part of this chapter as well.

To allow each window to have its own unique data associated with it (such as its own user-entered text or graphics), you'll want to know how to store a set of information with each window. In addition, you'll also want to know how to later retrieve that information. These topics are all covered in this chapter.

Opening and Closing Windows

You already know how to open a window in a Mac OS X nib-based program—Chapter 2, "Overview of Mac OS X Programming," demonstrated that technique. First, create a window resource in your project's nib file. Then, in your project's source code file, call `CreateNibReference` to open the nib file and `CreateWindowFromNib` to get a reference to the window resource. Show the newly opened window by calling ShowWindow:

```
IBNibRef    nibRef;
OSStatus    err;
WindowRef   window;

err = CreateNibReference( CFSTR("main"), &nibRef );

err = CreateWindowFromNib( nibRef, CFSTR("MainWindow"), &window );

ShowWindow( window );
```

You also know how your program implements window closing. To close a window, your program does nothing—the Carbon Event Manager handles a click of the window's Close button for you. So, knowing these facts, what's left to learn about opening and closing windows? Actually, there's plenty, as you'll see in this section.

Opening Multiple Windows of the Same Type

Your program might enable more than one window to be open at any given time. Those windows might be of the same type, as in the case of a word processor enabling any number of new, empty document windows to be opened. Typically, such a program enables new windows of the same type to be opened by choosing New from the File menu.

Implementing the New Menu Item in a Nib File

To have your program respond to a user's choosing the New menu item, you'll need to assign that menu item a command. You do that by assigning a command to the New menu item in the menu bar resource of your project's nib resource file. That involves opening the nib file, clicking the New menu item, choosing Show Info from the Tools menu, and then typing a four-character command in the Command field of the Info window. The BeepWorld 2.0 example program from Chapter 3, "Events and the Carbon Event Manager," introduced this technique; several other example programs in that chapter further demonstrated how this is done. To build on this, Figure 4.1 shows what you'll see in Interface Builder if you were to assign nwin (for new window) as the command for the New menu item.

Implementing the New Menu Item in Source Code

To allow any number of identical windows to be opened, you'll package the window-opening code in an application-defined routine and then call that routine in response to the user's choosing the New menu item. The following is such a routine. Note that all its code has been lifted from the main routine shared by all Chapter 3 examples:

```
void CreateMyNewWindow( void )
{
   IBNibRef    nibRef;
```

```
    OSStatus    err;
    WindowRef   window;

    err = CreateNibReference( CFSTR("main"), &nibRef );
    err = CreateWindowFromNib( nibRef, CFSTR("MainWindow"), &window );
    DisposeNibReference( nibRef );

    ShowWindow( window );
}
```

Figure 4.1 Assigning a command to the New menu item.

Every time a program needs to open a new window, it should call the `CreateMyNewWindow` routine to do so. To call this routine in response to a New menu item selection, you'll need to have the call appear in the event handler that's invoked in response to a selection of the New menu item. Here's how that event handler might look:

```
#define    kNewWindowCommand    'nwin'

pascal OSStatus MyAppEventHandler( EventHandlerCallRef handlerRef,
                                   EventRef event, void *userData)
{
    OSStatus    result = eventNotHandledErr;
    HICommand   command;

    GetEventParameter( event, kEventParamDirectObject, typeHICommand,
                   NULL, sizeof (HICommand), NULL, &command);

    switch ( command.commandID )
    {
```

```
        case kNewWindowCommand:
            CreateMyNewWindow();
            result = noErr;
            break;
    }
    return result;
}
```

This routine responds to just one command—the `kNewWindowCommand` command that matches the command assigned to the New menu item in the nib resource file (see Figure 4.1). This event handler gets invoked by the system in response to the user choosing New from the File menu. For the system to invoke this routine in that manner, it first needs to be installed in the Carbon Event Manager. Here's the code that takes care of that task:

```
EventTargetRef  target;
EventHandlerUPP handlerUPP;
EventTypeSpec   appEvent = { kEventClassCommand, kEventProcessCommand };

target = GetApplicationEventTarget( );
handlerUPP = NewEventHandlerUPP( MyAppEventHandler );
InstallEventHandler( target, handlerUPP, 1, &appEvent, 0, NULL );
```

As discussed in Chapter 3, the event that defines a command has an event class of `kEventClassCommand` and an event kind of `kEventProcessCommand`. Use that class and kind in the declaration of an event specification, and then use that `EventTypeSpec` in the installation of the event handler routine. The preceding code snippet does that for an application-defined event handler routine named `MyApplicationEventAHandler`.

One line in the code might have caught your eye—the line that makes use of the call to `GetApplicationEventTarget`. That routine was mentioned in Chapter 3, but most of that chapter's target discussions—and all of that chapter's target examples—relied on the related routine— `GetWindowEventTarget`. Here, however, I'm specifying that the application itself, rather than a window, be the target associated with the event handler routine.

The target is typically the object affected by the event, but choosing the target of an event handler is *not* a process that's set in stone. Being the analytical, methodical people that we programmers are, don't we just hate ambiguous situations like that? As an example of this "looseness" in choosing a target, consider that if you specify that a window should be the target, and you then alter your code so that the application is instead the target, the results might be the same.

Here's why the preceding scenario is possible: If you're writing a handler for a command generated by a button, your first inclination might be to select the button itself to be the target. After all, the button seems to be the target of the user's click of the mouse button. The button, though, is generally not the target of such an action. In short, your goal in choosing a target is to select the object that will be *affected* by an event's action. In this example, it's unlikely that the button itself will be affected by a click of the button. Instead, the affected object will probably be (but not always) the window that holds the button. For instance, clicking a window's Draw button might draw something in that window. The button *initiates* the action, but the window is the *target* of the action.

An event is processed in a *containment hierarchy* that starts at a specific object and works its way up to the application itself. A program should attempt to handle an event at the lowest level first and then, failing that, pass the event up a level. The Carbon Event Manager holds standard event handlers that take care of a number of different event types at a number of different levels in this event hierarchy.

It's best to define an event to be targeted to its lowest level, and then have your program attempt to handle the event at that level. If your program can't handle the event at that level, the event should then be passed to the system where the Carbon Event Manager will attempt to handle it. Looking back at the general format of an event handler reminds you of this event-handling technique:

```
pascal OSStatus MyEventHandler( EventHandlerCallRef handlerRef,
                                EventRef event, void *userData)
{
    OSStatus    result = eventNotHandledErr;

    // attempt to handle the event here and if we can, then tell the
    // Carbon Event Manager that by setting result to noErr:
    result = noErr;

    // if the event *can't* be handled, then we notify the Carbon Event
    // Manager of this fact by sending it the value eventNotHandledErr:
    return result;
}
```

I want my program to handle the New menu item. Choosing this item doesn't act on any existing window. It creates a new window, so it makes sense to name the application itself as the target of the event. The `GetWindowEventTarget` routine requires a window as its argument, and a target is returned. The `GetApplicationEventTarget` needs no argument. That makes sense. A program might have any number of windows that possibly could be a window target, but a program has only one application (itself) that can be the application target.

When installing an event handler for an event that has a window as the target, it often makes sense to use a reference to the window as the user data, like this:

```
InstallEventHandler( target, handlerUPP, 1, &windowEvent,
                     (void *)window, NULL );
```

When installing the event handler for an event that has the application as its target, you might not want to pass along any user data. In such a case, simply use a value of 0 as the second-to-last argument:

```
InstallEventHandler( target, handlerUPP, 1, &appEvent, 0, NULL );
```

MultipleSameTypeWindow Program

The purpose of the MultipleSameTypeWindow program is to demonstrate how a program implements the New menu item to cause any number of windows of the same type to be opened.

The MultipleSameTypeWindow program gathers the code from this section's discussion and presents it as an application that has a functioning New menu item. Each time a user chooses New from the File menu, a new window opens. As per the program name, each new window is identical to the previously opened window. Figure 4.2 shows that each window holds a couple of paragraphs of text (determining the author of said text is left as an exercise for the reader). This figure also shows that each new window will open offset from the previously opened window.

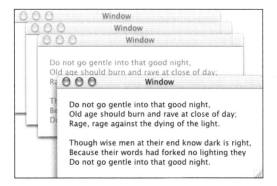

Figure 4.2   The windows displayed by the MultipleSameTypeWindow program.

Editing the Nib File

The project's nib file requires a window resource named MainWindow. Although I've opted to include a static text item in the window, the contents of the window are insignificant. Of more importance is the assignment of a command to the New menu item. Back in Figure 4.1, you saw how to do this. You can use any four-character code you want, but regardless of your choice, you need to take note of it so that you can define a matching constant in the project's source code.

Writing the Source Code

Example 4.1 holds the entire listing for the MultipleSameTypeWindow program. Most of this example's code has been discussed on earlier in this chapter. The exception is the code that offsets a new window from the previously opened window:

Example 4.1 **MultipleSameTypeWindow Source Code**

```
#include <Carbon/Carbon.h>

#define  kNewWindowCommand   'nwin'

pascal OSStatus MyAppEventHandler( EventHandlerCallRef handlerRef,
                                   EventRef event, void *userData );
void CreateMyNewWindow( void );

SInt16   gWindowStartTop  = 40;
SInt16   gWindowStartLeft = 15;

int main(int argc, char* argv[])
{
   IBNibRef          nibRef;
   OSStatus          err;
   EventTargetRef    target;
   EventHandlerUPP   handlerUPP;
   EventTypeSpec     appEvent = { kEventClassCommand,
                                  kEventProcessCommand };

   err = CreateNibReference( CFSTR("main"), &nibRef );
   err = SetMenuBarFromNib( nibRef, CFSTR("MainMenu") );
   DisposeNibReference( nibRef );

   CreateMyNewWindow();

   target = GetApplicationEventTarget( );
   handlerUPP = NewEventHandlerUPP( MyAppEventHandler );
   InstallEventHandler( target, handlerUPP, 1, &appEvent, 0, NULL );

   RunApplicationEventLoop();

   return( 0 );
}


pascal OSStatus MyAppEventHandler( EventHandlerCallRef handlerRef,
                                   EventRef event, void *userData)
{
   OSStatus   result = eventNotHandledErr;
   HICommand  command;

   GetEventParameter( event, kEventParamDirectObject, typeHICommand,
                  NULL, sizeof (HICommand), NULL, &command);

   switch ( command.commandID )
   {
     case kNewWindowCommand:
```

continues

Example 4.1   **Continued**

```
CreateMyNewWindow();
        result = noErr;

break;
    }
    return result;
}


void CreateMyNewWindow( void )
{
    IBNibRef      nibRef;
    OSStatus      err;
    WindowRef     window;

    err = CreateNibReference( CFSTR("main"), &nibRef );
    err = CreateWindowFromNib( nibRef, CFSTR("MainWindow"), &window );
    DisposeNibReference( nibRef );

    MoveWindow ( window, gWindowStartLeft, gWindowStartTop, TRUE );
    ShowWindow( window );

    if ( gWindowStartTop < 200 )
    {
        gWindowStartLeft += 20;
        gWindowStartTop  += 20;
    }
    else
    {
        gWindowStartLeft = 15;
        gWindowStartTop  = 40;
    }
}
```

A window's initial screen placement is defined by the nib window resource used as the window's template. Opening more than one window based on the same nib resource means that new windows appear directly on top of one another. The result of this stacking is that the user might not even be aware that a new window has indeed appeared on screen. The MultipleSameTypeWindow program handles this potential dilemma by opening a new window and then offsetting that window.

The Carbon API routine MoveWindow moves a window to the specified location. The coordinates listed as the second and third arguments to this routine serve to define the new upper-left corner for the window named in the first argument. The final argument to MoveWindow is a Boolean value that specifies that position of the window in the layer of open application windows. A value of TRUE means the window will become the active window. A value of FALSE means the window should retain its current position (which might or might not mean that the window is the active [frontmost] window).

The global variable pair `gWindowStartLeft` and `gWindowStartTop` are used to provide the screen coordinates for the upper-left corner of the first new window. After a window is opened, these global values are incremented so that the next new window appears slightly below and to the right of the previously opened window. So that the windows don't cascade completely offscreen, the global variable values are reset to their initial values after several windows have been opened.

Opening and Closing a Window by Showing and Hiding It

The previous discussion centered on programs that enable multiple windows of the same type to be opened. An application that uses such a technique is usually document-based. A typical document-based program is a word processor or a graphics application.

Other types of applications, however, might enable only one or two windows to appear on screen. A program of this type usually isn't document-based. An example of this type of program is a utility application that displays a window in which the user carries out some calculation. Figure 4.3 provides an example of an application that displays only one window and that doesn't enable multiple copies of this one window to be opened.

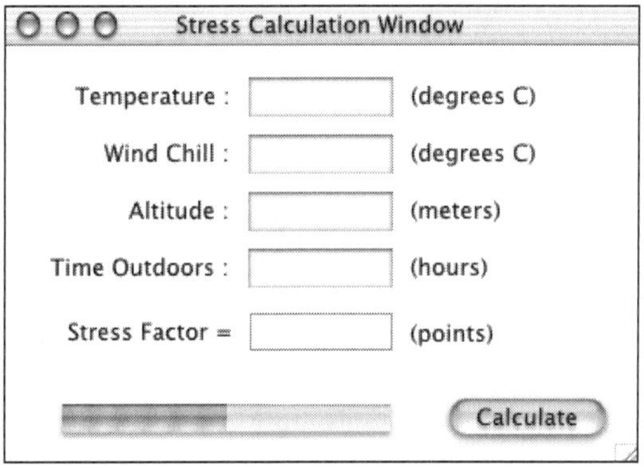

Figure 4.3   An example of a window that isn't document-based.

In a program such as the one pictured in Figure 4.3, there's no need to open multiple copies of the same window. If you're developing such an application, and you want the user to be able to open and close your program's window, it might make sense to open the window at program startup, and then simply hide and reshow this same window rather than actually closing and re-creating a new window.

In such a program, there's no need to open multiple copies of the same window. If you're developing such an application, and you want the user to be able to open and close your program's window, it might make sense to open the window at program startup, and then simply hide and reshow this same window rather than actually closing and re-creating a new window. Doing this means that each time the user chooses the New menu item, your program doesn't have to open the nib file and receive a refererence to the file, copy the window resource to memory and get a reference to that memory, and then close the nib file. Instead, create the window once and let it sit around, perhaps hidden some or even much of the time, for the duration of the program's execution.

This technique of opening a window and then closing it by hiding it rather than actually destroying it also is a good way to preserve a window's state. That might be helpful for a particular application. For instance, if the window has a number of interface items such as radio buttons, checkboxes, or text boxes, and the user enters values in these items, hiding the window won't work because the window loses those values. These values might represent information the user would prefer not to re-enter— something the user that would need to do if the window was "really" closed and then later opened as a new window.

A program that displays a window like the one pictured in Figure 4.3 might enable its File menu items New and Close, but use the items simply to show and hide the program's one window. That way, the window can be created at program start up and need not be created each time the user closes and then opens the window.

The previous example program, MultipleSameTypeWindow, assigned a command to the New menu item so that choosing that menu item results in a new window opening. To have the New menu item show a hidden window rather than open a new window, you'll do the same. In the MultipleSameTypeWindow program, I gave the New menu item a command of `nmai`. You can give that menu item the same command here as well.

By now, you should be accustomed to adding a command to a menu item. If you need a little help, however, refer back to Figure 4.1 to see how this is done. You'll also want to give the Close menu item a command as well. If you use `nmai` for "new main window," you might want to use `cmai` for "close main window." Keep in mind that the functionality of a menu item is determined in your code, not in the nib resource file or by the name of the menu item. Thus, the four-character command you assign to a menu item, as well as the action that results from a selection of a menu item, is entirely up to you.

Your code now has two command constants: one for the New menu item and one for the Close menu item:

```
#define  kNewMainWindowCommand    'nmai'
#define  kCloseMainWindowCommand  'cmai'
```

A single command-handling event handler routine will handle both commands. As you read in the section describing the MultipleSameTypeWindow program, sometimes it makes sense to have an event handler installed at the application level rather than at a lower level (such as for a particular window level).

The following code is another example of an event handler being installed with the application as the target. Having the event handler act at the application level is especially important here because after a window is hidden, an event handler can't show it again (the Carbon Event Manager won't respond properly to act on the window that isn't present on the screen). Here's how the installation of the event handler might look:

```
EventTargetRef  target;
EventHandlerUPP handlerUPP;
EventTypeSpec   appEvent = { kEventClassCommand, kEventProcessCommand };

target = GetApplicationEventTarget( );
handlerUPP = NewEventHandlerUPP( MyAppEventHandler );
InstallEventHandler( target, handlerUPP, 1, &appEvent,
                    (void *)window, NULL );
```

In this chapter's MultipleSameTypeWindow program, the action of the New menu item was implemented in the event handler by calling an application-defined routine that actually opened a new window:

```
switch ( command.commandID )
{
   case kNewWindowCommand:
      CreateMyNewWindow();
      result = noErr;
      break;
}
```

Now we'll replace the call to the application-defined CreateMyNewWindow routine with a call to the Carbon routine ShowWindow:

```
switch ( command.commandID )
{
   case kNewMainWindowCommand:
      ShowWindow( window );
      result = noErr;
      break;
   case kCloseMainWindowCommand:
      HideWindow( window );
      result = noErr;
      break;
}
```

You've already worked with the Carbon routine ShowWindow. Look at any source code listing in this book and you'll see that a call to this routine always appears after a window is created from a call to CreateWindowFromNib. ShowWindow is used to show, or display, a previously hidden window (a window created from a nib resource starts out as invisible).

MenuCloseOneWindow Program

The purpose of the MenuCloseOneWindow program is to demonstrate how a program can simply show and hide an existing window in response to the user opening and closing the window.

The MenuCloseOneWindow displays a single window like the one shown in Figure 4.2. Once again, the content of the window is unimportant to the example at hand, so I've opted to simply reuse the nib resource from the MultipleSameTypeWindow program. This window will be displayed and hidden in response to selections of the New and Close menu items, giving the illusion that the window is actually being opened and closed.

Note that clicking the window's Close button generates an event that *isn't* handled by the program's own event handler. Instead, a Carbon Event Manager standard event handler takes care of that task, as it has in all previous examples in this book. What that means is that closing the window by clicking its Close button really does close the window; it doesn't just hide it. If you use the window's Close button to close the window, choosing New from the File menu won't reopen the window (the attempt to show the now-disposed-of window fails). Later in this chapter, the MenuButtonCloseWindows program solves this problem.

Editing the Nib File

The same nib resource file used for the MultipleSameTypeWindow project can be used here. The `MainWindow` window resource can have any (or no) content. The New menu item should have a command (`nmai` is used here), and the Close menu item should have a command (`cmai` is used in this example).

Writing the Source Code

The MenuCloseOneWindow source code is similar to the MultipleSameTypeWindow source code. The important changes are the addition of a second `#define` to match the command given to the Close menu item, the addition of a second `case` label to the `switch` statement in the event handler, and the use of the Carbon routine `HideWindow` to carry out the action associated with the New and Close menu items. Example 4.2 holds the complete listing for the MenuCloseOneWindow program.

Example 4.2 **MenuCloseOneWindow Source Code**

```
#include <Carbon/Carbon.h>

#define   kNewMainWindowCommand     'nmai'
#define   kCloseMainWindowCommand   'cmai'

pascal OSStatus MyAppEventHandler( EventHandlerCallRef handlerRef,
                                   EventRef event, void *userData );

int main(int argc, char* argv[])
{
    IBNibRef        nibRef;
    OSStatus        err;
    WindowRef       window;
    EventTargetRef  target;
    EventHandlerUPP handlerUPP;
```

```
    EventTypeSpec  appEvent = {kEventClassCommand, kEventProcessCommand};

    err = CreateNibReference( CFSTR("main"), &nibRef );
    err = SetMenuBarFromNib( nibRef, CFSTR("MainMenu") );
    err = CreateWindowFromNib( nibRef, CFSTR("MainWindow"), &window );
    DisposeNibReference( nibRef );

    target = GetApplicationEventTarget( );
    handlerUPP = NewEventHandlerUPP( MyAppEventHandler );
    InstallEventHandler( target, handlerUPP, 1, &appEvent,
                         (void *)window, NULL );

    ShowWindow( window );

    RunApplicationEventLoop();

    return( 0 );
}


pascal OSStatus MyAppEventHandler( EventHandlerCallRef handlerRef,
                                   EventRef event, void *userData )
{
    OSStatus    result = eventNotHandledErr;
    HICommand   command;
    WindowRef   window;

    window = ( WindowRef )userData;

    GetEventParameter( event, kEventParamDirectObject, typeHICommand,
                       NULL, sizeof (HICommand), NULL, &command);

    switch ( command.commandID )
    {
       case kNewMainWindowCommand:
          ShowWindow( window );
          result = noErr;
          break;
       case kCloseMainWindowCommand:
          HideWindow( window );
          result = noErr;
          break;
    }
    return result;
}
```

Using Global Variables to Reference Windows

With the exception of the MultipleSameTypeWindow program, this book's discussions and examples have revolved around applications that display a single window. That simplicity is ideal for demonstrating how to implement specific programming tasks, but it doesn't represent the real world. The majority of applications are capable of displaying more than one window.

Multiple windows can be displayed in two ways. First, a program might allow the opening of more than one window of the same type. For instance, a word processor application lets a user repeatedly choose New from the File menu to open a new, empty document window that's identical to the window opened before it. You've seen how to do that in this chapter's MultipleSameTypeWindow example.

The second way to display multiple windows is to display two or more different types of windows. An example would be a graphics program that displays a window to which you can draw and a different window that holds a palette of drawing tools from which you can choose. Figure 4.3 illustrates this concept. Of course, a program can make use of both multiple window techniques—a graphics program might display one tool palette window and then enable any number of new, empty, identical drawing windows to be opened.

If a program enables numerous windows of the same type to appear at the same time, it doesn't make sense to attempt to track each window by way of its own window reference variable. You wouldn't know in advance how many such variables to allocate. However, when a program opens one or more windows and each is a *different type*, it becomes a practical matter to define a global window reference variable for each type. I'll cover this topic in this section because this technique simplifies the opening and closing of windows.

> **Note**
>
> The updating of window contents is another topic that lends itself well to global window reference variables, so you can expect to see examples later in this chapter in the "Updating Window Content" section.

To make use of global window references, declare a global `WindowRef` variable for each type of window your program uses. To make the reference global, declare it outside `main` or any other routine. You can give such a variable any name, but the commonly used convention in Macintosh programming is to start such a variable name with a lowercase `g` (for *global*).

Consider a program that displays two windows: one window is the main window and another window is the information window. The two `WindowRef` declarations might look like this:

```
#include <Carbon/Carbon.h>

WindowRef       gMainWindow;
WindowRef       gInfoWindow;
```

```
int main( int argc, char* argv[] )
{
   IBNibRef          nibRef;
   OSStatus          err;
   ...
```

Near the start of `main`, you'll want to create one instance of each window. Depending on your program, you also might want to show each window at startup as well:

```
err = CreateWindowFromNib( nibRef, CFSTR("MainWindow"), &gMainWindow );
err = CreateWindowFromNib( nibRef, CFSTR("InfoWindow"), &gInfoWindow );

ShowWindow( gMainWindow );
ShowWindow( gInfoWindow );
```

At this point, either window can be referenced at any time, from any routine. This is handy when updating (as you'll see later in this chapter) and closing a window:

```
HideWindow( gInfoWindow );
```

GlobalWindows Program

The purpose of the GlobalWindows program is to provide a simple example of how global variables can be used to reference windows. This program also illustrates the use of a *utility*, or *floating*, window.

Figure 4.4 shows the two windows displayed by the GlobalWindows program. Two global variables are used here—one to keep track of each window.

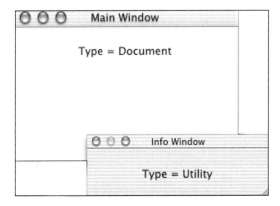

Figure 4.4 The windows displayed by the GlobalWindows program.

The GlobalWindows program includes a utility window titled *Info Window*. A program typically uses a utility window when the window's information needs to be easily accessible at any time. For instance, a graphics program might use a utility window to display its tool palette.

Notice that in comparison to the window titled *Main Window*, this utility window has a smaller title bar, smaller buttons in the title bar, and smaller text in its title. Additionally, this window cannot be minimized. Running the program also reveals that this window always remains the frontmost window. If you click the other window—the one titled *Main Window*—that Main Window will become active (its title bar will become highlighted). The Info Window, however, remains in front of the Main Window.

Editing the Nib File

The GlobalWindows program displays two types of windows, so the project requires two window resources in its nib file. To add a second window to a nib file, click the right-most button at the top of the Interface Builder palette window (that button displays a small window, as shown in Figure 4.5), click the window that includes three buttons in its title bar, and drag and drop that window onto the main.nib window. Name the new window by double-clicking its name in the main.nib window and typing the new name. In Figure 4.5, I've given the new window the name *InfoWindow*.

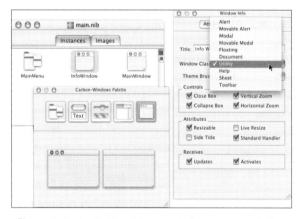

Figure 4.5   A nib file with two window resources in it.

By default, Interface Builder gives a new "three button" window a window type of Document. To change the window type, click the window in the main.nib window, and then choose Show Info from the Tools menu. Now click the Window Class pop-up menu and choose the preferred type.

In Figure 4.5, I'm changing the InfoWindow from a document window to a utility window. A floating window looks identical to a utility window, and it too remains in front of document windows. The primary difference between a utility window and a floating window is that the utility window is displayed in front of document windows *and* in front of floating windows.

Writing the Source Code

Example 4.3 shows the complete listing for the GlobalWindows program. Notice that no special handling of the utility window is necessary from the source code. After a window is defined as a utility window in the nib resource, the system knows how to handle its look and screen placement.

Example 4.3 **GlobalWindows Source Code**

```
#include <Carbon/Carbon.h>

WindowRef    gMainWindow;
WindowRef    gInfoWindow;

int main( int argc, char* argv[] )
{
   IBNibRef    nibRef;
   OSStatus    err;

   err = CreateNibReference( CFSTR("main"), &nibRef );
   err = SetMenuBarFromNib( nibRef, CFSTR("MainMenu") );
   err = CreateWindowFromNib(nibRef, CFSTR("MainWindow"), &gMainWindow);
   err = CreateWindowFromNib(nibRef, CFSTR("InfoWindow"), &gInfoWindow)
   DisposeNibReference( nibRef );

   ShowWindow( gMainWindow );
   ShowWindow( gInfoWindow );

   RunApplicationEventLoop();

   return( 0 );
}
```

Showing and Hiding Multiple Windows

Using global window reference variables along with the ShowWindow and HideWindow routines is a good technique to handle window opening and closing for a program that has a couple or a few different types of windows.

This chapter's MenuCloseOneWindow program displayed just one window, so it made sense to pass that window as the user data during the installation of the event handler:

```
target = GetApplicationEventTarget( );
handlerUPP = NewEventHandlerUPP( MyAppEventHandler );
InstallEventHandler( target, handlerUPP, 1, &appEvent,
                     (void *)window, NULL );
```

Within that program's event handler, the window was extracted from the user data and used in calls to ShowWindow and HideWindow to show and hide the one window:

```
window = ( WindowRef )userData;

GetEventParameter( event, kEventParamDirectObject, typeHICommand,
                   NULL, sizeof (HICommand), NULL, &command);

switch ( command.commandID )
{
   case kNewMainWindowCommand:
      ShowWindow( window );
      result = noErr;
      break;
   case kCloseMainWindowCommand:
      HideWindow( window );
      result = noErr;
      break;
}
```

A program that displays two windows, each of a different type, could declare a global variable for each, use two calls to CreateWindowFromNib to create an instance of each type of window, and then install the event handler without passing a reference to either window:

```
WindowRef       gTypeAWindow;
WindowRef       gTypeBWindow;

...

err = CreateWindowFromNib( nibRef, CFSTR("WindowA"), &gTypeAWindow );
err = CreateWindowFromNib( nibRef, CFSTR("WindowB"), &gTypeBWindow );

DisposeNibReference( nibRef );

target = GetApplicationEventTarget( );
handlerUPP = NewEventHandlerUPP( MyAppEventHandler );
InstallEventHandler( target, handlerUPP, 1, &appEvent, 0, NULL );
```

In the preceding snippet, note that the second-from-last InstallEventHandler argument is 0, whereas in all other examples, it's been a generic pointer to a window, as in (void *)window. This new code is meant to handle menu items that work with more than one particular window, so passing one particular window to the event handler wouldn't serve much of a purpose.

With the event handler receiving no reference to a window, how does it go about determining which window or windows to open or close? Two methods are used for the determination. For opening a window, a separate New menu item can exist for each type of window. That's a technique you find in a lot of programs, including Apple's Project Builder IDE. That program has a File menu that includes a New Project menu item for opening a new project window and a New File menu item for opening a new source code file.

Here's how the `switch` statement in an event handler could take care of the opening of two types of windows (which really is the *showing* of one of two previously created windows):

```
#define    kNewTypeAWindowCommand     'newA'
#define    kNewTypeBWindowCommand     'newB'

...

switch ( command.commandID )
{
   case kNewTypeAWindowCommand:
      ShowWindow( gTypeAWindow );
      result = noErr;
      break;
   case kNewTypeBWindowCommand:
      ShowWindow( gTypeBWindow );
      result = noErr;
      break;
```

Closing a window involves a different technique. In this case, the global window reference variables aren't needed. In a Macintosh program, it's common practice for the File menu to have a single Close menu item, regardless of the number of types of windows the program displays. In addition, it's common practice for that Close menu item to close the frontmost window, regardless of the type of window that the frontmost window might be. Thus, to implement the Close menu item, you'll determine which window is frontmost and then hide that window. Fortunately, the Carbon `FrontWindow` routine makes that task easy:

```
#define    kCloseFrontWindowCommand   'cfnt'

...

WindowRef     window;

...

case kCloseFrontWindowCommand:
   window = FrontWindow();
   HideWindow( window );
   result = noErr;
   break;
```

Combining this `case` section with the two `case` sections in the previous snippet (the `case` sections for the `kNewTypeAWindowCommand` label and the `kNewTypeBWindowCommand` label) results in an event handler that opens and closes (shows and hides) two types of windows. The next example program provides a complete example of how that's done.

MenuCloseTwoWindows Program

The purpose of the MenuCloseTwoWindows program is to demonstrate how to use the `ShowWindow/HideWindow` technique to open and close more than one type of window from the File menu. This chapter's MenuCloseOneWindow program used the `ShowWindow` and `HideWindow` routines to show and hide a single window. Here I'll use that same routine to show and hide two windows.

The MenuCloseTwoWindows program displays two New menu items—one for each of the program's two types of windows. To make it easy to distinguish between the windows, the program draws text in one and numbers in the other. Figure 4.6 shows the program's File menu and its two windows.

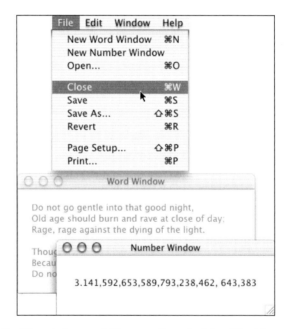

Figure 4.6   The windows and File menu from the MenuNewClose program.

To close a window, click it to make it active and then choose the Close menu item. To reopen a closed window, choose the appropriate New menu item. As in the MenuCloseOneWindow program, closing a window by clicking its Close button closes the window for good; choosing the corresponding New menu item can't reopen it. This chapter's MenuButtonCloseWindows program demonstrates how to integrate the Close button into the `ShowWindow/HideWindow` approach of opening and closing windows.

Editing the Nib File

The nib file requires a menu bar that includes a File menu with the items shown in Figure 4.6. In Interface Builder, edit the existing New item to say *New Word Window*, and then add a menu item beneath the New Word Window item. To add the new menu item to the existing File menu, follow these steps in Interface Builder:

1. Click the File menu in the menu bar window to expose the items in that menu.

2. Click the leftmost button running along the top of the palette window.

3. Click the blue box titled Item in the palette window and drag and drop this box under the New Word Window item in the File menu in the menu bar window.

4. Double-click the newly added item and type the name New Number Window for the menu item.

Now click the New Word Window item and choose Show Info from the Tools menu. Type nwrd (for new word window) in the Command field of the Info window, as shown in Figure 4.7. In a similar manner, give the New Number Window item a command of nnum (for new number window) and the Close item a command of cfnt (for close frontmost window).

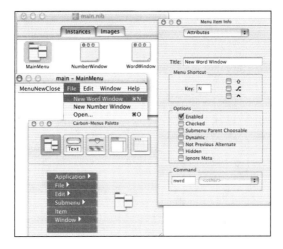

Figure 4.7   Assigning a command to a program's New menu item.

The nib file requires two window resources. Change the name of the existing window resource from MainWind to WordWindow by double-clicking its name in the main.nib window and typing the new name. Add a second window by clicking the right-most button in the palette window and then dragging and dropping a window onto the main.nib window. As shown in Figure 4.7, this new window should have the name NumberWindow.

Writing the Source Code

Example 4.4 provides the entire listing for the MenuCloseTwoWindows program. The three #defines have values that match the three commands assigned to the menu items in the nib file. Also note that the two calls to `CreateWindowFromNib` need to have window names that match the window resource names (`WordWindow` and `NumberWindow`). The two function calls also include the proper global window reference variables (`gWordWindow` and `gNumberWindow`) as arguments.

Example 4.4 **MenuCloseTwoWindows Source Code**

```
#include <Carbon/Carbon.h>

#define    kNewWordWindowCommand      'nwrd'
#define    kNewNumberWindowCommand    'nnum'
#define    kCloseFrontWindowCommand   'cfnt'

pascal OSStatus MyAppEventHandler( EventHandlerCallRef handlerRef,
                                   EventRef event, void *userData );
WindowRef    gWordWindow;
WindowRef    gNumberWindow;

int main( int argc, char* argv[] )
{
   IBNibRef        nibRef;
   OSStatus        err;
   EventTargetRef  target;
   EventHandlerUPP handlerUPP;
   EventTypeSpec   appEvent= {kEventClassCommand, kEventProcessCommand};

   err = CreateNibReference( CFSTR("main"), &nibRef );
   err = SetMenuBarFromNib( nibRef, CFSTR("MainMenu") );
   err = CreateWindowFromNib(nibRef, CFSTR("WordWindow"), &gWordWindow);
   err = CreateWindowFromNib(nibRef, CFSTR("NumberWindow"),
                             &gNumberWindow);
   DisposeNibReference( nibRef );

   target = GetApplicationEventTarget( );
   handlerUPP = NewEventHandlerUPP( MyAppEventHandler );
   InstallEventHandler( target, handlerUPP, 1, &appEvent, 0, NULL );

   ShowWindow( gWordWindow );
   ShowWindow( gNumberWindow );

   RunApplicationEventLoop();

   return( 0 );
}


pascal OSStatus MyAppEventHandler( EventHandlerCallRef handlerRef,
```

```
                                      EventRef event, void *userData)
{
   OSStatus    result = eventNotHandledErr;
   HICommand   command;
   WindowRef   window;

   GetEventParameter( event, kEventParamDirectObject, typeHICommand,
                 NULL, sizeof (HICommand), NULL, &command );

   switch ( command.commandID )
   {
      case kNewWordWindowCommand:
         ShowWindow( gWordWindow );
         result = noErr;
         break;
      case kNewNumberWindowCommand:
         ShowWindow( gNumberWindow );
         result = noErr;
         break;
      case kCloseFrontWindowCommand:
         window = FrontWindow();
         HideWindow( window );
         result = noErr;
         break;
   }
   return result;
}
```

Hiding a Window Using the Window's Close Button

Closing a window by clicking the window's Close button is a task normally handled by the Carbon Event Manager. To round out the show/hide technique, you'll want to have your program take control of this type of event so that the affected window can be hidden simply with a call to HideWindow, instead of deallocating its memory, as would be the case if the window were actually being closed.

The Chapter 3 program MyCloseWindow supplies you with the information you need to change the behavior of a window's Close button. You'll declare an event specification for a window close event, and then pass that specification to InstallEventHandler:

```
EventTypeSpec  windowEvent = { kEventClassWindow, kEventWindowClose };

...

err = CreateWindowFromNib( nibRef, CFSTR("WordWindow"), &window );

target = GetWindowEventTarget( window );
handlerUPP = NewEventHandlerUPP( MyWindowEventHandler );
```

```
InstallEventHandler( target, handlerUPP, 1, &windowEvent,
                     (void *)window, NULL );
```

In the MyCloseWindow program, the event handler routine
MyWindowEventHandler made a call to `SysBeep` in response to a window close
event. In Chapter 3, I promised that this technique of intercepting a window-related
event would be put to better use. Here's where that's done. In the following version of
MyWindowEventHandler, a call to `HideWindow` hides the affected window. The variable `result` then is assigned a value of `noErr` so that the Carbon Event Manager is
notified that the program's event handler took care of the event. If the code didn't
return this value, the window would be hidden and the Carbon Event Manager would
go ahead and *really* close the window.

```
pascal OSStatus MyWindowEventHandler( EventHandlerCallRef handlerRef,
                                      EventRef event, void *userData )
{
    OSStatus    result = eventNotHandledErr;
    UInt32      eventKind;
    WindowRef   window;

    window = ( WindowRef )userData;

    eventKind = GetEventKind( event );

    if ( eventKind == kEventWindowClose )
    {
        HideWindow( window );
        result = noErr;
    }
    return result;
}
```

MenuButtonCloseWindows Program

The purpose of the MenuButtonCloseWindows program is to provide a complete example of using the `ShowWindow`/`HideWindow` technique to enable more than one type of window to be opened and closed from the File menu and to be closed with a click on a
window's Close button. This program expands upon the previous example,
MenuCloseTwoWindows, so a few comparisons can be made between the two examples.

This program displays the same File menu and two windows that are displayed by
MenuCloseTwoWindows (refer to Figure 4.6). To create these interface elements, this
example uses the same nib file as the MenuCloseTwoWindows example. No changes
are needed.

Example 4.5 shows the complete source code listing for the
MenuButtonCloseWindows program. In the source code, #defines, the
`MyAppEventHandler` routine, and the global window reference variables all remain
unchanged from the source code of the MenuCloseTwoWindows program. This new

program adds a second event handler routine (`MyWindowEventHandler`) to the one event handler routine present in the MenuCloseTwoWindows program (`MyAppEventHandler`).

Note that Example 4.5 introduces the concept of using the same event handler routine for more than one target. To force a window's Close button to hide the window, each window installs the same event handler, `MyWindowEventHandler`, with itself as the target. A second example of using the same event handler for different windows can be found near the end of this chapter in the SameTypeWindowWithData example program.

Example 4.5 **MenuButtonCloseWindows Source Code**

```
#include <Carbon/Carbon.h>

#define    kNewWordWindowCommand     'nwrd'
#define    kNewNumberWindowCommand   'nnum'
#define    kCloseFrontWindowCommand  'cfnt'

pascal OSStatus MyAppEventHandler( EventHandlerCallRef handlerRef,
                                   EventRef event, void *userData );

pascal OSStatus MyWindowEventHandler( EventHandlerCallRef handlerRef,
                                      EventRef event, void *userData );

WindowRef    gWordWindow;
WindowRef    gNumberWindow;

int main( int argc, char* argv[] )
{
    IBNibRef         nibRef;
    OSStatus         err;
    EventTargetRef   target;
    EventHandlerUPP  handlerUPP;
    EventTypeSpec    appEvent= {kEventClassCommand, kEventProcessCommand};
    EventTypeSpec    windowEvent = {kEventClassWindow, kEventWindowClose};

    err = CreateNibReference( CFSTR("main"), &nibRef );
    err = SetMenuBarFromNib( nibRef, CFSTR("MainMenu") );
    err = CreateWindowFromNib(nibRef, CFSTR("WordWindow"), &gWordWindow);

    target = GetWindowEventTarget( gWordWindow );
    handlerUPP = NewEventHandlerUPP( MyWindowEventHandler );
    InstallEventHandler( target, handlerUPP, 1, &windowEvent,
                         (void *)gWordWindow, NULL );

    err = CreateWindowFromNib( nibRef, CFSTR("NumberWindow"),
                               &gNumberWindow );

    target = GetWindowEventTarget( gNumberWindow );
```

continues

Example 4.5   **Continued**

```
    handlerUPP = NewEventHandlerUPP( MyWindowEventHandler );
    InstallEventHandler( target, handlerUPP, 1, &windowEvent,
                         (void *)gNumberWindow, NULL );

    DisposeNibReference( nibRef );

    target = GetApplicationEventTarget( );
    handlerUPP = NewEventHandlerUPP( MyAppEventHandler );
    InstallEventHandler( target, handlerUPP, 1, &appEvent, 0, NULL );

    ShowWindow( gWordWindow );
    ShowWindow( gNumberWindow );

    RunApplicationEventLoop();

    return( 0 );
}


pascal OSStatus MyWindowEventHandler( EventHandlerCallRef handlerRef,
                                      EventRef event, void *userData)
{
    OSStatus    result = eventNotHandledErr;
    UInt32      eventKind;
    WindowRef   window;

    window = ( WindowRef )userData;


    eventKind = GetEventKind( event );

    if ( eventKind == kEventWindowClose )
    {
      HideWindow( window );
      result = noErr;
    }
    return result;
}


pascal OSStatus MyAppEventHandler( EventHandlerCallRef handlerRef,
                                   EventRef event, void *userData)
{
    OSStatus    result = eventNotHandledErr;
    HICommand   command;
    WindowRef   window;

    GetEventParameter( event, kEventParamDirectObject, typeHICommand,
                   NULL, sizeof (HICommand), NULL, &command );
```

```
   switch ( command.commandID )
   {
      case kNewWordWindowCommand:
         ShowWindow( gWordWindow );
         result = noErr;
         break;
      case kNewNumberWindowCommand:
         ShowWindow( gNumberWindow );
         result = noErr;
         break;
      case kCloseFrontWindowCommand:
         window = FrontWindow();
         HideWindow( window );
         result = noErr;
         break;
   }
   return result;
}
```

Updating Window Content

A window's content can come from resources in a nib file. Up to this point in the book, that's always been the case. If a window included a button, it was from a button item added to the window resource. If a window included text, it was from a static text item added to the window resource.

The Carbon Event Manager, by way of its standard event handlers, knows how to update a window to properly draw all its resource-related content. The code so far in this book verifies this. None of the example programs includes any code to update a window; yet, when an example program is run and its window is obscured and then returned to full view, the window's contents are correctly redrawn.

Your program likely will include one or more windows that include content generated from resource items. However, your program also might include one or more windows that include dynamic content—text, graphics, and pictures. The system will handle *resource-related* window content updates for you, but the updating of *code-generated* window content is up to you.

Introduction to Window Updating

Here's how your program will handle window updating: you write a routine that draws the window's content, and then you make sure that the routine gets called when a window update event occurs. That's a bit of an oversimplification, but it sums up nicely how window updating works, and it hints that this task won't be difficult to handle.

A window's content can be any combination of many entities: text, numbers, simple graphics, complex graphics, digitized images, movies, and on and on. The particulars of updating each type of content varies. The general approach to updating doesn't.

In this section of the chapter, I'll select one type of content—text—and examine how that content is updated. After you understand the updating technique for text, you'll be able to apply it to other types of content, such as graphics.

Drawing Text to a Window

The easiest way to display a small amount of text in a window is to use the Carbon `DrawString` routine. The `DrawString` routine was briefly mentioned in Chapter 3. `DrawString` accepts a Pascal-formatted string (a string prefaced by `\p`) as its one argument, and it then proceeds to draw that string to a specified window. Where that text is drawn depends on the current position of the graphics pen.

Graphics pen is the term given to a set of values that collectively specify how subsequent drawing should take place. For instance, the graphics pen specifies the thickness of lines that are drawn and the pixel location for the start of a drawing. In the case of drawing text, the starting location (the positioning of the graphics pen) is important. You set this starting position by calling the Carbon `MoveTo` routine.

As its name implies, `MoveTo` moves the graphics pen to a specified location. `MoveTo` accepts two arguments: the horizontal placement of the pen and the vertical placement of the pen. The upper-left corner of a window's content area is considered to have an x, or horizontal, value of 0, and a y, or vertical, value of 0. Thus, the following call to `MoveTo` would establish the starting point for drawing at 10 pixels in from the left edge of a window and 30 pixels down from the top of that window:

```
MoveTo( 10, 30 );
```

The WindowUpdate example program that follows this discussion includes a call to `MoveTo`. That call sets the graphics pen 30 pixels in from the left of the window and 60 pixels down from the top of that window. You can peek ahead at Figure 4.8 to see that example program's window and take note of where the *T* of the word *This* from the string *This is drawn from code!* starts. That string is the result of the following code:

```
MoveTo( 30,60 );
DrawString( "\pThis is drawn from code!" );
```

Updating Text

Now you know how to draw text in a window. However, drawing text once doesn't have anything to do with updating that text. If you include a call to `DrawString` in your program's main routine, the text might very well be drawn to your program's window. Obscure that window by dragging most of it offscreen and then reveal it again by dragging it back onscreen, and the result will be a window void of the text! This happens because the call to `DrawString` needs to be made each time the window needs to be updated (or redrawn or refreshed). Your program can become aware of when a window needs updating by watching for a window update event. Such an event has a class of `kEventClassWindow` and a kind of `kEventWindowDrawContent`:

```
EventTypeSpec    windowEvent ;
```

```
windowEvent.eventClass = kEventClassWindow;
windowEvent.eventKind  = kEventWindowDrawContent;
```

Now is as good a time as any to point out that the previous method of defining an event—declaring the event specification variable and then assigning values to each of its two members—isn't the only way of defining that event. An alternate means of accomplishing the same task is to perform the assignment at the time of the declaration:

```
EventTypeSpec   windowEvent = { kEventClassWindow,
                                kEventWindowDrawContent };
```

Regardless of how the event is defined, the next step is to use the event in the installation of a window event handler. In the following code, it's done to install an event handler routine named `WindowEventHandler` for a window that's already been created with a call to `CreateWindowFromNib`:

```
EventTargetRef   target;
EventHandlerUPP  handlerUPP;
EventTypeSpec    windowEvent = { kEventClassWindow, kEventWindowDrawContent };

target = GetWindowEventTarget( window );
handlerUPP = NewEventHandlerUPP( WindowEventHandler );
InstallEventHandler( target, handlerUPP, 1, &windowEvent,
                     (void *)window, NULL );
```

Now let's take a look at the event handler. This routine should extract the affected window from the `userData` argument so that the proper window can be updated. Call `GetEventKind` to verify that the event is a window update event, and then call an application-defined `UpdateWindow` routine to carry out the actual updating.

```
pascal OSStatus WindowEventHandler( EventHandlerCallRef handlerRef,
                                    EventRef event, void *userData)
{
   OSStatus   result = eventNotHandledErr;
   UInt32     eventKind;
   WindowRef  window;

   window = ( WindowRef )userData;

   eventKind = GetEventKind( event );

   if ( eventKind == kEventWindowDrawContent )
   {
      UpdateWindow( window );
   }
   return result;
}
```

Before moving on to the code that makes up the `UpdateWindow` routine, take another look at the `if` statement in the preceding `WindowEventHandler` function. Recall from previous event handlers that after an event is handled, `result` is set to `noErr` to let the Carbon Event Manager know that it does *not* have to handle the event. *The preceding routine doesn't do that.* The effect of this is that `result` keeps its initial value of `eventNotHandledErr`, which gets returned to the Carbon Event Manager. That means that the Carbon Event Manager won't be aware of the handling of the event, and it too will handle the event using its standard event handler for this type of event.

Building on this concept, your `UpdateWindow` routine will update the content of the window for which your program's code is responsible. This content might be created by calls to `DrawString`. Your `UpdateWindow` routine won't update resource-related content. As you've done in the past, you'll leave that up to the system. By telling the Carbon Event Manager that the update event *wasn't* handled, you're letting the Carbon Event Manager know that it should go forth with its normal updating of resource-related window content.

Now comes the `UpdateWindow` routine. There is no one way to write to a routine; it's truly application-specific. A program that draws one line of text in a window will have an `UpdateWindow` routine that might include just a single call to `MoveTo` and a single call to DrawString. A program that draws text, graphics, and pictures in a window will have an `UpdateWindow` routine that could include dozens of calls to a variety of QuickDraw graphics routines. (QuickDraw is the topic of Chapter 7, "QuickDraw Graphics.") Two points will generally hold true, though: the function needs to know which window to update and that window's port needs to be set:

```
void UpdateWindow( WindowRef window )
{
    SetPortWindowPort( window );

    // code to draw the contents of the window goes here
}
```

Before a program starts calling drawing routines, it should specify where that drawing is to take place. On a Macintosh, drawing takes place in a *port*. In Macintosh programming parlance, a port is a data structure that defines a drawing environment.

The computer screen itself is considered a port. That makes it possible for the system to direct drawing of the desktop to the monitor. Each window has a port, which makes it possible for your program to specify to which window drawing should take place. If you don't specify the port in which drawing is to take place, the results will be unpredictable. Your drawing *might* work as you intended, or it might not. The Carbon `SetPortWindowPort` routine lets you specify the port to which to draw. Pass this routine a reference to a window and all subsequent drawing routines will operate in the port of that window.

WindowUpdate Program

The purpose of the WindowUpdate program is to demonstrate a technique for updating the application-defined content of a window.

Figure 4.8 shows the results from running the WindowUpdate program. As you can surmise from the content of the window, this program demonstrates the updating of content derived from resources (a static text item in a window resource) and from code (a string of text drawn from a call to `DrawString` in an update routine).

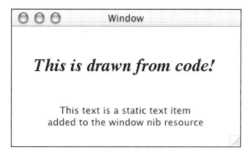

Figure 4.8   The window displayed by the WindowUpdate program.

The nib file holds a window with one static text item, as shown in Figure 4.9. It isn't important what text appears in the static text item. In fact, it isn't even important what kind of resource item appears in the window. What is important, however, is that you can verify that the program updates resource-related content and code-created content.

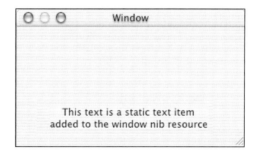

Figure 4.9   The window resource from the UpdateWindow nib file.

As shown in the program source listing in Example 4.6, the program uses the technique of responding to an event of class `kEventClassWindow` and kind `kEventWindowDrawContent`. When such an event occurs, the event handler calls this application-defined routine:

```
void UpdateWindow( WindowRef window )
{
   FMFontFamily      fontFamily;

   SetPortWindowPort( window );

   fontFamily = FMGetFontFamilyFromName( "\pTimes" );
   TextFont( fontFamily );
   TextFace( bold + italic );
```

```
    TextSize( 24 );
    MoveTo( 30, 60 );
    DrawString( "\pThis is drawn from code!" );
}
```

`UpdateWindow` could simply draw a line of text in the system font, but I've opted to take this opportunity to demonstrate the use of a few Carbon routines that alter the characteristics of the drawn text. Back in Figure 4.8, you saw the line of text that results from the call to `UpdateWindow`. The font used in the drawing is set with a call to `TextFont`. Before calling `TextFont`, call `FMGetFontFamilyFromName` to get a `FMFontFamily` reference to the desired font. Pass `FMGetFontFamilyFromName` the name of the font of interest. Even though you're programming in C, this routine is expecting the font name in the form of a Pascal string, so preface the name with \p.

To change the face, or style, of drawn text, call `TextFace`. Use Apple-defined constants alone or in conjunction with one another as the argument to `TextFace`. The values `bold`, `italic`, and `normal` are three of the constants. Chapter 7 lists the others. To change the size of text that's drawn by calls to `DrawString`, you'll use the `TextSize` routine. Pass `TextSize` the size in points.

After calls to characteristic-changing routines such as `TextFont`, `TextFace`, and `TextSize`, all subsequent drawing of text takes place with the newly specified look. To draw text with a different look, call any one of the same routines, as illustrated in the following code:

```
    TextFace( bold );
    MoveTo( 10, 30 );
    DrawString( "\pThis text is bold." );
    TextFace( italic );
    MoveTo( 10, 50 );
    DrawString( "\pThis text appears is italic." );
```

Example 4.6   **UpdateWindow Source Code**

```
#include <Carbon/Carbon.h>


pascal OSStatus WindowEventHandler( EventHandlerCallRef handlerRef,
                                    EventRef event, void *userData );


void UpdateWindow( WindowRef window );

int main(int argc, char* argv[])
{
    IBNibRef         nibRef;
    OSStatus         err;
    WindowRef        window;
    EventTargetRef   target;
    EventHandlerUPP  handlerUPP;
    EventTypeSpec    windowEvent = { kEventClassWindow,
                                     kEventWindowDrawContent };
```

```
    err = CreateNibReference( CFSTR("main"), &nibRef );
    err = SetMenuBarFromNib( nibRef, CFSTR("MainMenu") );
    err = CreateWindowFromNib( nibRef, CFSTR("MainWindow"), &window );
    DisposeNibReference( nibRef );

    target = GetWindowEventTarget( window );
    handlerUPP = NewEventHandlerUPP( WindowEventHandler );
    InstallEventHandler( target, handlerUPP, 1, &windowEvent,
                         (void *)window, NULL );

    ShowWindow( window );

    RunApplicationEventLoop();

    return( 0 );
}


pascal OSStatus WindowEventHandler( EventHandlerCallRef handlerRef,
                                    EventRef event, void *userData)
{
    OSStatus    result = eventNotHandledErr;
    UInt32      eventKind;
    WindowRef   window;

    window = ( WindowRef )userData;

    eventKind = GetEventKind( event );

    if ( eventKind == kEventWindowDrawContent )
    {
        UpdateWindow( window );
    }
    return result;
}


void UpdateWindow( WindowRef window )
{
    FMFontFamily    fontFamily;

    SetPortWindowPort( window );

    fontFamily = FMGetFontFamilyFromName( "\pTimes" );
    TextFont( fontFamily );
    TextFace( bold + italic );
    TextSize( 24 );
    MoveTo( 30,60 );
    DrawString( "\pThis is drawn from code!" );
}
```

Updating Multiple Windows

This chapter's MenuButtonCloseWindows example created two windows, each tracked by a global window reference variable. The program defined one window event handler and then installed that same handler for each window. In that example, the event handler responded to a window close event so that a click of a window's Close button would result in the hiding of the window instead of the actual disposing of the window. If a program that used global window references instead wanted to watch for update events, a similar technique could be used. Instead of a window close event, you would define a window update event:

```
EventTypeSpec  windowEvent = { kEventClassWindow,
                                     kEventWindowDrawContent };
```

You would then create one window and install the event handler for that window:

```
WindowRef    gWindowType1;

err = CreateWindowFromNib( nibRef, CFSTR("MainWindow"), &gWindowType1 );

target = GetWindowEventTarget( gWindowType1 );
handlerUPP = NewEventHandlerUPP( MyWindowEventHandler );
InstallEventHandler( target, handlerUPP, 1, &windowEvent,
                     (void *)gWindowType1, NULL );
```

You would do this for each type of window, making sure that the establishment of the target and the installation of the event handler routine used the same window reference. This was done in the preceding code; `gWindowType1` appears in calls to both `GetWindowEventTarget` and `InstallEventHandler`.

The window event handler should determine if the window-related event is of the `kEventWindowDrawContent` kind and, if it is, call the appropriate application-defined update routine. In the `userData` argument, the window event handler will have received a reference to the affected window. That's the window that should be passed to the update routine. Here's the pertinent part of the window event handler routine:

```
window = ( WindowRef )userData;

eventKind = GetEventKind( event );

if ( eventKind == kEventWindowDrawContent )
{
   if ( window == gWindowType1 )
      UpdateWindowType1();
   else if ( window == gWindowType2 )
      UpdateWindowType2();
}
```

Each update routine should hold the code necessary to redraw one type of window. The next program, MultipleWindowUpdate, provides an example.

MultipleWindowUpdate Program

The purpose of the MultipleWindowUpdate program is to expand on the single-window updating technique described in the previous example program, WindowUpdate.

As shown in Figure 4.10, MultipleWindowUpdate displays two windows, each with a different line of text in it. The program uses the technique of keeping track of each window by means of global window reference variables, as described in this chapter's "Using Global Variables to Reference Windows" section. An example of updating multiple windows of the same type so that each can hold different information (such as document windows created by choosing New from the File menu) can be found in this chapter's "Window Data and Multiple Windows" section.

Figure 4.10   The windows displayed by the MultipleWindowUpdate program.

The nib file for this project requires two window resources. This example uses a document window and a utility window, but you're free to change the window types. In the nib file, the windows should be named `MainWindow` and `InfoWindow`. If you use different names, you'll need to change the arguments to calls to `CreateWindowFromNib` to match your names. Both windows are empty. Their content will be created in window update routines in the source code. The program doesn't make use of any of the menu items, so you can leave the menu bar resource unchanged.

Example 4.7 contains the entire listing for the example program. Here you see an example of the multiple window updating technique described in the previous section: a global variable is declared for each of two window types, and a single event handler is used to invoke the proper update routine for the window that needs to be redrawn. The code that comprises each update routine is similar to the code discussed in the previous example, WindowUpdate.

Example 4.7   **MultipleWindowUpdate Source Code**

```
#include <Carbon/Carbon.h>


pascal OSStatus MyWindowEventHandler( EventHandlerCallRef handlerRef,
                                      EventRef event, void *userData );
void UpdateMainWindow( void );
void UpdateInfoWindow( void );

WindowRef    gMainWindow;
WindowRef    gInfoWindow;

int main(int argc, char* argv[])
{
    IBNibRef         nibRef;
    OSStatus         err;
    EventTargetRef   target;
    EventHandlerUPP  handlerUPP;
    EventTypeSpec    windowEvent = { kEventClassWindow,
                                     kEventWindowDrawContent };

    err = CreateNibReference( CFSTR("main"), &nibRef );
    err = SetMenuBarFromNib( nibRef, CFSTR("MainMenu") );
    err = CreateWindowFromNib(nibRef, CFSTR("MainWindow"), &gMainWindow);

    target = GetWindowEventTarget( gMainWindow );
    handlerUPP = NewEventHandlerUPP( MyWindowEventHandler );
    InstallEventHandler( target, handlerUPP, 1, &windowEvent,
                         (void *)gMainWindow, NULL );

    err = CreateWindowFromNib(nibRef, CFSTR("InfoWindow"), &gInfoWindow);

    target = GetWindowEventTarget( gInfoWindow );
    handlerUPP = NewEventHandlerUPP( MyWindowEventHandler );
    InstallEventHandler( target, handlerUPP, 1, &windowEvent,
                         (void *)gInfoWindow, NULL );

    DisposeNibReference( nibRef );

    ShowWindow( gMainWindow );
    ShowWindow( gInfoWindow );

    RunApplicationEventLoop();

    return( 0 );
}


pascal OSStatus MyWindowEventHandler( EventHandlerCallRef handlerRef,
                                      EventRef event, void *userData)
```

```
{
   OSStatus    result = eventNotHandledErr;
   UInt32      eventKind;
   WindowRef   window;

   window = ( WindowRef )userData;

   eventKind = GetEventKind( event );

   if ( eventKind == kEventWindowDrawContent )
   {
      if ( window == gMainWindow )
         UpdateMainWindow();
      else if ( window == gInfoWindow )
         UpdateInfoWindow();
   }
   return result;
}


void UpdateMainWindow( void )
{
   FMFontFamily    fontFamily;

   SetPortWindowPort( gMainWindow );

   fontFamily = FMGetFontFamilyFromName( "\pTimes" );
   TextFont( fontFamily );
   TextFace( bold + italic );
   TextSize( 36 );
   MoveTo( 30,60 );
   DrawString( "\pMain Window" );
}


void UpdateInfoWindow( void )
{
   FMFontFamily    fontFamily;

   SetPortWindowPort( gInfoWindow );

   fontFamily = FMGetFontFamilyFromName( "\pArial" );
   TextFont( fontFamily );
   TextFace( bold );
   TextSize( 18 );
   MoveTo( 60,35 );
   DrawString( "\pInfo Window" );
}
```

Associating Information with Windows

You've seen that it's easy to use Interface Builder to define windows that display information such as text or pictures. Using a window resource to define the content of a window is a great technique for creating a window for data input, such as a window used as a spreadsheet, or for creating a window that displays information for the user to view, such as an About window that reveals copyright information about a program.

On the other hand, a window resource isn't always useful for defining a window that will have dynamic content. For example, you might use a window resource to define the content of a window that displays a picture of the program's creator (that would be you). However, if your program opens a window that enables the user to add one or more pictures of his or her own choosing, defining that window's content in advance is impossible. For situations in which the user creates window content during program execution, a nonresource solution is in order.

Experienced Mac Programmer

Of course, it is possible to set up dynamic content display in a window resource. In the past, you might have used a user item in a WIND resource (or a user pane in a window nib resource) to provide a means of adding window content during runtime. That's sidestepping the issue a bit, though. In this section, I'm leading up to a means of creating multiple, complex windows, such as those that would be found in a program that enables the user to add text, numbers, and pictures in various combinations at various locations within each window.

A window can display any kind of information. Text, numbers, or pictures are common entities making up the content of a window. A window also can display a QuickTime movie, or it can "hold" a sound. In addition, depending on what features a programmer wants to provide, a program can hold any combination of these entities.

A program that supports the display of just one type of content can enable each of its windows to display different forms of that same content. For instance, a text editor that enables only the entry of text will enable each open window to hold different passages of text. Thus, when it comes to associating information with windows, there are a few techniques to master.

You'll want to know the simplest technique first: how to associate one piece of information, such as a number, with a single window. Beyond that you'll want to know how to associate different types of information, such as several numbers, a picture, and a string of text, with a single window. Finally, you'll want to know how to make sure that the information associated with different windows is tracked. For instance, when two windows in the text editor program you're developing need updating, you'll want to make sure that the correct text gets displayed in the proper window. In this section, you'll see how your program's windows can include all these features.

Associating a Single Variable With a Window

To associate data with a window, you'll rely on the Carbon `SetWindowProperty` routine. To retrieve a window's data, you'll use the corresponding `GetWindowProperty` routine.

Setting a Window's Data

The `SetWindowProperty` routine accepts a pointer to the data to associate with the window; thus, that data can be as trivial as a single variable (such as an `int` variable that holds a number) or as complex as a large structure (that might have numerous fields to hold text, pictures, movies, and so forth).

I'll start out simple by demonstrating how to use `SetWindowProperty` to associate one piece of information with a window. Here's the prototype for `SetWindowProperty`:

```
OSStatus SetWindowProperty( WindowRef        window,
                            PropertyCreator  propertyCreator,
                            PropertyTag      propertyTag,
                            UInt32           propertySize,
                            void *           propertyBuffer );
```

The `window` parameter is a reference to the window with which to associate the data. This parameter is the variable returned by `CreateWindowFromNib` when the window was created.

The `propertyCreator` is a creator code, which is typically the application's signature. When you build an application, you have the option of providing it with a four-character code. This code is used by the desktop to relate document files created by your application to your application. For instance, if you double-click a Microsoft Word file on the desktop, the system knows to open that file in Microsoft Word. If you don't provide your application with a signature, you can pass 0 as the `propertyCreator` value.

The `propertyTag` is a four-character identifier that you provide for this one piece of data. Later, when it comes time to retrieve this data (with a call to the `GetWindowProperty` routine), you'll use the same `propertyTag`. You can use any four characters you want for this value.

The `propertySize` tells `SetWindowProperty` the size of the data. This size is in bytes, so you can use `sizeof` to get this value. For instance, if the data consists of just one integer, you could pass `sizeof( int )` here. If the data is a structure, you'll use `sizeof` with the structure type, as in `sizeof( MyWindDataStruct )`. The MoreWindowInfo example program that follows the WindowInfo example program provides an example of using a structure to hold window data.

Finally, it's time to consider the data. The `propertyBuffer` is a generic pointer that points to the memory that holds the data to associate with the window. For a single piece of data, such as an integer, you'll pass the address of the integer variable, as in `&theNumber`. For a structure, you'll first create a handle to the structure and then pass a pointer to that handle. Don't worry; that process isn't as complicated as it sounds! This chapter's "Associating a Window with a Structure" section provides an example of how to do this.

This following snippet of code provides a look at how `SetWindowProperty` can be used to associate a single value—an integer—to a window:

```
UInt32     windowNumber = 99;
WindowRef  window;
...

err = CreateWindowFromNib( nibRef, CFSTR("MainWindow"), &window );

...

SetWindowProperty( window, 0, 'test', sizeof( UInt32 ), &windowNumber );
```

This example associates the number 99 with the window created from the previous call to `CreateWindowFromNib`. The program isn't using an application signature, so a value of 0 is passed as the second argument. I somewhat arbitrarily chose test as the four-character property tag. The characters that make up the tag aren't important, as long as the exact same characters are used in the `GetWindowProperty` call that will follow.

The `UInt32` data type is a commonly used Carbon data type for a variable that's to hold an unsigned integer. Using `sizeof` with this data type provides the size in bytes of this type. Prefacing the data-holding variable name with `&` sends the address of the `windowNumber` variable to `SetWindowProperty`.

Retrieving a Window's Data

After associating data with a window, you'll eventually want to retrieve that data. If the data consists of information about the content of the window (such as text or graphics that are displayed in the window), this is when you'll want to update the window.

On the other hand, if the data consists of other information, such as user-entered numbers, the time to retrieve the window data might be when the user specifies that some calculation involving the data is to take place. In any case, you'll use the Carbon routine `GetWindowProperty` to retrieve previously stored window information:

```
OSStatus  GetWindowProperty( WindowRef        window,
                             PropertyCreator  propertyCreator,
                             PropertyTag      propertyTag,
                             UInt32           bufferSize,
                             UInt32 *         actualSize,
                             void *           propertyBuffer );
```

If you take a look back at the prototype for the `SetWindowProperty` routine in the "Setting a Window's Data" section, you'll see that most of the parameters for that routine match those of `GetWindowProperty`. The first parameter, `window`, is the window to examine for associated data. The `propertyCreator` and `propertyTag` are each four-character strings that should match the corresponding arguments previously passed to `SetWindowProperty` for this same window. The `bufferSize` is the size, in bytes, of the data to retrieve. This argument should match the `propertySize` argument passed to `SetWindowProperty` for this window. `actualSize` is a pointer to a variable.

GetWindowProperty uses this variable to hold the actual size of the data to retrieve. This size should of course match the bufferSize, so if you aren't interested in this actualSize, you can pass a value of NULL here. Finally, the propertyBuffer is a generic pointer to the memory that will, upon completion of GetWindowProperty, hold the window's data.

The following snippet shows how to retrieve the data associated with a window. I've included the call to SetWindowProperty to emphasize that a call to SetWindowProperty must precede a call to GetWindowProperty (or else there will be no data to retrieve) and to demonstrate how similar the arguments to the two routines are. After you've figured out how to call SetWindowProperty for your particular situation, you then know how to call GetWindowProperty.

```
UInt32      windowNumber = 99;
WindowRef   window;
UInt32      theNumber;
...

err = CreateWindowFromNib( nibRef, CFSTR("MainWindow"), &window );

...

// associate the data (99) in variable windowNumber with a window:
SetWindowProperty( window, 0, 'test', sizeof( UInt32 ), &windowNumber );

...

// retrieve the data (99) from the window and store it in theNumber:
GetWindowProperty( window, 0, 'test', sizeof( UInt32 ),
                   NULL, &theNumber );
```

WindowInfo Program

The purpose of the WindowInfo program is to demonstrate the use of SetWindowProperty and GetWindowProperty to associate data with a window, and then to retrieve that data from a window. This program associates a single integer value with a window. The next example in this chapter, MoreWindowInfo, demonstrates associating a structure with a window.

WindowInfo displays one window with the number *2* written to it. It isn't important what number is used. I'm simply showing how data can be assigned to a window, and then later retrieved during the updating of the window. This program doesn't make use of any menu items, and the window that displays the number is initially empty, so providing details about the project's nib file are unimportant. Simply make sure there's a window named MainWind in the nib file and you're all set to go.

Example 4.8 provides the entire source code listing for the WindowInfo program. After creating a new window, the program calls SetWindowProperty to associate the number 2 with the window. The one event the program looks for is an update event, as discussed in this chapter's "Updating Window Content" section. When an update event occurs, `MyWindowEventHandler` is invoked. That routine calls the application-defined routine UpdateWindow to redraw the window's contents. To do this, the window's data (the number 2) is retrieved and that data is drawn to the window.

In previous examples, you've seen that `DrawString` is used to draw a string of text to a window. Because this program's window has a number associated with it, and because I want to draw that number to the window, a conversion needs to take place. The Carbon routine `NumToString` accepts an integer as its first argument and returns the string version of that number in the second argument. Here's how variable windowNumber gets its value:

```
UInt32      windowNumber;

GetWindowProperty( window, 0, 'test', sizeof( UInt32 ),
                   NULL, &windowNumber );
```

In the following code, `NumToString` is called to convert the integer value in the variable windowNumber to a string held in variable numberStr:

```
Str255      numberStr;

NumToString( windowNumber, numberStr );
```

Now `DrawString` can be called to draw the string, with the result being the number 2 being written to the window:

```
DrawString( numberStr );
```

Example 4.8   **WindowInfo Source Code**

```
#include <Carbon/Carbon.h>


pascal OSStatus MyWindowEventHandler( EventHandlerCallRef handlerRef,
                                      EventRef event, void *userData );

void UpdateWindow( WindowRef window );

int main( int argc, char* argv[] )
{
    IBNibRef          nibRef;
    OSStatus          err;
    WindowRef         window;
    EventTargetRef    target;
    EventHandlerUPP   handlerUPP;
    EventTypeSpec     windowEvent = { kEventClassWindow,
                                      kEventWindowDrawContent };
    UInt32            windowNumber = 2;

    err = CreateNibReference( CFSTR("main"), &nibRef );
    err = SetMenuBarFromNib( nibRef, CFSTR("MainMenu") );
```

```
    err = CreateWindowFromNib( nibRef, CFSTR("MainWindow"), &window );

    target = GetWindowEventTarget( window );
    handlerUPP = NewEventHandlerUPP( MyWindowEventHandler );
    InstallEventHandler( target, handlerUPP, 1, &windowEvent,
                         (void *)window, NULL );

    SetWindowProperty( window, 0, 'test', sizeof(UInt32), &windowNumber);

    DisposeNibReference( nibRef );

    ShowWindow( window );

    RunApplicationEventLoop();

    return( 0 );
}


pascal OSStatus MyWindowEventHandler( EventHandlerCallRef handlerRef,
                                      EventRef event, void *userData)
{
    OSStatus    result = eventNotHandledErr;
    UInt32      eventKind;
    WindowRef   window;

    window = ( WindowRef )userData;

    eventKind = GetEventKind( event );

    if ( eventKind == kEventWindowDrawContent )
    {
        UpdateWindow( window );
    }
    return result;
}


void UpdateWindow( WindowRef window )
{
    FMFontFamily    fontFamily;
    UInt32          windowNumber;
    Str255          numberStr;

    SetPortWindowPort( window );

    GetWindowProperty( window, 0, 'test', sizeof( UInt32 ),
                       NULL, &windowNumber );

    NumToString( windowNumber, numberStr );
    fontFamily = FMGetFontFamilyFromName( "\pTimes" );
```

continues

Example 4.8   **Continued**

```
    TextFont( fontFamily );
    TextFace( bold + italic );
    TextSize( 36 );
    MoveTo( 150,60 );
    DrawString( numberStr );
}
```

Associating a Structure with a Window

Using a single piece of information, such as a number, as the data to associate with a window provides a good look at how `SetWindowProperty` and `GetWindowProperty` are used. However, if your program associates data with a window, it's going to associate more than one value with that window. `SetWindowProperty` and `GetWindowProperty` each work with only one piece of information. Bundling all your window's data into a single structure is how you get around this apparent limitation.

The first thing you need to do is to define a structure that includes the fields appropriate to storing whatever data is to be associated with your program's window. The following snippet defines a structure that holds one integer and one string. The structure your program needs will differ, but the techniques that I'll be describing still apply.

```
typedef struct
{
    UInt32    number;
    Str255    string;
} WindowData, **WindowDataHandle;
```

The preceding structure is given the data type name of `WindowData`. The code also defines the data type `WindowDataHandle`, which serves as a handle to the `WindowData` structure. A *handle*, which is a pointer to a pointer, is a data type commonly used in Macintosh programming.

Before associating a structure with a window, you'll want to declare a structure of type `WindowData` and then reserve the memory space necessary to hold such a structure. You can do that by using the Carbon routine `NewHandle`, which specifies the number of bytes to reserve. You can typecast the result so that instead of a generic handle, you have a handle that references a `WindowData` structure:

```
WindowDataHandle    windDataHndl;

windDataHndl = ( WindowDataHandle )NewHandle( sizeof( WindowData ) );
```

With memory reserved for the `WindowData` structure and a means to reference that memory, it's time to fill the structure's fields with values. For a numerical field like the number field, you dereference the handle twice. Dereferencing a handle once results in a pointer to the structure; dereferencing a handle a second time results in the structure itself. You then access the field of interest. Here the number field of the `WindowData` structure referenced by the `windDataHndl` variable is being assigned the value 5:

```
UInt32    theNumber = 5;

(**windDataHndl).number = theNumber;
```

Next, you assign a value to the `string` field of the structure. Assigning a string variable a value at the time of declaration is easy:

```
Str255    theString = "\pCopyright (c) 2001"
```

A `Str255` variable isn't a single value. It's actually an array of characters, so assigning a string variable *after* the string is declared is a little trickier. One way to do this is to use the Carbon `BlockMoveData` routine to transfer a block of memory (the block that holds an existing string) to another block of memory (the block pointed to by a different string variable). Here's an example of that technique:

```
Size    numBytes;

numBytes = theString[0] + 1;
BlockMoveData( theString, (**windDataHndl).string, numBytes );
```

The first argument to `BlockMoveData` is the source string, which is the string that holds a value that is to be copied to another string. The second argument is the destination string, which is the string that will hold the copied value when `BlockMoveData` has executed. The final argument is the number of bytes to copy, which are the bytes in the source string.

As mentioned, an `Str255` is an array. It's an array that can hold up to 255 characters, but it also can hold any number of characters less than that. The first element in the array holds the actual number of characters in the array. Thus, the byte size of an `Str255` variable is the number of characters in the array (as specified in element [0]) and one extra byte to account for the first count-holding element (element [0] itself). The variable `numBytes` holds the total byte length of the string.

After assigning values to the `number` and `string` fields of the structure, the structure can be used as the data to be associated with a window. A call to `SetWindowProperty` does that:

```
SetWindowProperty(window, 0, 'test', sizeof(WindowData), &windDataHndl);
```

The size of the data is simply the size of the structure; `sizeof` provides that value. The pointer to the data is a pointer to the structure's handle variable.

You've seen how a call to `GetWindowProperty` is made to retrieve a single value from a window. Using that routine with a structure works in a similar fashion. Before making the call, you will need to allocate storage space for the structure to retrieve. You can do this by setting up a structure to be used before the call to `SetWindowProperty`:

```
WindowDataHandle    windDataHndl;

windDataHndl = ( WindowDataHandle )NewHandle( sizeof( WindowData ) );
```

Alternately, you could declare a global `WindowDataHandle` variable, allocate memory for it (perhaps in `main`), and then use that variable for both setting and getting window data.

Recall that the first four `GetWindowProperty` arguments will be similar to the first four `SetWindowProperty` arguments. The fifth argument can be `NULL` if you don't need to verify that the actual data size matches the expected size. The sixth argument matches the last argument to `SetWindowProperty`. It's a pointer to a block of memory of the appropriate size to hold the retrieved data:

```
GetWindowProperty( window, 0, 'test', sizeof( WindowData ),
                    NULL, &windDataHndl );
```

After retrieving a handle to a structure, you need to dereference the handle to access the various members of the structure. Here's how that's done for the integer held in the `number` member of this example's structure:

```
UInt32    theNumber;

theNumber = (**windDataHndl).number;
```

For the string member in this example, you get the number of bytes in the string. With the following code, you can move that many bytes into a local string variable:

```
Size      numBytes;
Str255    theString;
numBytes = **windDataHndl).string[0] + 1;
BlockMoveData( (**windDataHndl).string, theString, numBytes );
```

Now that the structure members are stored in local variables, your program can use the window data. For example, the content of the window (such as text or pictures) could be associated with the window and then used in updating the window's contents. Such an example is discussed next.

MoreWindowInfo Program

The purpose of the MoreWindowInfo program is to expand on the technique demonstrated in the previous example, WindowInfo. In this program, a structure, rather than a single value, is associated with a window.

The MoreWindowInfo program displays the window shown in Figure 4.11. The text *And the number is...* comes from a string stored in the string member of a structure associated with the window. The number *5* comes from an integer stored in the same structure. When the window requires updating, the structure associated with the window is retrieved, the structure's string is drawn to the window, and the structure's integer is converted to a string and drawn to the window.

Just like the previous example, WindowInfo, the MoreWindowInfo program doesn't use any menu items and the program's window starts out empty. That means that you don't need to put any work into the nib file. If the nib file has a window named MainWind, you're all set.

The source code listing for MoreWindowInfo appears in Example 4.9. The `struct` used to hold window data is the same structure we just described. It consists of a `number` member and a `string` member. In Example 4.9, a single global variable is used in all instances in which a structure of this type needs to be used. This means that memory for the structure is allocated just once (in `main` in this example). The structure is used as a temporary holding place of sorts to store data to assign to a window and to hold data just retrieved from a window.

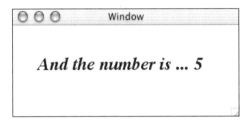

Figure 4.11 The window displayed by the MoreWindowInfo program.

Example 4.9 **MoreWindowInfo Source Code**

```
#include <Carbon/Carbon.h>


pascal OSStatus MyWindowEventHandler( EventHandlerCallRef handlerRef,
                                      EventRef event, void *userData );

void UpdateWindow( WindowRef window );

typedef struct
{
    UInt32   number;
    Str255   string;
} WindowData, **WindowDataHandle;

WindowDataHandle    gWindDataHndl;

int main( int argc, char* argv[] )
{
    IBNibRef          nibRef;
    OSStatus          err;
    WindowRef         window;
    EventTargetRef    target;
    EventHandlerUPP   handlerUPP;
```

continues

Example 4.9 **Continued**

```
EventTypeSpec      windowEvent = { kEventClassWindow,
                                   kEventWindowDrawContent };
  UInt32           theNumber = 5;
  Str255           theString = "\pAnd the number is ...";
  Size             numBytes;

  err = CreateNibReference( CFSTR("main"), &nibRef );
  err = SetMenuBarFromNib( nibRef, CFSTR("MainMenu") );
  err = CreateWindowFromNib( nibRef, CFSTR("MainWindow"), &window );

  target = GetWindowEventTarget( window );
  handlerUPP = NewEventHandlerUPP( MyWindowEventHandler );
  InstallEventHandler( target, handlerUPP, 1, &windowEvent,
                       (void *)window, NULL );

  gWindDataHndl = (WindowDataHandle)NewHandle( sizeof( WindowData ) );
  (**gWindDataHndl).number = theNumber;
  numBytes = theString[0] + 1;
  BlockMoveData( theString, (**gWindDataHndl).string, numBytes );

  SetWindowProperty( window, 0, 'test', sizeof( WindowData ),
                     &gWindDataHndl );

  DisposeNibReference( nibRef );

  ShowWindow( window );

  RunApplicationEventLoop();

  return( 0 );
}


pascal OSStatus MyWindowEventHandler( EventHandlerCallRef handlerRef,
                                      EventRef event, void *userData)
{
  OSStatus   result = eventNotHandledErr;
  UInt32     eventKind;
  WindowRef  window;

  window = ( WindowRef )userData;

  eventKind = GetEventKind( event );

  if ( eventKind == kEventWindowDrawContent )
  {
    UpdateWindow( window );
  }
  return result;
```

```
    }


    void UpdateWindow( WindowRef window )
    {
        FMFontFamily    fontFamily;
        UInt32          theNumber;
        Str255          numberStr;
        Size            numBytes;
        Str255          theString;

        SetPortWindowPort( window );

        GetWindowProperty( window, 0, 'test', sizeof( WindowData ),
                           NULL, &gWindDataHndl );

        theNumber = (**gWindDataHndl).number;
        numBytes = (**gWindDataHndl).string[0] + 1;
        BlockMoveData( (**gWindDataHndl).string, theString, numBytes );

        NumToString( theNumber, numberStr );
        fontFamily = FMGetFontFamilyFromName( "\pTimes" );
        TextFont( fontFamily );
        TextFace( bold + italic );
        TextSize( 24 );
        MoveTo( 35,60 );
        DrawString( theString );
        MoveTo( 250,60 );
        DrawString( numberStr );
    }
```

Window Data and Multiple Windows

A common situation is for a program to enable the user to open multiple windows of the same type, and for each of these open windows to hold different data. A word processor, for instance, enables any number of documents to open, and each can hold different text. To create a program of this type, you can use the New menu item to open a new window and then use `SetWindowProperty` and `GetWindowProperty` to assign and retrieve data unique to that window.

This chapter's "Opening Multiple Windows of the Same Type" section describes how to use the New menu item to enable any number of windows of the same type to be opened. In short, you can assign the New menu item a command in the menu bar of the nib file, and then install an application-level event handler that responds to that command. In the event handler, you'll call an application-defined routine that opens a new window. This chapter's MultipleSameTypeWindow program introduces this technique.

If each new window is to have some initial information assigned to it, you can do that in the routine that creates the window. A call to SetWindowProperty does the trick. In addition, to ensure that each window is properly updated, you can install an event handler in that same window-creating routine.

The following code snippet provides an abbreviated version of a CreateMyNewWindow routine that performs these tasks. This routine creates a window, assigns the number 10 to it, and installs an event handler that responds to an update event. For a look at a complete CreateMyNewWindow routine that creates a window, assigns unique data to it, and then installs an event handler, refer to the "SameTypeWindowWithData Program" section of this chapter.

```
void CreateMyNewWindow( void )
{
   IBNibRef        nibRef;
   OSStatus        err;
   WindowRef       window;
   EventTargetRef  target;
   EventHandlerUPP handlerUPP;
   EventTypeSpec   windowEvent = { kEventClassWindow,
                   kEventWindowDrawContent };
   SInt16          number = 10;

   err = CreateNibReference( CFSTR("main"), &nibRef );
   err = CreateWindowFromNib( nibRef, CFSTR("MainWindow"), &window );

   target = GetWindowEventTarget( window );
   handlerUPP = NewEventHandlerUPP( MyWindowEventHandler );
   InstallEventHandler( target, handlerUPP, 1, &windowEvent,
                   (void *)window, NULL );

   DisposeNibReference( nibRef );

   SetWindowProperty( window, 0, 'test', sizeof( SInt16 ), &number );

   // offset and show window here
}
```

SameTypeWindowWithData Program

Sure, it's a somewhat unwieldy name, but a title of *SameTypeWindowWithData* certainly lets you know the purpose of this example program. This program demonstrates how to create multiple windows of the same type, each with its own associated data.

The SameTypeWindowWithData program has a New menu item that creates a new window. By way of a call to SetWindowProperty, each new window gets a randomly generated number associated with it. By way of a call to GetWindowProperty, each window is properly updated (that is, each window has the correct number drawn to it any time the window becomes obscured and then revealed). Figure 4.12 shows the program after the New menu item has been selected a few times.

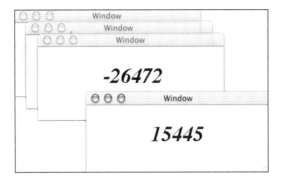

Figure 4.12   The windows displayed by the SameTypeWindowWithData program.

The nib file for this project requires a single empty window named `MainWind`. You'll give the New menu item a command by assigning it a command of `nwin` so that the command corresponds to the `#define` that will be used in the source code. This chapter's "Opening Multiple Windows of the Same Type" section provides an example of assigning this same command to the New menu item.

Example 4.10 provides the complete listing for the SameTypeWindowWithData program. From other examples in this chapter, you're familiar with most of this code.

The application event handler watches for the command generated by a selection of the New menu item. The two global variables are used in the staggering of each new window. Refer back to this chapter's MultipleSameTypeWindow example to review either of these two techniques.

The `CreateMyNewWindow` routine is invoked by the application event handler in response to choosing the New menu item. To provide each new window with data, `SetWindowProperty` is called. Rather than simply assigning the same value to each window, `CreateMyNewWindow` calls the Carbon routine `Random` to generate a random number to assign to the new window. That way, each window will (most likely) have a different number assigned to it.

When you run the program, you should choose New several times to create a number of windows. Move the windows about because changing the ordering forces updates. As you do this, you'll see that the program properly updates each window by redrawing the correct number to that window. The `Random` function requires no arguments. Just call it and the routine returns an integer value in the range of –32767 to +32767.

Example 4.10   **SameTypeWindowWithData Source Code**

```
#include <Carbon/Carbon.h>


#define    kNewWindowCommand    'nwin'
```

continues

Example 4.10 **Continued**

```
pascal OSStatus MyAppEventHandler( EventHandlerCallRef handlerRef,
                                   EventRef event, void *userData );


pascal OSStatus MyWindowEventHandler( EventHandlerCallRef handlerRef,
                                      EventRef event, void *userData );

void  CreateMyNewWindow( void );
void UpdateWindow( WindowRef window );

SInt16   gWindowStartTop  = 40;
SInt16   gWindowStartLeft = 15;

int main( int argc, char* argv[] )
{
    IBNibRef          nibRef;
    OSStatus          err;
    EventTargetRef    target;
    EventHandlerUPP   handlerUPP;
    EventTypeSpec     appEvent = { kEventClassCommand,
                                   kEventProcessCommand };

    err = CreateNibReference( CFSTR("main"), &nibRef );
    err = SetMenuBarFromNib( nibRef, CFSTR("MainMenu") );
    DisposeNibReference( nibRef );

    CreateMyNewWindow();

    target = GetApplicationEventTarget( );
    handlerUPP = NewEventHandlerUPP( MyAppEventHandler );
    InstallEventHandler( target, handlerUPP, 1, &appEvent, 0, NULL );

    RunApplicationEventLoop();

    return( 0 );
}


pascal OSStatus MyAppEventHandler( EventHandlerCallRef handlerRef,
                                   EventRef event, void *userData)
{
    OSStatus    result = eventNotHandledErr;
    HICommand   command;

    GetEventParameter( event, kEventParamDirectObject, typeHICommand,
                  NULL, sizeof (HICommand), NULL, &command);

    switch ( command.commandID )
    {
```

```
      case kNewWindowCommand:
         CreateMyNewWindow();
         result = noErr;
         break;
   }
   return result;
}

void CreateMyNewWindow( void )
{
   IBNibRef          nibRef;
   OSStatus          err;
   WindowRef         window;
   EventTargetRef    target;
   EventHandlerUPP   handlerUPP;
   EventTypeSpec     windowEvent = { kEventClassWindow,
                                     kEventWindowDrawContent };
   SInt16            randomNum;

   err = CreateNibReference( CFSTR("main"), &nibRef );
   err = CreateWindowFromNib( nibRef, CFSTR("MainWindow"), &window );

   target = GetWindowEventTarget( window );
   handlerUPP = NewEventHandlerUPP( MyWindowEventHandler );
   InstallEventHandler( target, handlerUPP, 1, &windowEvent,
                        (void *)window, NULL );

   DisposeNibReference( nibRef );

   randomNum = Random();

   SetWindowProperty( window, 0, 'test', sizeof( SInt16 ), &randomNum );

   MoveWindow ( window, gWindowStartLeft, gWindowStartTop, TRUE );

   ShowWindow( window );

   if ( gWindowStartTop < 200 )
   {
      gWindowStartLeft += 20;
      gWindowStartTop  += 20;
   }
   else
   {
      gWindowStartLeft = 15;
      gWindowStartTop  = 40;
   }
}
```

continues

Example 4.10 **Continued**

```
pascal OSStatus MyWindowEventHandler( EventHandlerCallRef handlerRef,
                                      EventRef event, void *userData)
{
   OSStatus    result = eventNotHandledErr;
   UInt32      eventKind;
   WindowRef   window;

   window = ( WindowRef )userData;

   eventKind = GetEventKind( event );

   if ( eventKind == kEventWindowDrawContent )
   {
      UpdateWindow( window );
   }
   return result;
}


void UpdateWindow( WindowRef window )
{
   FMFontFamily   fontFamily;
   SInt16         windowNumber;
   Str255         numberStr;

   SetPortWindowPort( window );

   GetWindowProperty( window, 0, 'test', sizeof( SInt16 ),
                      NULL, &windowNumber );

   NumToString( windowNumber, numberStr );
   fontFamily = FMGetFontFamilyFromName( "\pTimes" );
   TextFont( fontFamily );
   TextFace( bold + italic );
   TextSize( 36 );
   MoveTo( 110,60 );
   DrawString( numberStr );
}
```

For More Information

The following web site offers more information on some of the topics presented in this chapter:

- **Random number generation:**

    http://developer.apple.com/techpubs/macosx/Carbon/graphics/QuickDraw/
    QuickDraw_Manager/Functions/Random.html

5

Controls

A *CONTROL* IS AN ITEM WITH WHICH a program's user can interact. By clicking a control such as a push button, a user can initiate some immediate action, as you've seen in several of the example programs in previous chapters. Other types of controls also can be acted on by the user, but these controls generally modify a setting instead of causing an immediate action to take place. Examples of such controls are radio buttons, text input fields, and checkboxes. In this chapter you'll see how to create and manage controls of these types. In learning about these control types, you'll see how a control can be assigned either a command signature (as you've done in previous chapters) or a control ID.

Command Signatures and Control IDs

Some controls, such as radio buttons and checkboxes, usually don't initiate any action when clicked. The control's state might change—for instance, a checkbox will become checked if it was unchecked—but the act of clicking the control won't generally cause a change in the program. Instead, the program examines the state of such a control at a later time (such as when a Done button is clicked) and *then* an action might be initiated. It is this clicking of a button that more often causes an immediate action. These two different types of behavior that a control can exhibit explain why one control is assigned a command signature and another control is assigned a control ID.

Consider the window resource shown in Figure 5.1. It includes a static text item (the *Select a beep option, then click the Beep button* string), a push button control (the button titled *Beep*), and a radio button group control (all three radio buttons comprise a single control).

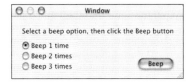

Figure 5.1   A window that includes a push button and a radio button group.

The push button is the type of control usually assigned a command signature (also referred to as a command). You've worked with commands before, so you know that a command is a four-character constant assigned to a control. Assigning a command signature to an item in a resource file enables a program's code to respond to the user's selection of that item. It's important to note that assigning a command signature to a control doesn't give the program any indication of which control has been selected by the user. For instance, if you assign each of two buttons a command of `beep`, the program responds the same way to a click on either button, and the program won't know or care which button initiated the action.

You've also seen that you can assign a menu item the same command as a button, and again, the program properly responds in the same manner to either a click on the button or a selection of the menu item. Again, the program won't know, or care, which action generated the command. Figure 5.2 shows the push button being assigned a command signature of `beep`.

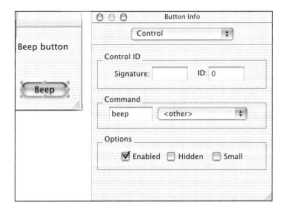

Figure 5.2   Assigning a command signature to a push button control.

The radio button group control pictured in Figure 5.1 is the type of control that is usually assigned a control ID rather than a command. A control ID consists of two components: a signature and an ID. The signature is a four-character constant, and the ID is an integer value. Be aware that there's the potential for confusion here. The control ID is composed of two parts: a signature and an integer. The integer is referred to as the ID. Thus, a *control ID* is the combination of two identifiers, while the *ID* is one of those identifiers. Tricky wording, to be sure. Figure 5.3 shows a control ID with a signature of SPRB and an ID of 1 being assigned to the radio button group.

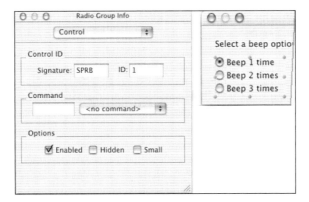

Figure 5.3   Assigning a control ID to a radio button group control.

The four-character constant used for the signature is typically the same as the program's creator code, which is the application signature. As discussed further in Chapter 10, "Bundles and Icons," each program that's released to the public should have its own creator code, and that creator code should be registered with Apple. In such a case, any four characters can be used as the signature. This chapter's RadioButtonGroup example program provides more information about creator codes, and the specific process of registering such a code with Apple is described in Chapter 10.

> **Note**
> This book's examples haven't been assigned creator codes—it's a bit unlikely that any of them will ship as commercial products!

The commonly used convention for assigning control IDs to a program's controls is to use the same four-character constant as the signature for every control ID and to use a unique integer value as the ID of every control ID. For instance, if I were to add two more controls that each required a control ID to the window pictured in Figure 5.1, their control IDs might each have a signature of SPRB, while their IDs would have values of 2 and 3. By giving each control that requires a control ID a unique value, your program can identify that particular control. This isn't possible if your program assigns only a command to a control.

When should you assign a control ID rather than a command to a control? The answer is this: when your program needs to access a particular control. When will your program need to access a control? Typically when the program needs to get, or set, the control's value.

Consider the window pictured in Figure 5.1. The value of a radio button group is a number that identifies which radio button is currently on (only one radio button in a group can be on at any given time). In this case, the program will need to get the value of the radio button group control when the user clicks the Beep button. When the user clicks the Beep button, the program accesses the radio button group control, determines which radio button is on, and then uses that information to sound the appropriate number of beeps. For the radio button group, a command won't do. The program needs a *unique* identifier for this control so that it can access the control. A control ID is unique; a command might not be.

In this chapter, you'll read about push buttons, bevel buttons, and even pictures used as buttons. A button is usually assigned a command. This chapter also covers radio button groups, text input fields, and checkboxes. Each type of control usually has a control ID assigned to it.

Buttons

Some types of controls have more than one state. For such a control, the program needs to examine the control to determine its state. This need to know about the particular control means that the program has to access the particular control. This is the reason for associating a unique identifier (a control ID) to some controls.

Note, however, that a button *isn't* such a control. A program doesn't have to examine a button to determine its state. The program knows that a button always is waiting to be clicked. Thus, there's no need to assign a unique identifier to it. Instead, a command signature usually is assigned to a button. This command doesn't have to be unique to the button. If it makes sense for the program to have more than one means of issuing the command, other controls and menu items can be assigned the same command.

You've been working with buttons and commands for a while now. BeepWorld, the very first example program in Chapter 3, "Events and the Carbon Event Manager," included a push button that had a command assigned to it. Thus, you know that from a resource standpoint, a command signature is assigned to a button by adding a four-character command to a button item on a window in a nib resource. In addition, you know that from a code standpoint, a command is dealt with by installing an event handler that specifically responds to a command event.

Button Types

To this point, the buttons that have been included in the example programs have all been push buttons. A push button is the most common type of button, but you should know that Interface Builder makes it easy to include other varieties of buttons in your programs as well. Figure 5.4 shows a window resource that includes a few different types of buttons.

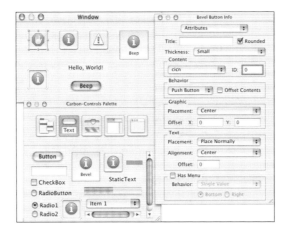

Figure 5.4   Several types of buttons in a window resource.

Along the top of the window in Figure 5.4 are four *bevel buttons*. From the left side of the window, the first three bevel buttons are all the same type. They each were created by dragging and dropping the smaller square button from the palette to the window.

The right-most, larger button in the row of four buttons in the window also is a bevel button. It was created by dragging and dropping the larger square button from the palette to the window. The icon that appears in any one of these buttons is set in the item's Info window. Enter a value of 0, 1, or 2 in the ID field of the Info window (as shown on the right side of Figure 5.4) to have the button display one of the three small color icons that are a part of any main.nib file. In Interface Builder, you can see those icons by clicking the Images tab in the file's main.nib window.

The last new button in the window resource is called an *imagewell*. It appears at the lower-left corner of the window in Figure 5.4. Drag and drop the small square button from the bottom of the palette to the window to add this item to the window. The icon displayed by this button is selected in the same way as it is for the other types of icon buttons. You enter an ID of 0, 1, or 2 in the button's Info window. Note that any of these buttons can be assigned a command in the same way that a push button is assigned one—click the item to select it, bring up the Info window, and enter a four-character command in the Command field of the Control pane of that window.

Another way to create a button is to add a picture to a window resource and give that picture a command. How to add a picture to a window resource was described in the "Adding a Picture to the HelloWorld Program" section of Chapter 2, "Overview of Mac OS X Programming." In short, you first add a picture file to the project, add a PICT item to the window, and then drag the picture from its place under the Images tab of the main.nib window to the window resource.

To turn a picture item into a button, select the picture item and choose Show Info from the Tools menu. With Attributes selected from the Info window's pop-up menu, uncheck the Don't Track checkbox. This step is important. If you leave this checkbox checked, the program won't track the user's mouse actions as related to the picture item, and a click on the picture item won't get registered. Your last step is to choose Control from the Info window's pop-up menu and enter a four-character command in the Command field. Voilá! You've got a picture that behaves like a button!

IconButtons Program

The purpose of the IconButtons program is to demonstrate how different types of buttons can be added to a window. The IconButtons program displays the window shown in Figure 5.5. Clicking any of the six buttons in the window produces the same result—a single beep.

Figure 5.5   The window displayed by the IconButtons program.

Use the Chapter 3 BeepWorld project as the basis for this project. Open the main.nib file and enlarge the window resource to accommodate the extra buttons. Now click the bevel button on the palette and drag and drop it on the window resource. Use the Attribute pane in the button's Info window to enter an ID of 0. The result is the display of the stop sign icon on the button.

Your next step is to select the Control pane in the Info window and assign a command of beep to the bevel button. Create any or all the other buttons in a similar manner. Experiment by dragging different types of buttons to the window resource and trying different ID values. The source code supports the beep command, so as long as you give any button that command, it will behave in the same way as the original button, which is the Beep push button.

The source code for the IconButtons program is *identical* to the source code developed for the Chapter 3 BeepWorld program. Rather than repeat the source code here, I'll summarize how the code works. To see the entire listing, refer to Example 3.3 back in Chapter 3.

The BeepWorld (and now the IconButtons) source code defines the constant kBeepCommand to be the same four characters (beep) as the command assigned to the Beep button. The program defines an event specification for a command event (an event with a class of kEventClassCommand and a kind of kEventProcessCommand) and installs an event handler with the program's window as the target, the application-defined routine CommandEventHandler as the event handler, and the command event as the event to which to respond. The CommandEventHandler routine responds only to an event with the command of beep, and it does so by invoking the application-defined BeepCommandHandler routine to call SysBeep.

Radio Buttons

Radio buttons are small, round buttons that come in groups. Unlike a checkbox, which is used to turn on or off an option, a radio button never appears without at least one other such button. This is because radio buttons are used to choose one (and only one) option from a set of two or more options. Thus radio buttons are used in mutually exclusive situations. When one button is on, all others in the set should be off.

A radio button group is a control consisting of two or more radio buttons. This type of control typically has a control ID, rather than a command, associated with it. When the user has finished making a selection from a set of radio buttons, your program will want to know something about this set of controls. Mainly, your program needs to know which button is now on so that some corresponding parameter can be set in the program. Thus your program needs to know about a particular control.

The control ID is how your program interacts with a control. This is unlike a user's selection of a push button, which initiates some prescribed action. Your program usually doesn't need to know anything about the control. It doesn't even need to know that it was a control that triggered an event. It could be a menu-item selection. That's why a command is associated with a control such as a push button, and a control ID is associated with a control such as a radio button group.

Radio Button Groups and the Nib Resource

Radio buttons are added to a window in a nib file. Radio buttons can be added individually. Back in Figure 5.4, you saw an individual radio button control labeled RadioButton near the lower-left of the palette window. Radio buttons also can be added collectively and treated as a single control using the radio button group item. Figure 5.4 shows this control appearing in the lower-left of the palette window as two radio buttons labeled Radio1 and Radio2.

In most situations, the radio group is the route to take. This control takes on all the responsibility of tracking the user's actions with the control. As the user clicks one radio button in a group, the control turns off the previously on button and then turns on the newly selected button. Your source code does not need to include any button-handling code. Instead, your source code is responsible only for getting (reading) the control to see which button the user selected as the final choice.

To add a radio button group to a window resource, drag and drop the radio button group item from the palette to the window. A radio button group starts with two radio buttons, as shown in Figure 5.6. To add more buttons to the group, select the group, choose Show Info from the Tools menu, and change one or both values in the Size section of the Attributes pane.

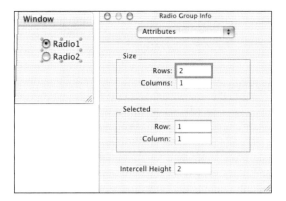

Figure 5.6 Setting the number of radio buttons in a radio button group control.

Figure 5.7 shows a radio button group with three radio buttons. The title of a button is changed by double-clicking the original title (such as on Radio1) and typing a new title (such as Beep 1 time).

To associate a control ID with a radio button group, select the group in the window and display the Info window. From the Control pane, enter a four-character signature in the Signature field and an integer in the ID field. The Command field is left blank. Figure 5.7 provides an example.

Radio Button Groups and Source Code

In response to the user clicking on a radio button, your program's code does nothing. The tracking of the user's interaction with a radio button control is the system's responsibility. Besides being extremely helpful to us programmers (thanks, Apple), this way of handling a control makes sense. Your program doesn't need to respond to, or even know about, the user's clicks on radio buttons. The user can click and click on these buttons and these actions don't matter to your program. Your program cares only about the user's final choice, which is the radio button that's on at the time the user specifies that his choice has been made.

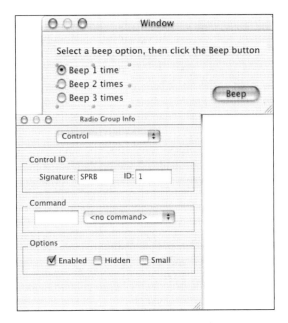

Figure 5.7 Setting the control ID of a radio button group control.

The final choice specification usually comes in the form of a click on a push button, such as an OK or Done button. In Figure 5.7, the user would click the Beep button when satisfied with his or her "number of beeps" choice. In that example, only when the user clicks the Beep button would the program need to examine the state of the radio button group control to determine which radio button is on.

You'll start your source code handling of a radio button group by defining a constant that matches the control signature and a constant that matches the control ID. These values match the values assigned to the control in the nib file. Using the radio button control pictured in Figure 5.7, those constants might look like this:

```
#define    kControlSignature    'SPRB'
#define    kRadioGroupControlID    1
```

Next, define a constant for each radio button in the radio button group. Each radio button in a radio button group has a value. Starting from the top (from the top-left if there is more than one column of radio buttons in the group) and going down, the values of the radio buttons start with the number 1 and increase consecutively. Referring to the example in Figure 5.7, here's how those constants could look:

```
#define    kBeep1Time    1
#define    kBeep2Time    2
#define    kBeep3Time    3
```

Note that the button numbering has nothing to do with the purpose of a button. For instance, if your program had a radio button group for selecting one color of three possible choices, your button constants would still have the values 1, 2, and 3.

Now install an event handler. Even though the radio button control doesn't have a command associated with it, the event handler will be one that responds to commands. Again, this is because it's usually a command (such as the one generated by the Beep button in the current example) that triggers the examining of the radio button group control. The following snippet holds the setup of such an event handler. Note that there's no new code in this snippet to discuss. The code has been used in many of the previous example programs that handled button or menu commands.

```
WindowRef          window;
OSStatus           err;
EventTargetRef     target;
EventHandlerUPP    handlerUPP;
EventTypeSpec      cmdEvent = { kEventClassCommand, kEventProcessCommand };

target = GetWindowEventTarget( window );
handlerUPP = NewEventHandlerUPP( CommandEventHandler );
InstallEventHandler( target, handlerUPP, 1, &cmdEvent,
                    (void *)window, NULL );
```

The event handler routine will be in the style of other handlers that respond to commands. Here, however, your program is watching for a click on the Beep button, not for any action associated with the radio button group. With that in mind, the event handler could look like this:

```
pascal OSStatus CommandEventHandler( EventHandlerCallRef handlerRef,
                                    EventRef event, void *userData)
{
    OSStatus       result = eventNotHandledErr;
    HICommand      command;
    WindowRef      window;

    window = ( WindowRef )userData;

    GetEventParameter( event, kEventParamDirectObject, typeHICommand,
                    NULL, sizeof (HICommand), NULL, &command);

    switch ( command.commandID )
    {
        case kBeepCommand:
            BeepCommandHandler( window );
            result = noErr;
            break;
    }
    return result;
}
```

Now we need to go to the heart of the matter. When the Beep button is clicked, the event handler invokes the application-defined routine `BeepCommandHandler`. Regardless of the purpose of your program's radio button group, the setup is similar. You need to watch for the action that signals that the user has finished with the radio button group, determine which radio button is on, and respond in a manner appropriate for the selected radio button.

Determining which radio button in a group is on is done by first accessing the radio button group control. A couple of new data types and a couple of new Carbon routines help you do that. You begin by declaring a `ControlHandle` variable that's to be used to reference the control and a `ControlID` variable that holds the control's signature and ID:

```
ControlHandle   numBeepsRadioButtonGroup;
ControlID       numBeepsControlID = { kControlSignature,
                                      kRadioGroupControlID };
```

Here the `ControlID` variable uses the previously defined constants `kControlSignature` ('SPRB') and `kRadioGroupControlID` (1). To obtain a handle to the radio button group control, call the `GetControlByID` routine:

```
GetControlByID( window, &numBeepsControlID,
                &numBeepsRadioButtonGroup );
```

You'll need to tell `GetControlByID` the window that holds the control (your program may have more than one window that displays a control). You'll also pass `GetControlByID` the control ID of the control. The combination of the signature and ID are unique to your program, so this information always specifies one and only one of your program's controls. Using that information, `GetControlByID` returns a handle to the specified control. After `GetControlByID` executes, your program can use this handle (`numBeepsRadioButtonGroup` in this example) to access the control. Here *accessing* the control means determining its value. Calling `GetControl32BitValue` returns the value of a control:

```
SInt32      numBeepsValue;

numBeepsValue = GetControl32BitValue( numBeepsRadioButtonGroup );
```

What the value of a control represents varies by the type of control. For a radio button group, the value corresponds to the radio button that's on. In the preceding code snippet, if `GetControl32BitValue` returns the number 1, the first radio button (the top button, or the top-left button in a multicolumn arrangement of controls) is the one that was on at the time the Beep button was clicked. If the number returned is 2, the second button—the middle of the three buttons—is the one that was on. You see the pattern. Now, all that's left to do is to use this control value in a switch statement, taking the appropriate action for the radio button that was on:

```
switch ( numBeepsValue )
{
  case kBeep1Time:
```

```
      // beep once
      break;
   case kBeep2Time:
      // beep twice
      break;
   case kBeep3Time:
      // beep thrice
      break;
   }
```

Obviously, the handling of the radio button choice is very application-specific. Other sets of radio buttons have other purposes. For instance, if your program's set of buttons was used to set a color from among four choices, the code would have four case labels and each label would set the same color-specifying variable to an appropriate value.

RadioButtonGroup Program

The purpose of the RadioButtonGroup program is to demonstrate how to include a set of radio buttons in a window. Figure 5.8 shows what the program's window looks like.

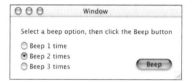

Figure 5.8   The window displayed by the RadioButtonGroup program.

In keeping with my pattern of picking a program name that hints at the purpose of the example program, I've named this program RadioButtonGroup. However, when it's complete (surely still more beeps can be added), I'll name the shipping version of this program SuperBeep. In preparation for that day, I've registered with Apple a creator code, or application signature, for this program. This is the book's first example that uses a control ID with a control, so it's as good a time as any to enhance the example by demonstrating what you'd do if you were developing a program that might actually be unleashed on the public!

The control ID consists of a four-character signature and an ID. Although not mandatory, Apple does suggest that the four-character signature match the program's four-character creator code. I visited Apple's site, determined that the creator code of SPRB was available, and registered that creator code for the SuperBeep program. Chapter 10 provides more information about creator codes and registering them. Now, for any one of the program's controls that requires a control ID, I'll use SPRB as the signature part of the control ID. Figure 5.7 illustrates this for the program's one control.

Note

I didn't *have* to register a creator code for this application to add a control to it. In addition, if you're creating numerous example and test programs (as in this book), you aren't going to want to go to Apple and register a creator code for each. By default, Project Builder assigns a creator code of ???? (four question marks) to an application built from a project. If you want to, go ahead and use that creator code for the signature part of the control ID for the controls in your test programs. Only if your program will become public do you need to register a creator code to ensure that the user's Mac OS X desktop properly associates related documents to your program. In case you haven't already guessed, *none* of this book's example programs result in shipping products, so there's no point in using up several available creator codes. That's right—even the super-charged SuperBeep application will never go public. Apparently my marketing research was poorly done, and I've overestimated the demand for a Mac OS X application that does little more than beep!

Editing the Nib File

This is another project based on the BeepWorld project from Chapter 3. Make a copy of that project, open the main.nib file, and add a radio button group control item to the window. You also can add a static text item as I've done in Figure 5.7. Set the control's signature to SPRB and give its ID a value of 1. You'll soon create corresponding constants in the source code. This control doesn't need a command, but make sure the Beep button has the command of beep associated with it.

Writing the Source Code

Example 5.1 provides the entire listing for the RadioButtonGroup program. Most of the source code was discussed in the overview of radio button groups. After looking over the BeepCommandHandler routine, you might notice that the routine could have been written in a much more succinct way. Right now, the routine calls GetControlByID to get a handle to the radio button group control. It then calls GetControl32BitValue to determine which radio button is on. Last, it enters a switch statement that looks like this:

```
switch ( numBeepsValue )
{
   case kBeep1Time:
      SysBeep( 1 );
      break;
   case kBeep2Time:
      SysBeep( 1 );
      SysBeep( 1 );
      break;
   case kBeep3Time:
      SysBeep( 1 );
      SysBeep( 1 );
      SysBeep( 1 );
      break;
}
```

Because the number of beeps sounded happens to match the value of the radio button (radio button number 1 specifies one beep should be played, and so forth), the entire `switch` statement could be replaced by these few lines of code:

```
SInt16    x;

for ( x = 1; x <= numBeepsValue; x++ )
    SysBeep( 1 );
```

Although that approach is the one to take in a "real" program, the intent here is to show the basic approach used to handle a radio button selection. In most cases, the button number will have nothing to do with the action that's to take place. For instance, if a set of radio buttons existed to enable the user to choose a United States currency, a for loop wouldn't cut it. Instead, the `switch` statement would be appropriate:

```
#define   kDollar1     1     // 1st radio button
#define   kDollar5     2     // 2nd radio button
#define   kDollar10    3     // 3rd radio button
#define   kDollar20    4     // 4th radio button
#define   kDollar50    5     // 5th radio button

Int32     dollarValue;

switch ( dollarValue )
{
   case kDollar1:
      dollarDenomination = 1;
      break;
   case kDollar5:
      dollarDenomination = 5;
      break;
   case kDollar10:
      dollarDenomination = 10;
      break;
   case kDollar20:
      dollarDenomination = 20;
      break;
   case kDollar50:
      dollarDenomination = 50;
      break;
}
```

Example 5.1   **RadioButtonGroup Source Code**

```
#include <Carbon/Carbon.h>


#define   kBeepCommand          'beep'
#define   kControlSignature     'SPRB'
#define   kRadioGroupControlID    1
#define   kBeep1Time              1
```

```
#define   kBeep2Time              2
#define   kBeep3Time              3

pascal OSStatus CommandEventHandler( EventHandlerCallRef handlerRef,
                                     EventRef event, void *userData );

pascal void    BeepCommandHandler( WindowRef window );


int main( int argc, char* argv[] )
{
   IBNibRef          nibRef;
   WindowRef         window;
   OSStatus          err;
   EventTargetRef    target;
   EventHandlerUPP   handlerUPP;
   EventTypeSpec     cmdEvent;

   cmdEvent.eventClass = kEventClassCommand;
   cmdEvent.eventKind  = kEventProcessCommand;

   err = CreateNibReference( CFSTR("main"), &nibRef );

   err = SetMenuBarFromNib( nibRef, CFSTR("MainMenu") );

   err = CreateWindowFromNib( nibRef, CFSTR("MainWindow"), &window );

   DisposeNibReference( nibRef );

   target = GetWindowEventTarget( window );
   handlerUPP = NewEventHandlerUPP( CommandEventHandler );
   InstallEventHandler( target, handlerUPP, 1, &cmdEvent,
                        (void *)window, NULL );
   ShowWindow( window );

   RunApplicationEventLoop();

   return( 0 );
}


pascal OSStatus CommandEventHandler( EventHandlerCallRef handlerRef,
                                     EventRef event, void *userData)
{
   OSStatus     result = eventNotHandledErr;
   HICommand    command;
   WindowRef    window;

   window = ( WindowRef )userData;
```

continues

Example 5.1   **Continued**

```
GetEventParameter( event, kEventParamDirectObject, typeHICommand,
                   NULL, sizeof (HICommand), NULL, &command);

  switch ( command.commandID )
  {
     case kBeepCommand:
        BeepCommandHandler( window );
        result = noErr;
        break;
  }
  return result;
}


pascal void BeepCommandHandler( WindowRef  window )

{
   ControlHandle   numBeepsRadioButtonGroup;
   ControlID       numBeepsControlID = { kControlSignature, kRadioGroupControlID
};
   SInt32          numBeepsValue;

   GetControlByID( window, &numBeepsControlID, &numBeepsRadioButtonGroup );

   numBeepsValue = GetControl32BitValue( numBeepsRadioButtonGroup );

   switch ( numBeepsValue )
   {
      case kBeep1Time:
         SysBeep( 1 );
         break;
      case kBeep2Time:
         SysBeep( 1 );
         SysBeep( 1 );
         break;
      case kBeep3Time:
         SysBeep( 1 );
         SysBeep( 1 );
         SysBeep( 1 );
         break;
   }
}
```

Checkboxes

A checkbox is a control that enables a user to turn something on or off. If a checkbox is checked, the control is considered to be "on"—if the checkbox is unchecked, the control is considered to be "off." Figure 5.9 shows a window that includes a single checkbox.

Figure 5.9   A window that includes a checkbox control.

Like a radio button group, a checkbox needs some unique identifier associated with it so that your program can determine its state. So, like a radio button group, a control will normally have a control ID, rather than a command, associated with it. When the user has signaled that he or she is satisfied with the state of a checkbox (usually by clicking a button, such as a Done button), your program determines whether the checkbox is on or off. The control ID you assign to the checkbox provides your program with access to this control.

Implementing a checkbox in a window is similar to implementing a radio button group in a window. If you've read the previous section of this chapter, you know the basics of working with a checkbox control. If you're planning on adding a set of radio buttons to a window in your program, you might consider reading the "Radio Buttons" section first to get more background information on controls that use control IDs.

Checkboxes and the Nib Resource

A checkbox is added to a window resource by clicking the checkbox control located at the left edge of the palette (see Figure 5.4) and dragging and dropping that item onto the window. To assign a control ID to the checkbox, select it and then choose Show Info from the Tools menu. Enter a signature and an ID in the Info window. In Figure 5.10, the checkbox titled *Mute speakers* has a control ID consisting of a signature of LxZZ and an ID of 3.

Different programmers use different schemes for choosing control IDs, but one common practice is for a programmer to assign each program control that require a control ID the same signature. Per Apple's convention, this signature matches the program's creator code (its application signature). Thus, you can guess that the resources pictured in Figure 5.10 belong to a program with a creator code of LxZZ.

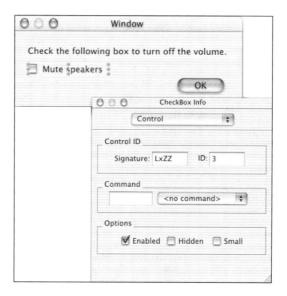

Figure 5.10   Setting the control ID of a checkbox control.

You should further note that the control's signature identifies the program to which the control belongs, and the control's ID identifies that one control from possibly many controls that the program uses. Thus, each control that requires a control ID should have a unique ID.

The window in Figure 5.10 has just one control that requires a control ID—the checkbox. Yet, the ID portion of the checkbox control ID has a value of 3. This provides a hint that the program that uses this window has other controls in other windows. Perhaps another window resource includes two controls: one with an ID of 1 and the other with an ID of 2.

Checkboxes and Source Code

Like a radio button group control, a checkbox control frees your program from the pains of tracking the user's involvement with the control. When the user clicks a checkbox, the system is responsible for toggling the checkbox to its opposite state. Only when the user has signaled that his or her choice is final do you need to be concerned with accessing the checkbox control.

To access a checkbox control, you use the same two routines described in this chapter's "Radio Buttons" section. A call to GetControlByID is used to obtain a handle to the checkbox control, and that handle is subsequently passed to GetControl32BitValue to obtain the value (the state) of the checkbox. For the checkbox pictured in Figure 5.10, that code would look like this:

```
#define    kControlSignature      'LxZZ'
#define    kMuteCheckboxControlID    3
```

```
ControlHandle   muteCheckbox;
ControlID       muteControlID = { kControlSignature, kMuteCheckboxControlID };
UInt32          muteValue;

GetControlByID( window, &muteControlID, &muteCheckbox );
muteValue = GetControl32BitValue( muteCheckbox );
```

If the value returned by `GetControl32BitValue` is a 1, consider the checkbox to be checked, or on. If the returned value is 0, that checkbox is unchecked, or off. With the current state of the checkbox known, your program can respond accordingly. In the example shown here, that would mean turning off the speaker volume of the user's computer if `muteValue` is 1 (the mute checkbox is checked) or turning on the speaker volume if `muteValue` is 0 (the mute checkbox is unchecked).

CheckboxDemo Program

The purpose of the CheckboxDemo program is to provide an example of how a program makes use of a checkbox control.

Figure 5.9 shows the window displayed by the CheckboxDemo program. If the one checkbox is checked at the time that the OK button is clicked, the program turns the speakers of the user's computer off. If the checkbox is unchecked at the time the button is clicked, the program restores the speaker volume to the level it was at when the CheckboxDemo program was launched.

CheckboxDemo introduces a couple of new routines unrelated to the handling of controls. The Carbon routine `GetDefaultOutputVolume` queries the system to determine the current volume level of the user's computer. The corresponding `SetDefaultOutputVolume` function changes the volume of the user's computer to a specified level. Both functions are called from within the `main` routine:

```
SInt32   gUserVolumeLevel;

int main( int argc, char* argv[] )
{
    ...

    GetDefaultOutputVolume( &gUserVolumeLevel );

    RunApplicationEventLoop();

    SetDefaultOutputVolume( gUserVolumeLevel );

    return( 0 );
}
```

Shortly after application startup, `GetDefaultOutputVolume` is called to get the current volume level of the user's computer. That level is retained in the global variable `gUserVolumeLevel`. When the program is about to exit (when `RunApplicationEvenLoop` returns), the speaker volume is restored to its initial setting.

The CheckboxDemo program is capable of muting the speakers of the user's computer, so what would happen if the program *didn't* include this speaker volume code in main? If the user checked the mute checkbox, clicked the OK button, and then quit the program, the speaker volume would remain off.

Note that a Macintosh user typically makes a *systemwide change*, which is a change that affects the system, not just one program. These changes include changing speaker volume or monitor resolution by choosing System Preferences from the Apple menu. Unless a program exists specifically to serve as a utility that alters systemwide settings, that program shouldn't make lasting changes to the user's computer. When the user quits a program, he or she typically expects the computer to be in the same state as it was before the program was launched. In the spirit of that expectation, CheckboxDemo is capable of muting the user's speakers. CheckboxDemo is a simple application that exists to demonstrate a programming technique. It is *not* a full-fledged application that a user expects to be a speaker-volume-adjusting utility! Being a good citizen of Mac OS X, CheckboxDemo is courteous enough to restore the speaker volume to the level it was at before the program launched.

GetDefaultOutputVolume accepts a single argument—a pointer to a SInt32 (signed 32-bit integer) variable. When GetDefaultOutputVolume returns this variable, it will hold a value between 0 and 256. A value of 0 signifies that the volume is off, and a value of 256 means the volume is set to its highest setting. Integral values within this range denote a volume level set proportional to the value. Thus, a value of, say, 128, would mean the volume level is at half its maximum setting.

In main, GetDefaultOutputVolume is used to capture the volume level of the user's Mac before the program has a chance to alter this level. After the event loop exits and the program is about to terminate, main calls SetDefaultOutputVolume to restore the volume to this initial level. SetDefaultOutputVolume accepts one argument—a value between 0 and 256. Again, a value of 0 mutes the speakers, and a value of 256 sets the speaker volume to its highest volume.

After the user clicks the OK button, the program responds to the command generated by the button by invoking the CommandEventHandler event handler, which in turn invokes the DoneCommandHandler routine to handle this one specific command. Here the program accesses the checkbox to determine its state:

```
ControlHandle    muteCheckbox;
ControlID        muteControlID = { kControlSignature,
                                   kMuteCheckboxControlID };
SInt32           muteValue;

GetControlByID( window, &muteControlID, &muteCheckbox );
muteValue = GetControl32BitValue( muteCheckbox );
```

A muteValue of 1 (the program defines the constant kCheckboxOn to this value) means the checkbox is checked, or on. In that case, the program calls SetDefaultOutputVolume to turn off the speakers on the user's computer:

```
if ( muteValue == kCheckboxOn )
    SetDefaultOutputVolume( kVolumeOffLevel );
```

As mentioned, `SetDefaultOutputVolume` sets the speaker volume level of the user's Mac. Here the level is set to 0, or off. For clarity, the program defines a constant for the speaker-off level. The constant `kVolumeOffLevel` has a value of 0.

If `GetControl32BitValue` instead returns a value of 0 (for thoroughness the program defines `kCheckboxOff` to this value, though that constant isn't used here), the checkbox is unchecked, or off. In that case, the speaker volume is set to the level at program startup:

```
else
    SetDefaultOutputVolume( gUserVolumeLevel );
```

After the volume level is set, a call to `SysBeep` is made to provide the user with some feedback. If the mute checkbox is checked at the time the OK button is clicked, no sound will be heard. If the checkbox is unchecked, a single beep at the volume noted at startup will be heard. Example 5.2 provides the complete listing for the CheckboxDemo program.

Example 5.2 **CheckboxDemo Source Code**

```
#include <Carbon/Carbon.h>


#define    kDoneCommand              'Done'
#define    kControlSignature         'LxZZ'
#define    kMuteCheckboxControlID      3
#define    kCheckboxOff                0
#define    kCheckboxOn                 1
#define    kVolumeOffLevel             0

pascal OSStatus CommandEventHandler( EventHandlerCallRef handlerRef,
                                     EventRef event, void *userData );

pascal void   DoneCommandHandler( WindowRef window );


SInt32   gUserVolumeLevel;

int main( int argc, char* argv[] )
{
    IBNibRef         nibRef;
    WindowRef        window;
    OSStatus         err;
    EventTargetRef   target;
    EventHandlerUPP  handlerUPP;
    EventTypeSpec    cmdEvent = { kEventClassCommand,
                                  kEventProcessCommand };
```

continues

Example 5.2   **Continued**

```
err = CreateNibReference( CFSTR("main"), &nibRef );

  err = SetMenuBarFromNib( nibRef, CFSTR("MainMenu") );

  err = CreateWindowFromNib( nibRef, CFSTR("MainWindow"), &window );

  DisposeNibReference( nibRef );

  target = GetWindowEventTarget( window );
  handlerUPP = NewEventHandlerUPP( CommandEventHandler );
  InstallEventHandler( target, handlerUPP, 1, &cmdEvent,
                       (void *)window, NULL );

  ShowWindow( window );

  GetDefaultOutputVolume( &gUserVolumeLevel );

  RunApplicationEventLoop();

  SetDefaultOutputVolume( gUserVolumeLevel );

  return( 0 );
}


pascal OSStatus CommandEventHandler( EventHandlerCallRef handlerRef,
                                     EventRef event, void *userData)
{
  OSStatus    result = eventNotHandledErr;
  HICommand   command;
  WindowRef   window;



 window = ( WindowRef )userData;



 GetEventParameter( event, kEventParamDirectObject,

                       typeHICommand, NULL,

                       sizeof (HICommand), NULL, &command);



 switch ( command.commandID )
```

```
   {
      case kDoneCommand:
         DoneCommandHandler( window );
         result = noErr;
         break;
   }
   return result;
}


pascal void DoneCommandHandler ( WindowRef  window )
{
   ControlHandle   muteCheckbox;
   ControlID       muteControlID = { kControlSignature,
                                     kMuteCheckboxControlID };
   SInt32          muteValue;

   GetControlByID( window, &muteControlID, &muteCheckbox );
   muteValue = GetControl32BitValue( muteCheckbox );

   if ( muteValue == kCheckboxOn )
      SetDefaultOutputVolume( kVolumeOffLevel );
   else
      SetDefaultOutputVolume( gUserVolumeLevel );

   SysBeep( 1 );
}
```

Text Input Fields

To accept user input, your program's window could use text input fields. This type
of control enables the user to type text in an outlined box. Although accepting user-
supplied text is the primary use of a text input field, such a control also can be used to
display text. If your window is to display a small amount of static text, a static text field
is the resource item to use. However, if your program instead will display a small
amount of dynamically created text, a text input field should be used.

If you peek ahead a bit at the description of the TextInputItems program, you'll see
that Figure 5.12 shows a window that includes a text input field to accept text (a user-
supplied string) and a text input field to display text (the user-supplied string converted to uppercase characters).

To work with a text input field, your program will add a text input field item to a
window resource, assign that field a control ID, and then access the control from
source code.

Text Input Fields and the Nib Resource

In a nib resource, dragging a text input field item from the palette to a window creates a text input field. The text input field is the framed white box located at the left edge of the palette, as shown back in Figure 5.4. A text input field is a control, so you'll assign a control ID to it so that your program can communicate with it. Figure 5.11 shows a window with three text input fields. In this figure, the top field is being given a control ID that consists of a signature of LxZZ and an ID of 1. This chapter's "Radio Buttons" section provides more details about control IDs.

Figure 5.11   A window resource that holds three text input controls.

> **Note**
>
> For aesthetic purposes, you can surround one or more text input fields with a border that displays a title. In Figure 5.11, the lower two text input fields are within a group box. One way to add a group box to a window is to drag the box from the palette to the window and then move and resize it to surround the text input item or items. You can click the middle of the three buttons along the top of the palette to see the pane that displays the group box.
>
> When boxing items, you need to be careful about the planes in which items lie. If you create a text input item and then add a group box that surround the text edit item, the result might be a window that doesn't enable the user to enter text in the text edit item. Instead, to ensure user input is possible, you can box items by selecting the items to group and then choosing Box from the Group In submenu of the Layout menu.

Text Input Fields and Source Code

From your source code, you'll access a text input field by obtaining a handle to the control and then using that handle in a call to the Carbon routine GetControlData.

  This chapter's discussion of radio buttons introduced the GetControlByID routine that's used to obtain a handle to a control. GetControlByID works with any type of control. Pass the routine the reference to the window in which the text input field resides, a pointer to the combination of the control's signature and ID (in the form of a `ControlID` variable), and a pointer to a variable where `GetControlByID` can place the control handle (in the form of a `ControlHandle` variable). For the text input field shown at the top of the window in Figure 5.12, the code to obtain a control handle could look like this:

```
#define   kControlSignature     'LxZZ'
#define   kStringInControlID        1

ControlHandle   stringInTextEdit;
ControlID       stringInControlID = { kControlSignature, kStringInControlID };

GetControlByID( window, &stringInControlID, &stringInTextEdit );
```

Now it's time to learn some new stuff. A control can have an integer as its value. You saw that in the discussion of radio button groups. For such a control, the `GetControl32BitValue` is used to obtain the control value. Another type of control might have something other than an integer for its value. A text input field is such a control. Its value is a string. For such controls, obtain the control's data using the `GetControlData` routine rather than the `GetControl32BitValue` function. Here's the prototype for `GetControlData`:

```
OSErr GetControlData( ControlRef       inControl,
                      ControlPartCode  inPart,
                      ResType          inTagName,
                      Size             inBufferSize,
                      void *           inBuffer,
                      Size *           outActualSize );
```

The `inControl` parameter is a handle to the control to be accessed. Pass the `ControlHandle` variable that was filled in by a previous call to `GetControlByID`. A `ControlHandle` is type `ControlRef`.

The `inPart` specifies the part of the control to be accessed. Some controls have different parts. Consider the time indicator control. It is a small digital clock that displays the current time (click the middle button in the row of buttons at the top of the palette in Interface Builder to see the time indicator control at the bottom of the palette). If your program uses such a control, it might have cause to access just a part of this control, such as the hour part, the minute part, and so forth. Apple defines several constants to be used in specifying what part of a control is to be accessed. For a time indicator, those would be the constants `kControlClockHourDayPart`, `kControlClockMinuteMonthPart`, `kControlClockSecondYearPart`, and `kControlClockAMPMPart`. For a text input field, there really is only one part to the control, so the data that's to be accessed isn't specific to that part of the control. Here you use the Apple-defined constant `kControlEntireControl`.

The `inTagName` is one of several constants defined in the ControlDefinitions.h header file. This constant supplies `GetControlData` with some specifics about the type of data that's to be accessed from the control. For a text input field, use the constant `kControlEditTextCFStringTag`.

The `inBufferSize` is the size in bytes of the information to be obtained. Use `sizeof` with the data type corresponding to the value in the control. For a text input field control, the value can be accessed as a `CFString` (the `CFString` type was discussed in Chapter 2).

The `inBuffer` is a pointer to a variable that is to hold the value returned by `GetControlValue`. If you're obtaining the data as a `CFString`, declare a variable of type `CFStringRef` and pass a pointer to that variable here.

In the `inBufferSize` parameter, you supply `GetControlValue` with the size of the data to obtain. Here in the `outActualSize` parameter, `GetControlValue` replies with the actual size of the data. This should match the `inBufferSize`, and if your program has no use for this information, you can pass `NULL` in place of a pointer to a variable of type `Size`.

Now it's time to move on to an example of an actual call to `GetControlData`. Assuming a control handle has been stored in variable `stringInTextEdit` by a call to `GetControlByID` (as shown in the previous snippet), the following code can be used to fill the variable `theString` with the text currently in the text input field referenced by the `stringInTextEdit` control handle:

```
CFStringRef    theString;

GetControlData( stringInTextEdit,
                kControlEntireControl,
                kControlEditTextCFStringTag,
                sizeof( CFStringRef ),
                &theString,
                NULL );
```

Now, what should be done with the obtained data? That's up to you and what you want your program to accomplish. Your program most likely will examine the user's information and base some decision on that information. As an alternate, your program might need to manipulate the user's input and then redisplay that altered value. In many cases, your program will want to supply some feedback, or some value, to the user in response to obtaining information from a text input field. You can do that by accessing a text input field and then drawing a string to it. To write to, rather than read from, a text input field, use the `SetControlData` routine:

```
OSErr SetControlData( ControlRef      inControl,
                      ControlPartCode inPart,
                      ResType         inTagName,
                      Size            inSize,
                      const void *    inData );
```

When you know how to use `GetControlData`, you know how to use `SetControlData`. The first three `SetControlData` parameters are identical to the first three `GetControlData` parameters. You pass a handle to the control to access, a constant representing the control part to access (again, `kControlEntireControl` for a text input field), and a constant specifying the type of data involved (again, the constant `kControlEditTextCFStringTag`).

The `SetControlData inSize` parameter is the same as the `GetControlData`
`inBufferSize` parameter. Use `sizeof( CFString )` again. The last parameter, `inData`, is
a pointer to the data to assign to the control. Again, use a pointer to a `CFStringRef`
variable. In `SetControlData`, where you're setting a control value rather than retrieving
a control value, this string needs to have been assigned a value *before* the function call.

The following is a call to `SetControlData`. Assume a handle to the control has been
obtained by a call to `GetControlByID`. Further assume that this handle is stored in the
`ControlHandle` variable `stringOutTextEdit`:

```
CFStringRef   theString = CFSTR( "Excellent idea!" );

SetControlData( stringOutTextEdit,
                kControlEntireControl,
                kControlEditTextCFStringTag,
                sizeof( CFStringRef ),
                &theString );
```

TextInputItems Program

The purpose of the TextInputItems program is to demonstrate how to get a value
from a text input field and how to set a value in a text input field.

Figure 5.12 shows the window displayed by the TextInputItems program. Type any
string in the top text input field, click the Convert to Uppercase button, and the program
converts the input string to uppercase and displays it in the bottom text input field.

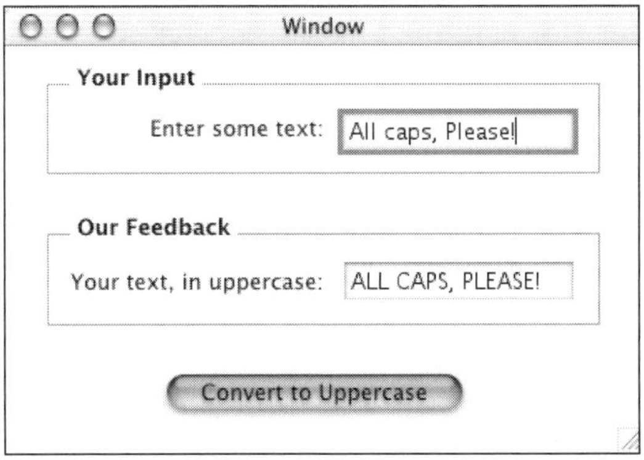

Figure 5.12   The window displayed by the TextInputItems program.

Editing the Nib File

The project's nib file requires a window resource that holds two text input fields. As
shown in Figure 5.13, the window resource also holds a number of other items,
including two group boxes, two static text items, and one push button. As far as

program functionality is concenred, all the other items, with the exception of the push button, are optional.

Figure 5.13   Associating a control ID with a text input control.

As shown in Figure 5.13, the upper of the two text input fields has a control ID that consists of a signature of UPPR and an ID of 1. The lower text input field has the same signature and an ID of 2. The Convert to Upper push button has a command of Cupr.

Like the signature of a control ID, a command can consist of a mix of uppercase and lowercase characters. Because Apple uses all lowercase characters in its predefined command constants (such as quit), you might consider including at least one uppercase character in your program's commands. I've done that here and will carry on with this system for the remainder of this book's examples.

The text input field that's used to receive the user's input is surrounded by a box that's created by clicking the text input field control and the static text item to the left of the control and then choosing Box from the Group In submenu in the Layout menu. The box surrounding the lower text input field, though, is created by dragging a group box from the palette to the window.

In this chapter's discussion of text input fields and the nib file, I've included a caveat regarding grouping text input field items. Using the group box item from the palette can result in enclosed text input fields that are "buried" within the group box. Such fields don't enable user input. That's why I opted to instead use the menu Box menu item for the upper group box. For a border around the *output* text edit item, though, you can go ahead and use the group box from the palette. It's actually best if the user *can't* enter text in this item. If the user does, it won't affect the program. When it comes time to place a string in the output text edit item, the program will replace the user's text. However, if the user is allowed to enter text in this box, it may be a source of confusion.

Writing the Source Code

The complete source code listing for the TextInputItems program appears in Example 5.3. Much of this code should look familiar to you. The TextInputItems program installs an event handler that responds to a command. This `CommandEventHandler` routine operates in a manner similar to other command-handling routines you've seen, including the one appearing in this chapter's radio button group example. Of interest is the routine called by `CommandEventHandler` in response to a `kUppercaseCommand` (the command issued by a click on the Convert to Uppercase button).

`MyCommandHandler` calls `GetControlByID` twice to obtain a handle to each of the two text input controls. A call to `GetControlData` is made to retrieve the user-entered string from the upper text input field. A call to `SetControlData` is made to display a string in the lower of the two text input fields. Rather than simply redisplaying the user's string, I've opted to include a quick, simple example of string manipulation using a Core Foundation String Services routine. These Carbon string-handling functions were introduced in Chapter 2.

Here you see that the `CFStringUppercase` is a routine that makes it easy to convert a string reference by a `CFStringRef` to all uppercase characters:

```
CFStringUppercase( theString, NULL );
```

The first `CFStringUppercase` parameter is the string to convert. Pass a `CFStringRef` variable that already has been assigned some value. The second parameter is a pointer to a supplementary data. As of this writing, this second parameter is unimplemented, and you should pass in a value of `NULL`, as shown in the preceding snippet.

After a control's look has been altered, your program should call `DrawOneControl` to update the display of the control. In this program, the look of the text input field used to hold the user's string doesn't get altered. The display of the typed characters is handled by the system, so that doesn't count. The look of the text input field used to provide feedback to the user, though, does get altered. The call to `SetControlData` draws a string to the control. To update that one control, call `DrawOneControl` with the control's handle as the only argument:

```
DrawOneControl( stringOutTextEdit );
```

Example 5.3 **TextInputItems Source Code**

```
#include <Carbon/Carbon.h>

#define    kUppercaseCommand      'Cupr'
#define    kControlSignature      'UPPR'
#define    kStringInControlID        1
#define    kStringOutControlID       2
```

continues

Example 5.3 **Continued**

```
pascal OSStatus CommandEventHandler( EventHandlerCallRef handlerRef,
                                     EventRef event, void *userData );

pascal void  MyCommandHandler( WindowRef window );

int main( int argc, char* argv[] )
{
   IBNibRef          nibRef;
   WindowRef         window;
   OSStatus          err;
   EventTargetRef    target;
   EventHandlerUPP   handlerUPP;
   EventTypeSpec     cmdEvent = { kEventClassCommand,
                                  kEventProcessCommand );

   err = CreateNibReference( CFSTR("main"), &nibRef );

   err = SetMenuBarFromNib( nibRef, CFSTR("MainMenu") );

   err = CreateWindowFromNib( nibRef, CFSTR("MainWindow"), &window );

   DisposeNibReference( nibRef );

   target = GetWindowEventTarget( window );
   handlerUPP = NewEventHandlerUPP( CommandEventHandler );
   InstallEventHandler( target, handlerUPP, 1, &cmdEvent,
                        (void *)window, NULL );

   ShowWindow( window );

   RunApplicationEventLoop();

   return( 0 );
}


pascal OSStatus CommandEventHandler ( EventHandlerCallRef handlerRef,
                                      EventRef event, void *userData)
{
   OSStatus     result = eventNotHandledErr;
   HICommand    command;
   WindowRef    window;

   window = ( WindowRef )userData;

   GetEventParameter( event, kEventParamDirectObject, typeHICommand, NULL,
                      sizeof (HICommand), NULL, &command);

   switch ( command.commandID )
```

```
      {
         case kUppercaseCommand:
            MyCommandHandler( window );
            result = noErr;
            break;
      }
      return result;
}


pascal void MyCommandHandler ( WindowRef  window )
{
   ControlHandle   stringInTextEdit;
   ControlHandle   stringOutTextEdit;
   ControlID       stringInControlID  = { kControlSignature,
                                          kStringInControlID };
   ControlID       stringOutControlID = { kControlSignature,
                                          kStringOutControlID };
   CFStringRef     theString;

   GetControlByID( window, &stringInControlID, &stringInTextEdit );
   GetControlByID( window, &stringOutControlID, &stringOutTextEdit );

   GetControlData( stringInTextEdit,
                   kControlEntireControl,
                   kControlEditTextCFStringTag,
                   sizeof( CFStringRef ),
                   &theString,
                   NULL );


   CFStringUppercase( theString, NULL );

   SetControlData( stringOutTextEdit,
                   kControlEntireControl,
                   kControlEditTextCFStringTag,
                   sizeof( CFStringRef ),
                   &theString );

   DrawOneControl( stringOutTextEdit );
}
```

For More Information

The following web sites provide extra information about some of this chapter's topics:

- **Control manager routines:**
  http://developer.apple.com/techpubs/macosx/Carbon/HumanInterfaceToolbox
  /ControlManager/Control_Manager/index.html

- **Control GUI guidelines:**
  http://developer.apple.com/techpubs/macosx/Carbon/HumanInterfaceToolbox
  /Aqua/aqua.html

6

Menus

M ENUS ENABLE A USER TO INTERACT with your program. You've seen that creating a new Project Builder project automatically provides your program with a few standard menus. However, you'll want to add other application-specific menus to the menu bar that your program displays. In this chapter, you'll read about creating and editing menus, including hierarchical menus. You'll also see how your program can access, disable, enable, or change the characteristics of any menu or menu item.

Menu Basics

Your program defines its menus (and items in those menus) in a menu bar resource in the project's main.nib file. Interface Builder makes it easy to add items to menus and to edit existing menu and submenu items. After your program's menu items are set up and assigned commands, your event-handling source code defines the response your program should have to a selection by the end user.

Adding New Menus and New Menu Items

To add a menu to a program, you'll use Interface Builder to add the menu and its items to the menu bar. You'll then add command-handling code to the project's source code file.

Menu and Menu Item Nib Resources

Adding a new menu and adding items to that menu are tasks easily accomplished in Interface Builder. Chapter 2, Overview of Mac OS X Programming," discusses adding a new menu to a menu bar in the nib resource file. Specifically, I walk you through adding a Sound menu with a Beep menu item. Chapter 3, "Events and the Carbon Event Manager," discusses adding a command signature to a menu item.

Now we're on to the next step: adding a new menu to a menu bar resource. To do so, click the blue Submenu box in the palette and drag that item to the menu bar. Determine between which two existing menus the new menu should go, position it between those menus, and drop it there. Then, double-click the menu name and type in a new name.

The new menu comes with one item. You can click the menu to expose its item, and then double-click that item and type a new name for it. To add a second item to the menu, click the blue Item box and drag and drop it under the first item in the menu. In Figure 6.1, a second item is being added beneath the Beep Once item in the Sound menu.

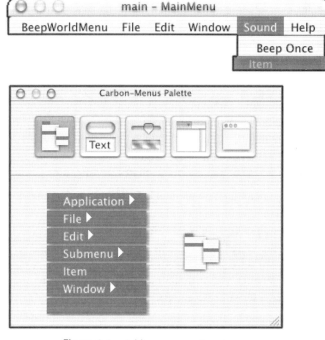

Figure 6.1   Adding a menu item to a menu.

When a menu item is selected by the user, that selection won't result in any action taking place unless the selected item has a command associated with it *and* the command is handled in the program's source code. In Figure 6.2, the Beep Once menu item is being assigned a command of **Bep1**. The program that uses this resource responds to a selection of the second item in the Sound menu. The second item needs a command too. The command can be any four characters, but a command of **Bep2** makes sense here.

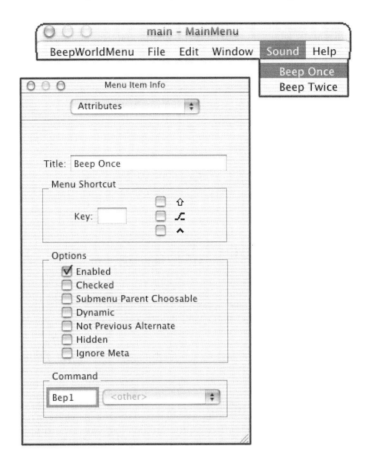

Figure 6.2 Assigning a command to a menu item.

Menu-Handling Source Code

To handle menu item selection, you'll write an event handler routine that calls `GetEventParameter` to extract the four-character command from the command-related event. The event handler has the following format:

```
pascal OSStatus CommandEventHandler( EventHandlerCallRef handlerRef,
                                      EventRef event, void *userData)
{
    OSStatus   result = eventNotHandledErr;
    HICommand  command;
```

```
GetEventParameter( event, kEventParamDirectObject, typeHICommand,
                   NULL, sizeof (HICommand), NULL, &command );

switch ( command.commandID )
{
  // case section for each command to handle
 }
return result;
}
```

The `switch` includes a `case` section for each command to be handled. For the two menu items shown in the Sound menu in Figure 6.2, those command will have constants like these:

```
#define  kBeep1Command  'Bep1'
#define  kBeep2Command  'Bep2'
```

Install the event handler using an `EventTypeSpec` that has a class of `kEventClassCommand` and a kind of `kEventProcessCommand`. The user data associated with the command is typically a window:

```
EventTargetRef   target;
EventHandlerUPP  handlerUPP;
EventTypeSpec    cmdEvent = { kEventClassCommand,
                             kEventProcessCommand };

target = GetWindowEventTarget( window );
handlerUPP = NewEventHandlerUPP( CommandEventHandler );
InstallEventHandler( target, handlerUPP, 1, &cmdEvent,
                     (void *)window, NULL );
```

When a command-related event occurs, the Carbon Event Manager invokes your program's event handler to handle the event.

NewMenuAndItems Program

The purpose of the NewMenuAndItems program is to provide an example that makes use of a new menu that includes more than one menu item. Its source code is listed in Example 6.1.

The menu that's handled by the program is the one pictured in Figure 6.2. Choosing the Beep Once menu item generates a `Bep1` command, while choosing the Beep Twice item produces a `Bep2` command. Both commands are handled within the program's `CommandEventHandler` routine. That routine calls the application-defined function `BeepCommandHandler`. This routine simply loops the appropriate number of times, playing the system sound once for each pass through the loop. Although this routine could have been eliminated in favor of simply calling `SysBeep` from the `CommandEventHandler`, the intent here is to provide the format for a more complicated program that that handles more commands and that does more than play the system sound.

Example 6.1   **NewMenuAndItems Source Code**

```
#include <Carbon/Carbon.h>


#define    kBeep1Command    'Bep1'
#define    kBeep2Command    'Bep2'

pascal  OSStatus  CommandEventHandler( EventHandlerCallRef handlerRef,
                                       EventRef event, void *userData );

pascal  void   BeepCommandHandler( UInt32 numBeeps );


int main( int argc, char* argv[] )
{
    IBNibRef          nibRef;
    WindowRef         window;
    OSStatus          err;
    EventTargetRef    target;
    EventHandlerUPP   handlerUPP;
    EventTypeSpec     cmdEvent = { kEventClassCommand,
                                   kEventProcessCommand };

    err = CreateNibReference( CFSTR("main"), &nibRef );

    err = SetMenuBarFromNib( nibRef, CFSTR("MainMenu") );

    err = CreateWindowFromNib( nibRef, CFSTR("MainWindow"), &window );

    DisposeNibReference( nibRef );

    target = GetWindowEventTarget( window );
    handlerUPP = NewEventHandlerUPP( CommandEventHandler );
    InstallEventHandler( target, handlerUPP, 1, &cmdEvent,
                         (void *)window, NULL );

    ShowWindow( window );

    RunApplicationEventLoop();

    return( 0 );
}


pascal OSStatus CommandEventHandler( EventHandlerCallRef handlerRef,
                                     EventRef event, void *userData)
{
    OSStatus    result = eventNotHandledErr;
    HICommand   command;
    UInt32      numBeeps;
```

continues

Example 6.1   **Continued**

```
GetEventParameter( event, kEventParamDirectObject, typeHICommand,
                   NULL, sizeof (HICommand), NULL, &command);

    switch ( command.commandID )
    {
       case kBeep1Command:
          numBeeps = 1;
          BeepCommandHandler( numBeeps );
          result = noErr;
          break;
       case kBeep2Command:
          numBeeps = 2;
          BeepCommandHandler( numBeeps );
          result = noErr;
          break;
    }
    return result;
}


pascal void BeepCommandHandler ( UInt32 numBeeps )
{
    UInt32    x;

    for ( x = 1; x <= numBeeps; x++ )
       SysBeep( 1 );
}
```

Adding a Submenu to a Menu

A submenu, or hierarchical menu, is a menu-within-a-menu. When the cursor moves over the submenu name, a menu drops down and the user chooses an item from the submenu by moving the cursor over the item of interest and then releasing the mouse button.

A submenu is created in Interface Builder using the Submenu item from the palette. First bring the menu bar to the forefront and click the menu that's to receive the submenu. With the menu items displayed, drag the Submenu item from the palette and drop it on the menu. If you've missed your mark and the submenu ends up with an incorrect placement in the menu, just click it and drag and drop it at its proper position between the existing menu items. In Figure 6.3, a submenu it being added after the Beep Twice item in the Sound menu in the menu bar resource of a nib file.

Supply the submenu with a name by double-clicking the submenu and typing the new name. The new submenu comes with one item. You can rename it by double-clicking it and typing a name. To add another menu item, display the submenu contents by clicking the submenu name, clicking Item in the palette, and then dragging and dropping the item to the displayed submenu. In Figure 6.4, an item is being added beneath the Soft menu item in the Volume submenu.

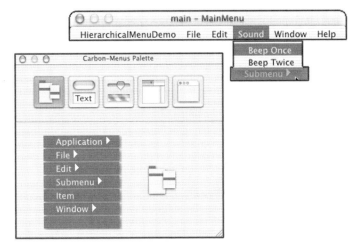

Figure 6.3 Adding a submenu to a menu

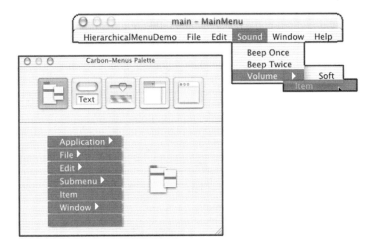

Figure 6.4 Adding a menu item to a submenu.

A menu item in a submenu is given a command in exactly the same way any other menu item is given a command: you make the item active and then enter the command in the item's Info window. In Figure 6.5, the Loud menu item in the Volume submenu is given the command vmHI (for volume high).

Figure 6.5   Assigning a command to an item in a submenu.

The handling of a submenu item is the same as the handling of any other menu item. You just include event-handling code for the item's command. The next example program provides a demonstration of this. We discuss it next.

HierarchicalMenuDemo Program

The purpose of the HierarchicalMenuDemo program is to demonstrate the workings of a program that includes a submenu.

The HierarchicalMenuDemo program includes the Volume submenu in the Sound menu pictured in Figure 6.5. In creating the submenu, the Soft item was given a command of `vmLO` and the Loud item was given a command of `vmHI`.

The code for HierarchicalMenuDemo is very similar to that of the previous program, NewMenuAndItems, so including the entire source code listing for the program is unnecessary. Instead, I'll point out the new code that's added to the NewMenuAndItems code.

NewMenuAndItems defined two constants. One is for the Beep Once menu item command and one is for the Beep Twice menu item command. HierarchicalMenuDemo uses those same two constants and adds two more command constants. Now that the Sound menu has a Volume hierarchical menu that holds two menu items, there are a total of four menu items that have commands, as shown in the following code:

```
#define   kBeep1Command        'Bep1'
#define   kBeep2Command        'Bep2'

#define   kVolumeLowCommand    'vmLO'
#define   kVolumeHighCommand   'vmHI'
```

Choosing either item from the Volume submenu results in a change in the volume level of the user's computer. SetDefaultOutputVolume, which is a routine discussed in the CheckboxDemo program in Chapter 5, "Controls," accepts a value in the range of 0 (volume off) to 256 (maximum volume level). I'll use 64 (somewhat arbitrarily) for the low volume setting, and I'll use the maximum volume value of 256 for the high volume setting:

```
#define   kVolumeLowLevel       64
#define   kVolumeHighLevel      256
```

The global variable gUserVolumeLevel keeps track of the volume level of the user's machine at program startup:

```
SInt32    gUserVolumeLevel;
```

In main, gUserVolumeLevel is used to get the volume level before any alteration is made to it. It is used again to restore the volume level before quitting. This code is similar to that which was used in the Chapter 5 CheckboxDemo program:

```
int main( int argc, char* argv[] )
{
    ...

    GetDefaultOutputVolume( &gUserVolumeLevel );

    RunApplicationEventLoop();

    SetDefaultOutputVolume( gUserVolumeLevel );

    return( 0 );
}
```

The event handler CommandEventHandler responds to selections of the Beep Once and Beep Twice menu items as it did in the NewMenuAndItems program. Here, however, the switch statement gains two new case sections, one for each submenu item. Note that the code doesn't distinguish between commands received from a hierarchical menu or a normal menu; a command is a command.

```
switch ( command.commandID )
{
   case kBeep1Command:
      numBeeps = 1;
      BeepCommandHandler( numBeeps );
```

```
            result = noErr;
            break;
        case kBeep2Command:
            numBeeps = 2;
            BeepCommandHandler( numBeeps );
            result = noErr;
            break;
        case kVolumeLowCommand:
            SetVolumeLevel( kVolumeLowLevel );
            result = noErr;
            break;
        case kVolumeHighCommand:
            SetVolumeLevel( kVolumeHighLevel );
            result = noErr;
            break;
    }
```

The application-defined `SetVolumeLevel` routine accepts an integer in the range of 0 to 256 and uses that value to change the volume level:

```
void  SetVolumeLevel( SInt32 volume )
{
    SetDefaultOutputVolume( volume );
    SysBeep( 1 );
}
```

Altering Menus Characteristics

A menu title, and the title of any or all the items in that menu, can be altered. The most common change to a menu or menu item is the disabling or enabling of it. If the function of a menu item, or an entire menu, doesn't make sense at a particular point in the running of your program, that menu item or menu should be disabled. For instance, if the user closes all your program's windows, you'll want some or all the items in the Window menu to be disabled.

Although the act of disabling and enabling are the main reasons your program will alter the look of a menu or menu item, there are other ways in which your program might want to alter a menu or menu item characteristic. Fortunately, the Carbon API makes it easy to change the font, size, or style of any menu item.

Accessing Menus and Menu Items

Before you change the look of a menu or menu item, you need to obtain access to it. That access comes in the way of a menu handle or menu reference. A menu handle has the data type `MenuHandle`, and a menu reference has the data type `MenuRef`. `MenuHandle` and `MenuRef` are the same type, so Carbon routines that list one type as the data type of a parameter will in fact accept an argument of either type.

To gain access to a menu, you need to give that menu an ID. That's something that hasn't been done in any of the previous examples in this book, so listen closely. To give a menu an ID, click the menu in Interface Builder, choose Show Info from the Tools menu, and then type an ID in the Menu ID field in the window's Attributes pane.

Figure 6.6 shows a Color menu being given an ID of 6. In this example, the Color menu is the sixth application menu from the left side of the menu bar (the program will automatically get the Apple menu added to the far left of its menu bar), so the menu is given an ID of 6. You are, however, free to choose your own numbering scheme for menus.

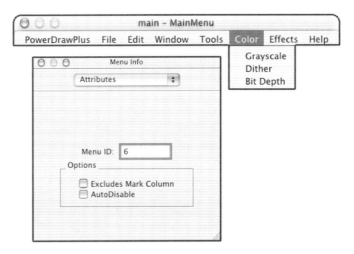

Figure 6.6 Assigning a menu ID to a menu.

After assigning a menu an ID, make a call to the Carbon routine `GetMenuHandle` to obtain a handle to the menu. Because you'll most likely access a menu from a variety of places in your program's code, it often makes sense to declare the menu handle as a global variable, obtain the handle early in the running of your program, and then use it whenever the menu, or an item in the menu, needs to be altered.

```
#define   kColorMenuID    6

MenuHandle    gColorMenu;

gColorMenu = GetMenuHandle( kColorMenuID );
```

After your program has a handle to a menu, it can access that menu and all the menu's items. You'll define constants that establish the item number of each item in a menu that might be altered. Doing this means that if you decide to rearrange a menu's items in Interface Builder, you need to make changes to menu-accessing code in just one place—the section of your program that defines the program's constants. For the Color menu shown in Figure 6.6, those constants might look like this:

```
#define   kColorMenuGrayscaleItemNum    1
#define   kColorMenuDitherItemNum       2
#define   kColorMenuBitDepthItemNum     3
```

In the next sections, you'll see how access to a menu makes it possible to enable and disable menu items (and an entire menu) and to change the characteristics of a menu item's title (such as its font, size, or style). All these techniques require that your program first obtain a handle to the menu that holds the item or items to alter.

Enabling and Disabling Menus and Menu Items

A program can disable any items in a menu, or even the entire menu. When a menu item is disabled, it appears lighter, or dimmer, than an enabled item. In addition, choosing the item produces no effect.

When one or more items in a menu are disabled, the title of the menu remains enabled so that the end user can access the remaining enabled items in that menu. However, an entire menu—including the menu title in the menu bar—can be disabled. To do that, your program can define the menu to be auto disabling in the project's nib file (Figure 6.6 shows the AutoDisable option), or it can explicitly disable the menu within the project's source code. If the menu is set to auto disable, any time all the items in that menu are disabled, the menu title itself will become disabled. If the menu isn't set to auto disable, all the items in the menu can be disabled and the menu title itself will remain enabled. In that case, the program's code could disable the menu title if desired.

Figure 6.7 shows a Sound menu that's been disabled. The top of the figure emphasizes that the menu title can be disabled, while the bottom of that same figure shows the dimmed appearance of disabled items within the menu.

Figure 6.7   A disabled menu and its disabled items.

Enabling and Disabling Menu Items in a Nib Resource

When you add a new menu item to a menu in your project's nib file, that menu item is enabled by default. Within the nib file, you can toggle that item's state from enabled to disabled easily. To do that, click the menu item, choose Show Info from the Tools menu, and then uncheck the Enabled checkbox in the Options section of the Attributes pane of the Info window. You can look back at Figure 6.2 or Figure 6.5 to see this checkbox.

Setting the state of a menu item in the nib file is good for *initially* enabling or disabling an entire menu or a menu item. For instance, if you add a menu item to the Window menu, you'll most likely have that item disabled initially if your program doesn't open any windows at launch. Regardless of which items you initially disable, there's a good chance that your application will need to disable one or more items as the program runs. As expected, that's done from within source code.

Enabling and Disabling Menu Items in Source Code

Disabling a menu item in the nib resource is fine for setting that item's initial state, but the bulk of menu item enabling and disabling work will be done in your program's code. Before attempting to alter a menu item, you need to get a handle to that item's menu. Consider the Color menu shown back in Figure 6.6, and the following constant definitions:

```
#define    kColorMenuID                   6
#define    kColorMenuGrayscaleItemNum     1
#define    kColorMenuDitherItemNum        2
#define    kColorMenuBitDepthItemNum      3
```

You now should declare a menu handle and call `GetMenuHandle` to get a handle to the desired menu:

```
MenuHandle    gColorMenu;

gColorMenu = GetMenuHandle( kColorMenuID );
```

To disable a menu item, call `DisableMenuItem`. Pass this Carbon routine a handle to the menu that holds the item to alter and the number of the item to alter. For instance, to disable the last menu item (the third item from the top of the menu), use this code:

```
DisableMenuItem( gColorMenu, kColorMenuBitDepthItemNum );
```

To enable a menu item, use the Carbon routine `EnableMenuItem`. It accepts the same arguments as `DisableMenuItem`. This call to `EnableMenuItem` enables the Dither menu item:

```
EnableMenuItem( gColorMenu, kColorMenuDitherItemNum );
```

Interestingly, a single call to `DisableMenuItem` can disable an entire menu. When a menu is disabled, its title is disabled, as are all the items in the menu. To disable an entire menu, pass a value of 0 as the number of the item to disable:

```
DisableMenuItem( gColorMenu, 0 );
```

To enable a menu and its contents, perform a similar trick using a call to `EnableMenuItem`, like this:

```
EnableMenuItem( gColorMenu, 0 );
```

DisableEnableMenu Program

The purpose of the DisableEnableMenu program is to demonstrate how to disable and enable individual menu items and an entire menu. Yes, you finally get to silence those annoying beeps that have appeared in so many previous examples!

DisableEnableMenu displays the menu bar and window shown in Figure 6.7. The six radio buttons are all part of one radio button group. To make a change to the state of a menu item in the Sound menu, or to change the state of the entire menu, click one of the buttons and then click the Do It button. Click the Sound menu to verify that the change in state took place. Note that disabling the entire menu renders ineffective enabling changes to individual items in that menu. For instance, if the Sound menu is disabled, an attempt to enable one of the items in that menu will fail.

The Sound menu is the same one found in this chapter's NewMenuAndItem program. Here, though, the menu has been assigned an ID. Figure 6.8 shows that the Sound menu has an ID of 4.

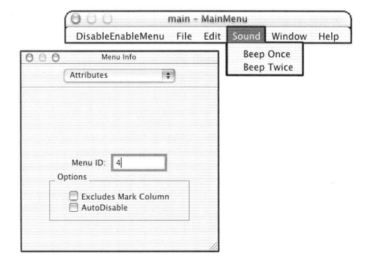

Figure 6.8　Assigning a menu ID to a program's Sound menu.

The program's window includes two controls: a radio button group and a push button. As shown in Figure 6.9, the radio button group has a control ID consisting of a signature of `abCD` (you can assume this is the program's creator code) and an ID of 1. The push button has a command of `SnMn` (for Sound menu). If you aren't familiar with controls and control IDs, refer to Chapter 5 in general and that chapter's "Radio Buttons" section in particular.

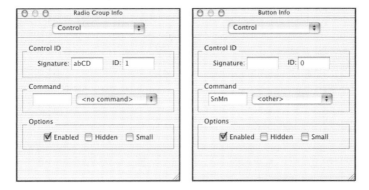

Figure 6.9 The control ID and command for two controls.

DisableEnableMenu is another program based on this chapter's NewMenuAndItems program, which means it's also another program that doesn't require a complete source code listing. Instead, we'll only take a look at the pertinent additions to NewMenuAndItems.

NewMenuAndItems defined two constants—one for the command associated with each of the two items in the Sound menu. Those contents appear here, but there's also a third command to watch for. It is the one associated with the Do It button:

```
#define    kBeep1Command              'Bep1'
#define    kBeep2Command              'Bep2'
#define    kAdjustSoundMenuCommand    'SnMn'
```

The radio button group has a control ID with a signature of abCD and ID of 1:

```
#define    kControlSignature          'abCD'
#define    kRadioGroupControlID       1
```

A call to GetControl32BitValue returns the number of the radio button that was on at the time the Do It button was clicked. The program defines a constant to match the six values GetControl32BitValue can return:

```
#define    kDisableSoundMenu          1
#define    kEnableSoundMenu           2
#define    kDisableBeepOnceItem       3
#define    kEnableBeepOnceItem        4
#define    kDisableBeepTwiceItem      5
#define    kEnableBeepTwiceItem       6
```

Accessing the Sound menu is dependent on using the menu's ID to obtain a menu handle for the menu. Changing the state of either item in that menu is dependent on knowing the item number of the item to change:

```
#define    kSoundMenuID               4
#define    kSoundMenuBeepOnceItemNum  1
#define    kSoundMenuBeepTwiceItemNum 2
```

A global variable is used to hold the handle to the Sound menu. In `main`, this variable is given its value by way of a call to `GetMenuHandle`:

```
MenuHandle    gSoundMenu;

...

gSoundMenu = GetMenuHandle( kSoundMenuID );
```

In the `CommandEventHandler` routine, the `switch` statement keeps its original two `case` sections to handle Sound menu item selections, and it gains one new `case` section to handle a click on the Do It button:

```
switch ( command.commandID )
{
   case kBeep1Command:
      numBeeps = 1;
      BeepCommandHandler( numBeeps );
      result = noErr;
      break;
   case kBeep2Command:
      numBeeps = 2;
      BeepCommandHandler( numBeeps );
      result = noErr;
      break;
   case kAdjustSoundMenuCommand:
      AdjustSoundMenu( window );
      result = noErr;
      break;
}
```

The handling of the Do It button necessitates a new routine—`AdjustSoundMenu`. The format of `AdjustSoundMenu` matches the format of `BeepCommandHandler`, which was in the Chapter 5 example program RadioButtonGroup.

As shown in the following code, a call to `GetControlByID` provides a reference to the radio button group control, and a call to `GetControl32BitValue` uses that reference to find which of the group's radio buttons was on. A `switch` statement provides the code to handle each button in the group. Each `case` section in this `switch` calls either `EnableMenuItem` or `DisableMenuItem` to enable or disable the item or menu included in the radio button title.

```
void  AdjustSoundMenu( WindowRef window )
{
   ControlHandle   adjustSndMenuRadioButtonGroup;
   ControlID       adjustSndMenuControlID = { kControlSignature,
                                              kRadioGroupControlID };
   SInt32          adjustSndMenuValue;

   GetControlByID( window, &adjustSndMenuControlID,
                   &adjustSndMenuRadioButtonGroup );
   adjustSndMenuValue = GetControl32BitValue(
```

```
                                    adjustSndMenuRadioButtonGroup );

      switch ( adjustSndMenuValue )
      {
         case kDisableSoundMenu:
            DisableMenuItem( gSoundMenu, 0 );
            break;
         case kEnableSoundMenu:
            EnableMenuItem( gSoundMenu, 0 );
            break;
         case kDisableBeepOnceItem:
            DisableMenuItem( gSoundMenu, kSoundMenuBeepOnceItemNum );
            break;
         case kEnableBeepOnceItem:
            EnableMenuItem( gSoundMenu, kSoundMenuBeepOnceItemNum );
            break;
         case kDisableBeepTwiceItem:
            DisableMenuItem( gSoundMenu, kSoundMenuBeepTwiceItemNum );
            break;
         case kEnableBeepTwiceItem:
            EnableMenuItem( gSoundMenu, kSoundMenuBeepTwiceItemNum );
            break;
      }
```

Changing the Characteristics of a Menu Item

Disabling or enabling a menu item involves obtaining a handle to the menu that holds
the item and then using that handle as an argument to a menu-altering Carbon routine. Disabling or enabling a menu item also involves changing the characteristic of
that menu item. To change some other characteristic of a menu item, first get a handle
to that menu. To change an item in the File menu, for instance, begin like this:

```
   #define   kFileMenuID    1

   MenuHandle   gFileMenu;

   gFileMenu = GetMenuHandle( kFileMenuID );
```

Now choose the appropriate Carbon routine that makes the required change. For
instance, to change the font used to display the name of the New menu item, call
SetMenuItemFontID. In the following code, the FMGetFontFamilyFromName routine is
called to get a FMFontFamily reference to the font of interest. You then pass
FMGetFontFamilyFromName the name of this font, with the name prefaced with \p to
specify that the name is in Pascal format. In this code, the font family is Times.

```
   FMFontFamily   fontFamily;

   fontFamily = FMGetFontFamilyFromName( "\pTimes" );
```

Now call `SetMenuItemFontID`. In the call, you pass the handle to the menu, the item number of the menu item to change (the New item appears first in the File menu), and the font family:

```
SetMenuItemFontID( gFileMenu, 1, fontFamily );
```

You can repeat the previous steps (get a menu handle and use that handle in a call to the appropriate menu–altering routine) for any change to a menu item's appearance.

To change the font of one menu item, call `SetMenuItemFontID`. To change the font of all items in a menu, call `SetMenuFont`. In the `SetMenuFont` routine, you pass a menu handle, a font family, and a constant specifying the point size of the font. For example, to change the font of all the items in the File menu to 24 point Times, use this code:

```
fontFamily = FMGetFontFamilyFromName( "\pTimes" );
SetMenuFont( gFileMenu, fontFamily, 24 );
```

You can change the style of a menu item's title by calling `SetItemStyle`. Pass this routine a handle to the menu that holds the item of interest, the number of the item of interest, and a constant that specifies the style to use. The following is a line that changes the Open menu item (the second menu item down from the top of the File menu) to italic:

```
SetItemStyle( gFileMenu, 2, italic );
```

There are eight constants for specifying menu item style: `normal`, `bold`, `italic`, `underline`, `outline`, `shadow`, `condense`, and `extend`. These constants can be used individually, or two or more constants can be combined, as shown in the following code:

```
SetItemStyle( gFileMenu, kFileMenuCloseItemNum, italic + bold );
```

MenuItemCharacteristics Program

The purpose of the MenuItemCharacteristics program is to provide an example of how to change the look of menu items.

MenuItemCharacteristics is a simple program that doesn't include any menus other than the ones supplied in the standard main.nib file that's part of any new nib-based project. The program doesn't include any event-handling code other than the call to `RunApplicationEventLoop`. You can see that the entire source code listing for this program (Example 6.2) consists of just a little more than two dozen lines of code. MenuItemCharacteristics exists simply to display some nonstandard menu items in the File menu. On the left of Figure 6.10, you see the program's File menu. On the right of that figure, you see the same File menu as it appears in a program that doesn't alter that menu.

The program makes a call to `SetMenuFont` to change the font of all the items in the File menu. Each item is set to be displayed in 24 point Courier. Then, a call to `SetMenuItemFontID` is made to change just the New menu item to Times. The Open menu item is set to appear in italics by way of a call to `SetItemStyle`. Finally, the Close menu item is set to appear in both italics and bold by combining the italic and bold constants in a call to `SetItemStyle`.

Figure 6.10   The File menu before and after being altered by a program.

Note

Menu item numbering includes blank items. For instance, Figure 6.10 shows that a blank space exists
between the Open and Close menu items in the File menu. This blank space is considered an item—item
number 3. That's why the constant for the Close menu item, kFileMenuCloseItemNum, has a value of 4.

Example 6.2   **MenuItemCharacteristics Source Code**

```
#include <Carbon/Carbon.h>


#define    kFileMenuID                1
#define    kFileMenuNewItemNum        1
#define    kFileMenuOpenItemNum       2
// blank (empty) item                 3
#define    kFileMenuCloseItemNum      4

#define    kBigFontSizePts            24


MenuHandle    gFileMenu;

int main( int argc, char* argv[] )
{
   IBNibRef       nibRef;
   WindowRef      window;
   OSStatus       err;
   FMFontFamily   fontFamily;

   err = CreateNibReference( CFSTR("main"), &nibRef );

   err = SetMenuBarFromNib( nibRef, CFSTR("MainMenu") );


   err = CreateWindowFromNib( nibRef, CFSTR("MainWindow"), &window );
```

continues

Example 6.2   **Continued**

```
    DisposeNibReference( nibRef );



    gFileMenu = GetMenuHandle( kFileMenuID );

    fontFamily = FMGetFontFamilyFromName( "\pCourier" );
    SetMenuFont( gFileMenu, fontFamily, kBigFontSizePts );

    fontFamily = FMGetFontFamilyFromName( "\pTimes" );
    SetMenuItemFontID( gFileMenu, kFileMenuNewItemNum, fontFamily );

    SetItemStyle( gFileMenu, kFileMenuOpenItemNum, italic );
    SetItemStyle( gFileMenu, kFileMenuCloseItemNum, italic + bold );

    ShowWindow( window );

    RunApplicationEventLoop();

    return( 0 );
}
```

Pop-Up Menus

A pop-up menu is a menu that exists in a window rather than in the menu bar. Figure 6.11 shows a pop-up menu. At the top of this figure, you see the pop-up menu before it's clicked. The bottom of the figure shows that this pop-up menu consists of four items, with the first item (Choose a shirt size) serving as the title of the menu itself.

Like a radio button group, a pop-up menu provides the user with a number of options from which the user picks one. Whether you should use a radio button group or a pop-up menu is up to you. There are no strict rules here. However, Apple does offer the following guideline: If a situation requires five or more options, you should use a pop-up menu rather than a radio button group.

Figure 6.11 shows a pop-up menu that uses the first menu item as a means of telling the user the purpose of the menu. Another way to do this is to place a static text item to the left of the pop-up menu, as shown in Figure 6.12.

Pop-Up Menu Nib Resource

Now it's time to announce this chapter's Mystery Menu question: When is a menu not a menu? To spare you the unbearable suspense you'd be subjected to should I hold off on the answer, I'll reveal it right here: a menu isn't a menu when it is a pop-up menu because a pop-up menu is actually a control. Thus, to use Interface Builder to add a pop-up menu to a window, you use the Controls pane of the palette. There you drag a pop-up menu control (it looks like a pop-up menu with Item 1 as its displayed menu item) from the palette to a window. Figure 6.13 shows a pop-up menu control being added to a window.

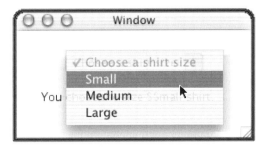

Figure 6.11 A pop-up menu in a window.

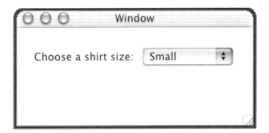

Figure 6.12 A pop-up menu with a static text caption.

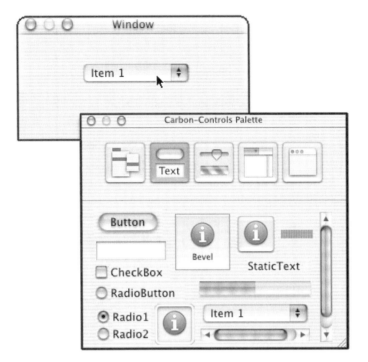

Figure 6.13   Adding a pop-up menu to a window.

A pop-up menu comes with one item; it has a title of Item 1. To edit this title, double-click it and type the new title. Now comes the interesting part. To add additional items to this control, you *don't* use the Controls pane of the palette. Instead, you use the Menus pane of the palette to drag and drop an item from the palette to the pop-up menu. This chapter's "Menu and Menu Item Nib Resources" section illustrates how this is done for a normal menu.

Each item in the pop-up menu should have a command associated with it. The possible exception is the first item. If you use that item as a menu title (as shown in Figure 6.11), it needs no command. In Figure 6.14, the Small item in the pop-up menu is given a command of pop1 (for the first selectable item in the pop-up menu). As with any item capable of having a command associated with it, the four-character naming scheme is up to you.

Pop-Up Menu Source Code

When the user chooses an item from a pop-up menu, that selection generates a command event, just as if the item resided in a standard menu in the menu bar. Your program responds to the command event as it would any other type of event generated by a command. The PopUpMenuDemo program provides an example of this.

Figure 6.14   Assigning a command to a pop-up menu item.

PopUpMenuDemo Program

The purpose of the PopUpMenuDemo program is to demonstrate the handling of a pop-up menu in a window.

Running the program displays the window shown in Figure 6.11. You can click the pop-up menu to reveal the items in that menu. Choosing the Small, Medium, or Large item results in a short string being drawn in the window. The string acknowledges which item was just selected. For instance, choosing Small results in the string *You chose the size Small shirt.* being drawn.

The first item, Choose a shirt size, serves as the menu's title and is disabled. Any menu item can be disabled by unchecking the Enabled checkbox in the Info window for that item. Figure 6.14 shows the Enabled checkbox checked for the Small menu item.

The three enabled menu items in the pop-up menu have commands of pop1, pop2, and pop3. The source code, shown in its entirety in Example 6.3, includes three constants corresponding to these commands.

The program's event handler calls GetEventParameter to extract the command from the event. If the command is either pop1, pop2, or pop3, the event handler responds by calling the application-defined `PopUpCommandHandler` routine. This is shown in the following code for the `pop1` event:

```
case kPopUpSizeSmallCommand:
    PopUpCommandHandler( window, kPopUpSizeSmallCommand );
    result = noErr;
    break;
```

The `PopUpCommandHandler` routine includes some code that's new to you. It's code that will be described in more depth in the next chapter of this book. Based on the menu item selected, the routine draws one of three strings to the window. Before drawing a string, `PopUpCommandHandler` clears the drawing area of text from a previous string by drawing a white rectangle. To work with a rectangle, you declare a variable of type `Rect` and then assign values to the rectangle's four coordinates. If the assignment is made at the time of declaration, the order of the coordinates is top, left, bottom, and right (`T`, `L`, `B`, and `R`):

```
//                      { T,  L,  B,   R }
Rect  whiteRect = { 60, 10, 90, 270 };
```

The preceding code creates a rectangle that has a top coordinate 60 pixels down from the top of the window to which the rectangle will eventually be drawn. The bottom coordinate is 90 pixels down. This establishes a rectangle 30 pixels in height. The left side of the rectangle is 10 pixels in from the left side of the window, while the right side of the rectangle is 270 pixels in from the left side (resulting in a rectangle 260 pixels across).

Declaring a `Rect` variable doesn't draw a rectangle. To do that, you must call `FrameRect` to frame a rectangle or `FillRect` to fill the rectangle. In the following code, `FillRect` is called to fill the `whiteRect` rectangle with a solid white pattern (which just happens to be the background pattern of a window):

```
Pattern white;

GetQDGlobalsWhite( &white );
FillRect( &whiteRect, &white );
```

The system predefines several patterns for your use. As will be discussed in detail in Chapter 7, "QuickDraw Graphics," these patterns reside in a QuickDraw global structure. To get a reference to one of these patterns, call the appropriate Carbon routine: `GetQDGlobalsWhite` to obtain a white pattern, `GetQDGlobalsBlack` to get a black pattern, and so forth. You then use that pattern in a call to `FillRect`. `FillRect` accepts a pointer to the rectangle to fill and a pointer to the pattern to use in the filling of said rectangle.

After filling the rectangle to effectively erase any previously drawn text, the program enters a `switch` statement where the appropriate string is drawn to the now-empty area in the bottom portion of the window.

Example 6.3   **PopUpMenuDemo Source Code**

```
#include <Carbon/Carbon.h>


#define    kPopUpSizeSmallCommand      'pop1'
#define    kPopUpSizeMediumCommand     'pop2'
#define    kPopUpSizeLargeCommand      'pop3'

pascal OSStatus CommandEventHandler( EventHandlerCallRef handlerRef,
                                     EventRef event, void *userData );

void PopUpCommandHandler ( WindowRef window, UInt32 command );


int main( int argc, char* argv[] )
{
   IBNibRef          nibRef;
   WindowRef         window;
   OSStatus          err;
   EventTargetRef    target;
   EventHandlerUPP   handlerUPP;
   EventTypeSpec     cmdEvent = { kEventClassCommand,
                                  kEventProcessCommand };

   err = CreateNibReference( CFSTR("main"), &nibRef );

   err = SetMenuBarFromNib( nibRef, CFSTR("MainMenu") );

   err = CreateWindowFromNib( nibRef, CFSTR("MainWindow"), &window );

   DisposeNibReference( nibRef );

   target = GetWindowEventTarget( window );
   handlerUPP = NewEventHandlerUPP( CommandEventHandler );
   InstallEventHandler( target, handlerUPP, 1, &cmdEvent,
                        (void *)window, NULL );

   ShowWindow( window );

   RunApplicationEventLoop();

   return( 0 );
}


pascal OSStatus CommandEventHandler( EventHandlerCallRef handlerRef,
                                     EventRef event, void *userData)
{
   OSStatus    result = eventNotHandledErr;
   HICommand   command;
   WindowRef   window;
```

continues

Example 6.3 **Continued**

```
    window = ( WindowRef )userData;

    GetEventParameter( event, kEventParamDirectObject, typeHICommand,
                       NULL, sizeof (HICommand), NULL, &command);

    switch ( command.commandID )
    {
       case kPopUpSizeSmallCommand:
          PopUpCommandHandler( window, kPopUpSizeSmallCommand );
          result = noErr;
          break;
       case kPopUpSizeMediumCommand:
          PopUpCommandHandler( window, kPopUpSizeMediumCommand );
          result = noErr;
          break;
       case kPopUpSizeLargeCommand:
          PopUpCommandHandler( window, kPopUpSizeLargeCommand );
          result = noErr;
          break;
    }
    return result;
}


void  PopUpCommandHandler( WindowRef window, UInt32 command )
{
//                      {  T,  L,  B,   R }
    Rect      whiteRect = { 60, 10, 90, 270 };
    Pattern   white;

    SetPortWindowPort( window );

    GetQDGlobalsWhite( &white );
    FillRect( &whiteRect, &white );
    MoveTo( 30, 80 );

    switch ( command )
    {
       case kPopUpSizeSmallCommand:
          DrawString( "\pYou chose the size Small shirt." );
          break;
       case kPopUpSizeMediumCommand:
          DrawString( "\pThe size Medium shirt was selected." );
          break;
       case kPopUpSizeLargeCommand:
          DrawString( "\pThat was the size Large shirt." );
          break;
    }
}
```

For More Information

The following web sites provide extra information about some of this chapter's topics:

- **Menu GUI guidelines:**

  `http://developer.apple.com/techpubs/macosx/Carbon/HumanInterfaceToolbox/`
  `Aqua/aqua.html`

- **Menu manager routines:**

  `http://developer.apple.com/techpubs/macosx/Carbon/HumanInterfaceToolbox`
  `/MenuManager/Menu_Manager/index.html`

7

QuickDraw Graphics

W HAT IS QUICKDRAW? You're asking that question just a little late. QuickDraw is a large set of Carbon API routines that enables programmers to draw simple shapes such as lines, rectangles, and ovals. All the programs in this book, as well as the programs you created, relied on QuickDraw. That's because QuickDraw is all about drawing, including the drawing of interface items such as windows and menus.

The routines in the Carbon API are conceptually categorized into separate areas. Each area consists of routines that, for the most part, work with a single programming topic. Each Carbon area can have a name that includes "Manager," such as Window Manager, Menu Manager, and Carbon Event Manager. On the other hand, some Carbon API areas don't include "Manager" in their names. QuickDraw is one such area.

In this chapter, you'll see how to draw shapes, as well as how to enhance the look of such shapes by filling them with monochrome or colored patterns.

QuickDraw Basics

So, you're ready to jump right into drawing a fancy shape such as an oval filled with a checkerboard pattern, right? No you aren't! Before drawing shapes, make sure that you know about the graphics grid that's used to define the size and window location of a shape. You also need to know how to go about setting drawing parameters, such as the thickness of the lines used to draw shapes. Topics such as these are covered in this section.

Coordinate System

When your program draws, it needs to specify where to draw. There are two components to this specification. Your program should specify the window to which to draw,
and it should specify where in that window the drawing is to take place.

Drawing always takes place in a port, which is a graphics entity used to hold information about a drawing. Every window has its own port, and the screen (monitor)
itself includes a port. The screen's port makes it possible for the desktop to be displayed. Note that the desktop isn't a window, yet it gets drawn to. A window's port
makes it possible to specify to which window to draw, in the event a program enables
more than one window at a time to be open.

You tell your program which port to draw to by passing to the SetPortWindowPort
routine the window in which the drawing will occur. Typically, this is done within a
window update routine, before any drawing takes place:

```
void UpdateWindow( WindowRef window )
{
    SetPortWindowPort( window );

    // now start drawing
}
```

Specifying where within a window a drawing should take place is done by specifying
the coordinates at which to draw. Macintosh windows make use of a coordinate grid
system. In this system, every pixel in the content area of a window is defined by a
coordinate pair. The content area is the area drawn to. This area excludes the window
title bar and scroll bars, if present.

The grid is a coordinate system that has a horizontal component and a vertical
component. The upper-left pixel in a window's content area has a horizontal component of 0 (zero pixels from the left side of the window) and a vertical component of 0
(zero pixels from the top of the window). The horizontal component of the pair is
specified first, followed by the vertical component. Thus, the upper-left pixel of a window is referred to as (0, 0).

To specify the pixel located 20 pixels in from the left side of the window, but still
in the uppermost row of pixels, you'd refer to the pixel as (20, 0). Figure 7.1 illustrates
this. In this figure, the circled pixel is 60 pixels in from the left side of the window and
20 pixels down from the top of the window, so to reference this one pixel, you'd use
the coordinate pair of (60, 20).

In Chapter 4, "Windows," the example program WindowUpdate used a graphics
grid. There, before a string of text was drawn, the MoveTo routine was called to specify
the starting point for drawing. That code specified that the drawing should start 30 pixels from the left side of the window and 60 pixels down from the top of the window:

```
MoveTo( 30, 60 );

DrawString( "\pThis is drawn from code!" );
```

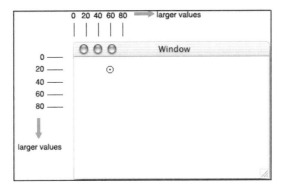

Figure 7.1 The coordinate system of a window.

The MoveTo routine specifies the starting location for drawing based on a coordinate pair global to the window. Another routine, Move, specifies the starting location based on the current drawing location. Here are the prototypes for those two routines:

```
void  MoveTo( SInt16 h, SInt16 v );
void  Move( SInt16 h, SInt16 v );
```

To see these routines used in conjunction with one another, consider this snippet:

```
MoveTo( 40, 80 );
Move( 70, 10 );
```

The call to MoveTo moves the starting location to the pixel 40 pixels in from the left side of the window and 80 pixels down from the top of the window. The call to Move moves the starting point 70 pixels to the left of its *current position* of 40 pixels in, and 10 pixels down from its *current position* of 80 pixels down. After both routines execute, the result is that the new starting position for drawing is at pixel (110, 90).

To use Move to move the starting position to the left or up, use negative values. For instance, to move the starting position left 10 pixels and up 20 pixels, call Move like this:

```
Move( -10, -20 );
```

Line and Shape Drawing and the Graphics Environment

Each port has its own *graphics environment*. That is, a port has a set of properties that a program makes use of when drawing to that port. Consider this snippet:

```
SetPortWindowPort( window );

MoveTo( 20, 60 );
LineTo( 120, 60 );
```

The preceding call to MoveTo specifies that the drawing should start 20 pixels from the left side of the window and 60 pixels down from the top of that window. LineTo is a drawing routine that draws a line from the current starting location to the specified ending location. The call to LineTo specifies that a line should be drawn from that starting point and extend to the point 120 pixels from the left side of the window and 60 pixels down from the top of the window. The result is a horizontal line 100 pixels in length. That line will be black, and it will have a thickness of one pixel. The line has these attributes because a graphics port has a graphics environment, and that environment assigns its various fields default values. One of those fields is line thickness, which is initially set to one pixel. Collectively, these fields that affect line and shape drawing make up a conceptual drawing device referred to as the *graphics pen.*

There are a few access routines that enable you to change the attributes of the graphics pen. You've already seen that Move and MoveTo move the graphics pen (though you might not have known that what was being affected by these routines was, in fact, the graphics pen). To change the pixel size of lines drawn in a port, call SetPortPenSize:

```
void SetPortPenSize( CGrafPtr   port,
                     Point      penSize );
```

A CGrafPtr is a pointer to a color graphics port, which is the type of port associated with a window. Rather than simply passing the WindowRef, you need to pass a pointer to the window's port. That's easy enough to do with the GetWindowPort routine. Assuming the window is a WindowRef variable, here's how you can change the size of the graphics pen so that it draws lines that have a height of 8 pixels and a width of 5 pixels:

```
Point   thePenSize = { 8, 5 };

SetPortPenSize( GetWindowPort( window ), thePenSize );
```

Use the PenNormal routine to return the current port's graphics pen to its initial, or default, state:

```
PenNormal();
```

Text Drawing and the Graphics Environment

The characteristics of text drawn to a window also are under the control of the port's graphics environment, though the graphics pen won't affect the look of the text. For instance, if you call SetPortPenSize to change the thickness of the graphics pen, the thickness of lines will be affected, but the thickness of the text won't be. To change the look of the text, use any of the following routines:

```
void TextFont( SInt16 font);
void TextFace( StyleParameter face );
void TextSize( SInt16 size );
```

TextFont establishes the font used in drawing text to the current graphics port. The font parameter specifies the font family ID. Each font is considered a family, and each family has an ID. A font family ID of 0 is used to represent the system font. This system font ID is the initial value that a graphics port uses for the display of text. Rather than trying to determine what ID is associated with any one font family, simply use the `FMGetFontFamilyFromName` routine to let the system supply your program with this information. Pass `FMGetFontFamilyFromName` the exact name of a font, prefaced with \p, and the routine returns the ID for that font. Use that value in a call to `TextFont`:

```
FMFontFamily     fontFamily;

fontFamily = FMGetFontFamilyFromName( "\pTimes" );
TextFont( fontFamily );
```

`TextFace` sets the style of the font in which text is drawn. The `face` parameter can be any one, or any combination, of the following constants: `normal`, `bold`, `italic`, `underline`, `outline`, `shadow`, `condense`, and `extend`. To set the face to one particular style, use the appropriate style constant. After the following call, all text drawn with `DrawString` will be in bold:

```
TextFace( bold );
```

To set the face to a combination of styles, use a plus (+) sign between each style:

```
TextFace( italic + underline + shadow );
```

To change the size of text drawn to a window, use the `TextSize` routine. Pass a size in points. A 12-point size is common and is considered a de facto standard for text. The initial setting for the text size is 0, which represents the size of the system font. This line of code sets the text size to twice the normal size:

```
TextSize( 24 );
```

GraphicsPortAndPen Program

The purpose of the GraphicsPortAndPen program is to provide an example of the effects of making changes to a window's graphics environment.

The GraphicsPortAndPen program draws three horizontal lines, making changes to the graphics pen between the drawing of each line. The program also draws three lines of text, making changes to the graphics environment before drawing each line of text. Figure 7.2 shows the window that this program displays.

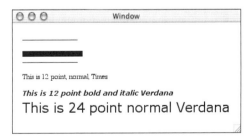

Figure 7.2 Altering a window's graphics environment affects line and text drawing.

Example 7.1 provides the source code for the GraphicsPortAndPen program. Most of the code that makes up this program was introduced in the WindowUpdate program found in Chapter 4. Of interest here is only the application-defined UpdateWindow routine. All the Carbon calls in UpdateWindow have been discussed on the preceding pages. One point worth discussing is the length of the three horizontal lines that UpdateWindow draws. Each line is drawn by calling Line. The Line routine draws a line of the specified length, regardless of where the current starting point is.

Notice in Figure 7.2 that the middle line is slightly longer than the other two lines, despite the fact that each line is drawn with the same arguments passed to Line. The reason the middle line is longer is that before it is drawn, the size of the graphics pen is set to a height and width of 10 pixels. It is the change in pixel width of the pen that affects the overall length of the line that's subsequently drawn. The call to Line does indeed draw a line 100 pixels in length, but because the pen's width is 10 pixels rather than 1, that extra width shows up after the line is drawn.

The bulk of the source code in all the examples in this chapter is similar. In fact, only the UpdateWindow routine in each program varies. All the rest of the code in each example is *identical*. For that reason, only this first example shows the entire source code listing. After this example, each following example shows only the routine that holds new code—the UpdateWindow routine.

Example 7.1   **GraphicsPortAndPen UpdateWindow Source Code**

```
#include <Carbon/Carbon.h>



pascal OSStatus WindowEventHandler( EventHandlerCallRef handlerRef,
                                    EventRef event, void *userData );

void UpdateWindow( WindowRef window );


int main(int argc, char* argv[])
{
   IBNibRef         nibRef;
   OSStatus         err;
   WindowRef        window;
   EventTargetRef   target;
   EventHandlerUPP  handlerUPP;
   EventTypeSpec    windowEvent = { kEventClassWindow,
                                    kEventWindowDrawContent };

   err = CreateNibReference( CFSTR("main"), &nibRef );

   err = SetMenuBarFromNib( nibRef, CFSTR("MainMenu") );

   err = CreateWindowFromNib( nibRef, CFSTR("MainWindow"), &window );

   DisposeNibReference( nibRef );
```

```
   target = GetWindowEventTarget( window );
   handlerUPP = NewEventHandlerUPP( WindowEventHandler );
   InstallEventHandler( target, handlerUPP, 1, &windowEvent,
                        (void *)window, NULL );

   ShowWindow( window );

   RunApplicationEventLoop();

   return( 0 );
}

pascal OSStatus WindowEventHandler( EventHandlerCallRef handlerRef,
                                    EventRef event, void *userData)
{
   OSStatus    result = eventNotHandledErr;
   UInt32      eventKind;
   WindowRef   window;

   window = ( WindowRef )userData;

   eventKind = GetEventKind( event );

   if ( eventKind == kEventWindowDrawContent )
   {
      UpdateWindow( window );
   }
   return result;
}


void UpdateWindow( WindowRef window )
{
   Point          thePenSize = { 10, 10 };
   FMFontFamily   fontFamily;

   SetPortWindowPort( window );

   MoveTo( 20, 30 );
   Line( 100, 0 );

   SetPortPenSize( GetWindowPort( window ), thePenSize );
   MoveTo( 20, 50 );
   Line( 100, 0 );

   PenNormal();
   MoveTo( 20, 70 );
   Line( 100, 0 );

   fontFamily = FMGetFontFamilyFromName( "\pTimes" );
   TextFont( fontFamily );
```

continues

Example 7.1 **Continued**

```
  TextFace( normal );
  MoveTo( 20, 100 );
  DrawString( "\pThis is 12 point, normal, Times" );

  fontFamily = FMGetFontFamilyFromName( "\pVerdana" );
  TextFont( fontFamily );                 '
  TextFace( bold + italic );
  MoveTo( 20, 130 );
  DrawString( "\pThis is 12 point bold and italic Verdana" );

  TextFace( normal );
  TextSize( 24 );
  MoveTo( 20, 160 );
  DrawString( "\pThis is 24 point normal Verdana" );
}
```

Defining and Drawing Shapes

Lines, rectangles, round rectangles, and ovals are the basic shapes used in drawing. Earlier in this chapter, you were introduced to line drawing. This section will expand on those previous line-related discussions. Here you'll also read about drawing rectangles and squares (a square is a rectangle with four sides of identical length), ovals and circles (a circle is an oval with identical horizontal and vertical diameters), and round rectangles (a round rectangle is a rectangle with rounded corners).

Drawing Lines

Line drawing is accomplished using the Line and LineTo routines. Thanks to this chapter's "Line and Shape Drawing and the Graphics Environment" section and the GraphicsPortAndPen example program, which introduced both of these routines, this "Drawing Lines" section can be brief.

To draw a line, you can move to a starting pixel coordinate and then call LineTo to specify the ending pixel for the line. Here a horizontal line is drawn from a point 30 pixels in from the left side of a window and 50 pixels down from the top of the window, to a point 100 pixels in from the left side of the window:

```
  MoveTo( 30, 50 );
  LineTo( 100, 50 );
```

Because the line runs from a horizontal point of 30 to a horizontal point of 100, the horizontal length of the line is 70 pixels. To specify a line of a specific length, use the Line routine rather than the LineTo function. Here *the same line* as previously described is drawn using Line:

```
  MoveTo( 30, 50 );
  Line( 70, 0 );
```

Defining and Drawing Rectangles

The rectangle is an important shape in its own right. You'll often use rectangles to frame graphics or text. The rectangle is important also because it is used to define some other shapes, including the square, the round rectangle (such as an interface push button), and, perhaps surprisingly, the oval and circle. (Remember that a circle is a special type of oval).

Before drawing a rectangle, you declare a variable of type `Rect` and then specify the coordinates of the four sides of the rectangle. The coordinates are pixel values and are given in terms of the port of the window to which the rectangle will be drawn. Each coordinate is in the system described in this chapter's "Coordinate System" section. For instance, a top coordinate of 50 means the top side of the rectangle will be drawn 50 pixels from the top of the window in which the rectangle appears. The following snippet defines the rectangle that's shown in Figure 7.3.

```
//              T,  L,   B,   R
Rect    theRect = { 50, 80, 110, 180 };
```

To define the coordinates of a rectangle *after* the rectangle has been declared, use the `SetRect` routine. Pass `SetRect` a pointer to a `Rect` variable, along with the four rectangle-defining coordinates. Of importance here is that the *order* of the assignment of the coordinates differs for an initialization and a call to `SetRect`. For initialization, the order is top, left, bottom, and right. For `SetRect`, the order is left, top, right, and bottom. The following snippet defines the same rectangle as the one previously defined:

```
Rect    theRect;
//                     L,  T,   R,   B
SetRect( &theRect, 80, 50, 180, 110 );
```

Figure 7.3 shows the rectangle `theRect` after it's drawn. Note, however, that the assignment of coordinates to a rectangle isn't enough to actually draw the rectangle. To do that, call the `FrameRect` routine, passing the function a pointer to a previously defined rectangle:

```
FrameRect( &theRect );
```

As its name implies, `FrameRect` draws just the frame of a previously defined rectangle. To draw a rectangle that's filled with a pattern, call `FillRect`. Here, a previously defined rectangle is being drawn with a dark gray pattern:

```
Pattern    thePattern;

GetQDGlobalsDarkGray( &thePattern );

FillRect( &theRect, &thePattern );
```

The `GetQDGlobalsDarkGray` routine is one of five access functions that returns a pattern to a program. The preceding snippet is included here to provide an example of how a shape can be filled with a pattern, but there are other ways for your program to make use of patterns as well.

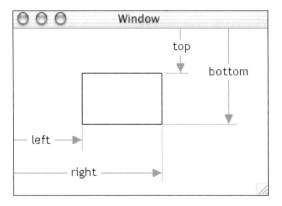

Figure 7.3 The pixel coordinates of a rectangle.

Note
This chapter's "Patterns" section provides you with all the details about using predefined system patterns and using patterns of your own creation.

Defining and Drawing Round Rectangles

The material in the preceding section is fundamental to the drawing of many types of shapes, so make sure you have a solid grasp of it. Our next step is to examine rectangles used with other types of shapes. Part of drawing a rectangle with rounded edges (like the one shown in Figure 7.4) involves first defining a rectangle. In the following code snippet, I'm defining the same rectangle used in the previous section and pictured in Figure 7.3.

```
Rect    theRect;
//                      L,  T,   R,   B
SetRect( &theRect, 80, 50, 180, 110 );
```

Now a call to FrameRoundRect draws the outline of the round rectangle:

```
//                          H,  V
FrameRoundRect( &theRect, 50, 50 );
```

The rectangle has the same size and window location as the one pictured back in Figure 7.3, but it has rounded corners. The degree of rounding of each corner is determined by the second and third arguments passed to FrameRoundRect. These two arguments define the horizontal and vertical diameter of a circle that is invisibly inscribed within the rectangle specified in the first FrameRoundRect argument. In Figure 7.4, I've gone ahead and drawn this circle in one of the four corners of the rectangle to illustrate how the circle diameters set the degree of roundness to a corner.

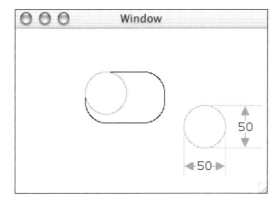

Figure 7.4   The pixel coordinates of a round rectangle.

As you read in the discussion of rectangles, a shape can be filled with a pattern using a fill routine. For a round rectangle, that routine is `FillRoundRect`:

```
Pattern    thePattern;

GetQDGlobalsDarkGray( &thePattern );

FillRoundRect( &theRect, &thePattern );
```

The `GetQDGlobalsDarkGray` pattern accessor routine is described in this chapter's "Patterns" section, and an example program that draws a round rectangle can be found in the "BasicShapes Program" section.

Defining and Drawing Ovals

The drawing of an oval is dependent on the defining of a rectangle. This chapter's "Defining and Drawing Rectangles" section tells you how to do that. To establish the coordinates of an oval, define a rectangle in which the oval will be inscribed. Here, I'm again defining the same rectangle used in the "Defining and Drawing Rectangles" section and pictured in Figure 7.3.

```
Rect    theRect;
//                    L,   T,   R,   B
SetRect( &theRect, 80, 50, 180, 110 );
```

Now a call to `FrameOval` draws the outline of the oval within the specified rectangle. The rectangle itself isn't drawn, though for clarity I've shown the rectangle in Figure 7.5:

```
FrameOval( &theRect );
```

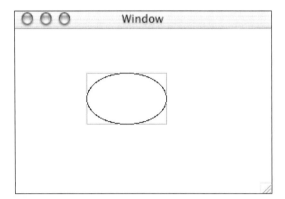

Figure 7.5   The outline of the oval.

Like other shapes, an oval can be filled with a pattern by using a fill routine. After obtaining a pattern, call `FillOval`:

```
Pattern    thePattern;

GetQDGlobalsLightGray( &thePattern );

FillOval( &theRect, &thePattern );
```

`GetQDGlobalsLightGray` and other pattern accessor routines are described in this chapter's "Patterns" section.

BasicShapes Program

The purpose of the BasicShapes program is to provide examples of how to frame and fill basic shapes such as a rectangle, oval, and round rectangle.

Figure 7.6 shows that when you run BasicShapes, you see a window that displays each of the three shapes discussed in this chapter. Example 7.2 shows that a call to `FillOval` fills the oval with a gray pattern. To fill the other two shapes, obtain a pattern and then follow the `SetRect` call with a call to `FillRect` or `FillRoundRect`.

Example 7.2   **BasicShapes UpdateWindow Source Code**

```
void UpdateWindow( WindowRef window )
{
    Rect       theRect;
    Pattern    thePattern;

    SetPortWindowPort( window );

    SetRect( &theRect, 40, 20, 180, 100 );
    FrameRect( &theRect );

    GetQDGlobalsGray( &thePattern );
```

```
    SetRect( &theRect, 120, 70, 220, 130 );
    FillOval( &theRect, &thePattern );
    FrameOval( &theRect );

    SetRect( &theRect, 50, 140, 140, 160 );
    FrameRoundRect( &theRect, 25, 25 );
}
```

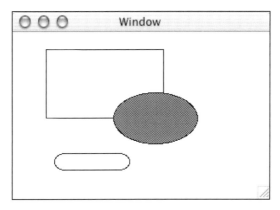

Figure 7.6 The window displayed by the BasicShapes program.

Patterns

Black lines? Empty rectangles? How boring. How "un-Macintosh"! Although I have managed to slip in a gray rectangle or two so far in this book, for the most part, things have been more drab than gray. Fortunately all that monochromeness was for the sake of brevity. I wanted to present short, concise examples of how to draw lines and shapes. Now that you know the basics, it's time to see how you can fill shapes with any of the dozens of predefined monochrome patterns present in the Mac OS X system software. It's also time to see how you easily can create your own colored patterns and use those patterns to fill lines and shapes.

QuickDraw Global System Patterns

When drawing a shape, such as a rectangle, you might want to simply frame the shape. On the other hand, you might want to fill that shape with a color or a pattern. As you'll see later in this chapter, you can define your own patterns. If you need a basic, monochrome pattern such as light gray or black, you can make use of one of the five predefined patterns that are available to all Mac programs.

To access one of the patterns, you need to know a little about a global data structure named `QDGlobals`. Here's how `QDGlobals` looks, as defined in the QuickDraw.h header file:

```
struct QDGlobals {
    char        privates[76];
    long        randSeed;
    BitMap      screenBits;
    Cursor      arrow;
    Pattern     dkGray;
    Pattern     ltGray;
    Pattern     gray;
    Pattern     black;
    Pattern     white;
    GrafPtr     thePort;
};
typedef struct QDGlobals    QDGlobals;
```

The members of this structure, with the exception of the array `privates`, are available to any program, including the one you're developing. To make use of one of the members of this structure, you use an accessor function. There's one such function for each member, except `privates`. Of most interest (in this chapter, anyway) are the five `Pattern` members. Each member defines a different monochrome pattern that your program can use in drawing lines and shapes. The access function for these five pattern members are as follows:

```
GetQDGlobalsWhite( Pattern * white );
GetQDGlobalsLightGray( Pattern * ltGray );
GetQDGlobalsGray( Pattern * gray );
GetQDGlobalsDarkGray( Pattern * dkGray );
GetQDGlobalsBlack( Pattern * black );
```

To get a pattern for use by your program, call the appropriate accessor function. Here a program gets a reference to the light gray pattern:

```
Pattern    thePattern;

GetQDGlobalsLightGray( &thePattern );
```

After you have a global pattern saved in a `Pattern` variable, you can use that pattern in the filling of shapes. The next section, "System Pattern List," describes a way to obtain still more system-defined monochrome patterns.

System Pattern List

The five patterns in the `QDGlobals` data structure come in handy. There will be times when you want to fill a shape with black, white, or a shade of gray, and these patterns are easy to access. However, there also will be times when you want the use of a more intricate pattern. In those cases, the system pattern list may help.

Every Mac system has 38 patterns, each stored in a pattern resource of type PAT. All these resources are collectively kept in a single pattern list resource of type PAT#. The

Carbon routine `GetIndPattern` is used to get a reference to a single pattern from a pattern list resource. Here's how `GetIndPattern` is called to provide a program with the use of one pattern from the list of 38 system patterns:

```
Pattern  thePattern;
short     thePatternListID = sysPatListID;
short     patternIndex = 12;

GetIndPattern( &thePattern, thePatternListID, patternIndex );
```

The first `GetIndPattern` parameter is a pointer to a variable of type `Pattern`. When `GetIndPattern` returns this variable, it will hold the desired pattern. The next parameter is the ID of the pattern list resource to access. It's possible to create your own list of patterns, so `GetIndPattern` needs to know which pattern list to access. The final `GetIndPattern` parameter is an index to the pattern to retrieve.

Pattern numbering in a list starts with the number 1. Figure 7.7 shows the 38 patterns and their associated index value. In the previous code snippet, the twelfth pattern in the list (the pattern that looks like bricks in Figure 7.7) is being sought.

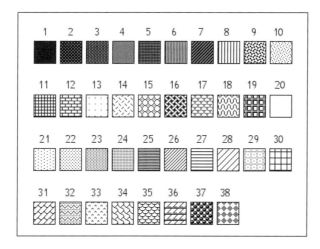

Figure 7.7   The patterns, with their index values, from the system pattern list.

After `GetIndPattern` finishes, the pattern variable (`thePattern` in the previous code snippet) can be used in the same way that a pattern obtained from the global variable `QDGlobals` can be used. An example of using a pattern to fill a shape appears in the following section of this chapter.

GlobalPatterns Program

The purpose of the GlobalPatterns program is to demonstrate how a program makes use of any of the five patterns that are part of the `QDGlobal` system data structure and any of the 38 patterns that are part of the system pattern list resource.

As shown in Figure 7.8, the GlobalPatterns program draws five rectangles along the top of the program's window. Each rectangle is filled in with one of the five system patterns. Beneath the top row are 38 smaller rectangles, each displaying one of the system patterns from the system pattern list resource.

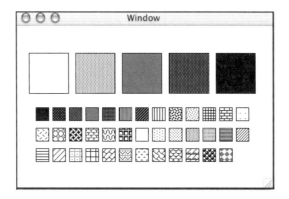

Figure 7.8   An example of the use of each of the five system patterns.

The GlobalPatterns program's `UpdateWindow` routine (shown in Example 7.3) uses a `for` loop to call each of the five `QDGlobal` pattern accessor routines, drawing and filling a rectangle in each pass through the loop. The program then uses a second `for` loop to call `GetIndPattern` 38 times, one time per pattern in the system pattern list resource. Each pass through the loop draws and fills one rectangle with one pattern.

Example 7.3   **GlobalPatterns UpdateWindow Source Code**

```
void UpdateWindow( WindowRef window )
{

    Rect      patternRect;
    Pattern   thePattern;
    short     thePatternListID = sysPatListID;
    short     x;

    SetPortWindowPort( window );

    SetRect( &patternRect, 20, 40, 80, 100 );

    for ( x = 1; x <= 5; x++ )
    {
        switch ( x )
```

```
      {
         case 1:
            GetQDGlobalsWhite( &thePattern );
            break;
         case 2:
            GetQDGlobalsLightGray( &thePattern );
            break;
         case 3:
            GetQDGlobalsGray( &thePattern );
            break;
         case 4:
            GetQDGlobalsDarkGray( &thePattern );
            break;
         case 5:
            GetQDGlobalsBlack( &thePattern );
            break;
      }

      FillRect( &patternRect, &thePattern );
      FrameRect( &patternRect );
      OffsetRect( &patternRect, 70, 0 );
   }

   SetRect( &patternRect, 30, 120, 50, 140 );

   for ( x = 1; x <= 38; x++ )
   {
      GetIndPattern( &thePattern, thePatternListID, x );

      FillRect( &patternRect, &thePattern );

      FrameRect( &patternRect );
      if ( x == 13 )

         SetRect( &patternRect, 30, 150, 50, 170 );

      else if ( x == 26 )
         SetRect( &patternRect, 30, 180, 50, 200 );

      else
         OffsetRect( &patternRect, 25, 0 );
   }
}
```

Color Pixel Patterns

The five system patterns held in the QDGlobals system variable and the 38 patterns
that make up the system pattern list resource are monochrome patterns. In many cases,
those patterns will suffice, but there certainly will come a time when you need to
make use of a color pattern. To do that, you'll create your own using a ppat (pixel
pattern) resource.

Interface Builder doesn't have a tool for creating pattern resources. For that chore, your best bet is to use Apple's free resource editing tool—ResEdit. If you don't already have ResEdit, you'll find a download link in the tools area of Apple's developer site at `http://developer.apple.com/tools/`.

ResEdit isn't a native Mac OS X application, so when you run it, you'll be running it in the Classic (Mac OS 9) environment. As for including ResEdit-created resources in your Project Builder projects that target Mac OS X, don't let the fact that ResEdit runs in Classic mode bother you. When you save a ResEdit resource to a file, that file can be included in a Project Builder project and that file's resources then can be accessed by your program's code.

To create a pixel pattern, or `ppat`, resource in ResEdit, choose Create New Resource from the Resource menu. Type `ppat` in the text box and click the OK button. Doing that creates a blank (all white) `ppat` resource with an ID of 128 and puts you in the `ppat` editor.

As shown in Figure 7.9, you can use a variety of tools and colors to create a colored pattern that is 8×8 pixels in size. In Figure 7.9, I've created a pattern that consists of diagonal lines (they're blue lines, in case you're curious). As you turn pixels on and off in the magnified view of the pattern in left box of the two boxes at the top of the pixel editor, the right-most box shows how the pattern will look when drawn at actual size in an area larger than 8×8 pixels.

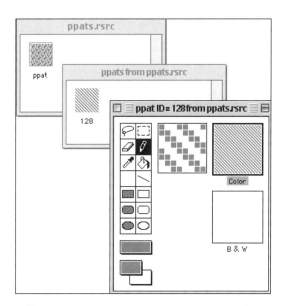

Figure 7.9 Creating a ppat resource in ResEdit.

After creating the ppat resource, choose Save from the File menu to save the file in which the resource is located. Note that you can store more than one ppat resource in the same file and that, in fact, you can save different types of resources in the same file as well. When it comes time for your code to access a particular resource from a resource file, it will be able to do so regardless of the file in which the resource resides. As long as the file is added to the project, the code will find it.

Speaking of adding a resource file to a project, that's what you do next. Before writing the code that accesses a resource, add the file that holds the resource to the project. Figure 7.10 shows that I've given the resource file that holds my ppat resource the name ppats.rsrc and that I have the file housed in the same folder as the project to which it's been added (the PixPatResource project). To add the resource file to a project, click the Resources folder under the Groups & Files heading in the project window and choose Add Files from the Project menu. As shown in Figure 7.10, the resource file name then appears along with the other project resource files (InfoPlist.strings and main.nib in Figure 7.10).

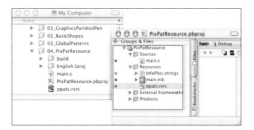

Figure 7.10   A resource file on disk and added to a project.

Earlier in this chapter (in the "System Pattern List" section), you saw that you can use the GetIndPattern routine to obtain a monochrome pattern (a pattern of type PAT) from a pattern resource list. To obtain a reference to a color pattern saved as a ppat resource, you use the Carbon routine GetPixPat. Pass GetPixPat the ID of a ppat resource and GetPixPat returns a handle to that pattern:

```
PixPatHandle  blueDiagonalPixPat;

blueDiagonalPixPat = GetPixPat( 128 );
```

After your program has a handle to a color pattern, it can use that handle in calls to other Carbon routines, including PenPixPat. The PenPixPat function sets the color state of the graphics pen, which means all subsequent drawing will take place using this new current pattern.

```
PenPixPat( blueDiagonalPixPat );
```

You've seen that the FillRect routine accepts two arguments: a rectangle to fill with a pattern and the pattern to be used in the filling of that rectangle. Another shape-filling routine is PaintRect. This routine, though, accepts only one argument—a rectangle to fill with a pattern. Unlike `FillRect`, which requires that a fill pattern be specified, `PaintRect` always uses the current graphics pen pattern, as set in a previous call to `PenPixPat`, as the fill pattern. This following code snippet defines a rectangle and then fills that rectangle with the diagonal blue line pattern to which the graphics pen was just set:

```
Rect    theRect;

SetRect( &theRect, 30, 50, 150, 120 );
PaintRect( &theRect );
```

If you prefer to specify the fill pattern each time you fill a rectangle with a colored pattern, you can use `FillCRect`. `FillRect` (without the `C` between `Fill` and `Rect`) accepts a monochrome pattern (type `Pattern`) as its second argument. `FillCRect` (with the `C`) accepts a handle to a color pixel pattern (type `PixPatHandle`) as its second argument. Rather than changing the graphic pen's color pattern with a call to `PenPixPat` and then calling `PaintRect` to fill a rectangle with this current pattern, the same patterned rectangle could be achieved by simply making a call to `FillCRect`:

```
// no need to call PenPixPat here

FillCRect( &theRect, blueDiagonalPixPat );
```

After your program is finished using a color pattern, it should dispose of the memory referenced by that handle. A call to the Carbon routine `DisposePixPat` takes care of that task:

```
DisposePixPat( blueDiagonalPixPat );
```

PixPatResource Program

The purpose of the PixPatResource program is to demonstrate how a program uses a programmer-defined color pattern resource (`ppat`) to draw patterned lines and shapes.

Figure 7.11 shows the window displayed by the PixPatResource program. To draw this patterned line and patterned rectangle, the program uses the `ppat` resource pictured back in Figure 7.9. As shown in the program's `UpdateWindow` routine (listed in Example 7.4), the filling of the rectangle is achieved by calling `GetPixPat` to set the graphics pen pattern to a handle that references a `ppat` resource and then calling `PaintRect`. The drawing of the patterned line is done with a call to the same `Line` routine used much earlier in this chapter.

After the graphics pen pattern is changed, even line drawing is affected. The program calls `PenSize` to increase the height and width of the line so that the line's pattern is more readily noticeable.

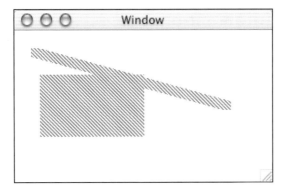

Figure 7.11 Drawings made with a pixel pattern.

Example 7.4 **PixPatResource UpdateWindow Source Code**

```
#define    kPixPatBlueDiagonal    128

void UpdateWindow( WindowRef window )
{
    PixPatHandle  blueDiagonalPixPat;
    Rect          theRect;

    SetPortWindowPort( window );

    blueDiagonalPixPat = GetPixPat( kPixPatBlueDiagonal );
    PenPixPat( blueDiagonalPixPat );

    PenSize( 10, 10 );
    MoveTo( 20, 20 );
    Line( 220, 60 );

    SetRect( &theRect, 30, 50, 150, 120 );
    PaintRect( &theRect );


    DisposePixPat( blueDiagonalPixPat );
}
```

For More Information

For more information about QuickDraw and Macintosh graphics, stop in at any of the following web sites:

- **ResEdit resource editor:** `http://developer.apple.com/tools/`
- **QuickDraw routines**: `http://
developer.apple.com/techpubs/macosx/Carbon/grahics/QuickDraw/quick-
draw.html`

8

Text and Localization

WHEN YOU DEVELOP A PROGRAM, you develop it using your native language. If your native language is English, your application has menus, buttons, and windows that display English text. This is all fine and well—if your target market is English-speaking. However, if your program is one that might find popularity among people that speak a language other than English, you'll want text displayed in the appropriate language. This chapter will help you accomplish that task.

If you think that your program will never be translated into a different language, you might be inclined to skip this chapter. Don't. Although at this moment you might not see the need to create alternate language versions of your program, that need might certainly arise in the near future. A corporate buyout, new marketing strategies, and other unforseen circumstances could result in justification of foreign language versions of your application. Because preparing your program for *internationalization* or *localization*, both of which are the translation of a program's text from one language to another, is surprisingly easy to do, it behooves you to set up your program for the day when localization might be an issue. In addition, even if you're sure your application will never be translated, the method used for localizing the text that's displayed in your program's windows is very useful for storing and displaying large amounts of text even if that text is never to be translated.

In the first section, you see how to localize interface text. The second section discusses localizing text that's displayed in a window.

Localized Resource Files

You've seen that a *resource file* holds the interface element of your programs. When you localize this resource file, you provide your application with the ability to display information in the user's native language. That is, if you originally create your project's nib file in English, and then localize that nib file for the Japanese language, your application becomes one that can display its menus, window titles, and so forth in both English and Japanese. It then becomes the user's choice as to which of these languages becomes the program's display language.

Choosing an Interface Language

When you launch an application on a Macintosh running Mac OS X, that application displays the text of interface elements (menu names and so forth) in English, by default. You can change this aspect of your Mac's behavior by specifying that you'd prefer that programs display the text of interface elements in a different language. To do that, run System Preferences from the Finder and click the International icon—it's pictured on the far left side of Figure 8.1. The International pane appears and you can click the Language tab to see a list of languages from which to choose. In Figure 8.1, I'm dragging Deutsch above English to change the preferred language of my Mac from English to German.

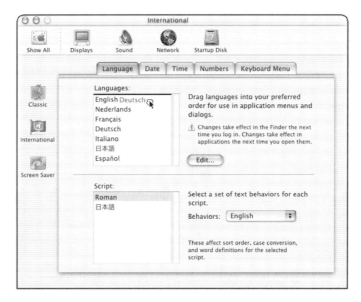

Figure 8.1   Using the International pane of
System Preferences to specify a different language.

So, I've set my preference for German. Now, whenever a program runs, the text of its interface elements will be displayed in German, if the developers of the application added a set of German resources to the English resources that were created for the application. If they didn't, I'll still see English.

To create a set of German resources, the developers need to create a localized main.nib file. We discuss that next.

> **Note**
>
> If you set your Mac to use a non-English language and then run one of the example programs from a previous chapter in this book, you'll still see interface element text displayed in English. That's because I didn't internationalize any of the example programs. My very short programs exist for the benefit of demonstrating one or two isolated topics, and they certainly aren't exercises in localization.

Creating a Localized Nib File

To create a version of your application localized for a different language, first completely develop the English version. Then make a copy of the main.nib file and edit any text that accompanies interface elements in the new version of the main.nib file.

In the past, you've opened a project's main.nib file by double-clicking the main.nib icon or name in the Groups & Files list of the project window. In doing so, you might not have noticed that this main.nib file isn't really a file, but a group of files. This group happens to initially hold just one file, but it's organized as a group nonetheless. To open the main.nib file only, you can click the triangle to the left of the main.nib icon. Doing so in our scenario reveals that the nib file has the title "English," as shown in the top project window of Figure 8.2.

The main.nib group lists the variants of the main.nib files in a project. So far, this group isn't much of a group at all. It has just one file, named English. The lower project window in Figure 8.2 shows that this group can hold other main.nib files. In this example, the second nib file is named German. To add a new localized main.nib file to this project, click main.nib in the Groups & Files list of the project window, and then choose Show Info from the Project menu. Click the Localization & Platforms dropdown list, and then click Add Localized Variant, as is being done in Figure 8.3.

Choosing the Add Localized Variant menu item from the Localization & Platforms pop-up menu displays a sheet requesting that you enter the name of the new locale (such as German, Spanish, Japanese, and so forth). Type the locale and click the OK button. Nothing appears to happen, but if you now look under the main.nib group in the project window, you will see that German has been added under English, as shown in the bottom project window of Figure 8.2.

Within the project, the new main.nib file is named German. If you look in the project's folder on your Desktop, you'll see that there is no nib file named German. Instead, there is a new main.nib file in a new folder—a folder named German.lproj—as shown in Figure 8.4. The nib file names of English and German (as shown back in

Figure 8.2) are names that Project Builder derives from the names of the project's lproj folders.

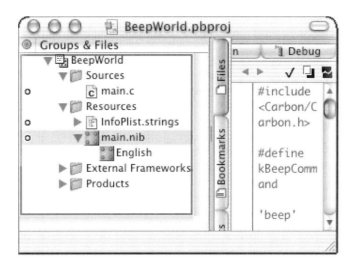

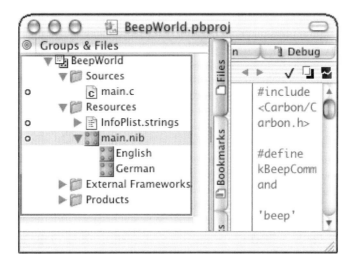

Figure 8.2 The top project has one main.nib file (English), and the bottom project has two main.nib files (English and German).

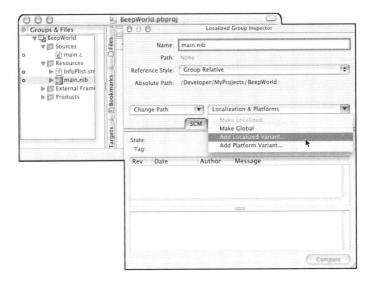

Figure 8.3   Creating a new localized main.nib file.

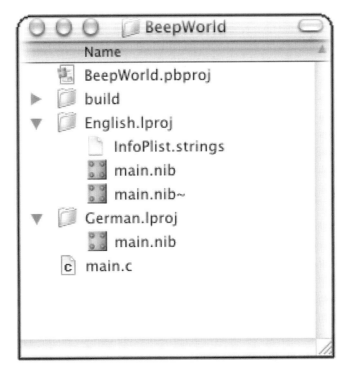

Figure 8.4   The new main.nib file goes into its own lproj folder.

Editing the New Localized Nib File

The project now holds two main.nib files; they are identical and both include English text. The next step is to open the new main.nib file and edit it such that the end result is a file that has all its interface text in German.

Consider the BeepWorld program from Chapter 3, "Events and the Carbon Event Manager." For a German version of that program, the program's window should display static text that says *Hallo, Welt!* instead of *Hello, World!*. Its button should have a title of *Signalton* instead of *Beep*. Figure 8.5 shows the window from the English version of BeepWorld's main.nib file (top) and the same window from the German version of BeepWorld's main.nib file (bottom).

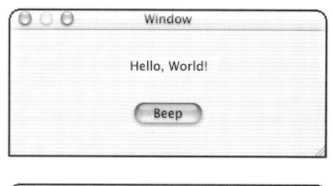

Figure 8.5   A simple example of localizing part of a program's interface.

For BeepWorld, you'd need to translate the text of each menu and menu item as well. Other more sophisticated applications would need far more extensive changes in the new main.nib file.

> **Note**
>
> Unfortunately, there's no magical Translate All Items To Different Language menu item in Interface Builder. The translation efforts fall on the shoulders of you or the translator you hire.

Despite the work involved, there is still a beauty to the Mac OS X internationalization method because, to convert an application from one language to another, you don't need to touch your source code. Thus, your code won't be littered with all kinds of `if (language == kEnglishLanguage)` style branches, and you won't need to use conditional compilation directives such as `#ifdef ENGLISH` throughout your code to enable the building of different versions of the same application. Instead, you develop your program in English, create a new copy of the main.nib file (using the Show Info menu item from the Project menu), and then edit that one resource file.

After making necessary changes to the localized main.nib file, save it, return to Project Builder, build the application as you've always done, and then run it. What happens? Nothing of interest—the program runs in its English version. To see the German interface, you need to change your computer's International setting to German in System Preferences and *then* run the program.

Localizing Window Content Text

An application might be able to display all its text as static text items in window resources. However, that's likely only for the most trivial of programs. An application also might be able to display all its text using the QuickDraw routine `DrawString`. That's unlikely too; `DrawString` isn't used for long passages of text, and the text resulting from its use isn't editable. `DrawString` typically is used for short strings that often are hard-coded into the program.

Instead of using static text resource items or calls to `DrawString` for displaying non-trivial amounts of text in a window, consider defining your program's text in string resources that then are stored in a single file that's easily readable from your source code.

The Localizable.strings file discussed in this section provides a powerful way for you to keep track of all the text your program displays, and it makes for an easy means for your application to access that text at any time. Thus, it's a good text-displaying solution even if you don't plan on localizing your application for another language.

Creating a Localizable.strings File

Just as your program can store interface items as resources to be retrieved and displayed by the program, so too can your program store strings as resources and retrieve and display their text within windows. To do this, you store the strings in a single Localizable.strings file that you add to your project. When you've added all the strings your program needs to the one Localizable.strings file, you can make a copy of this string-holding file and localize it to the language of your choosing.

Before jumping into localized files, though, you'll need to create the first, English language version of the Localizable.strings file. With your project open, choose New File from the File menu. Choose Empty File as the file type to add to the project, and then click the Set button to specify where the file should end up. Then, move to the project's English.lproj folder, choose it, and name the file Localizable.strings, as shown in Figure 8.6. Click the Finish button and a new, empty text file is added to the project. The file should end up in the project's Resources group (see Figure 8.7). If it ends up elsewhere, just drag and drop it on the Resources folder.C

Figure 8.6   Creating a new Localizable.strings file.

Storing Text in the Localizable.strings File

The Localizable.strings file is a text file that holds one or more strings. Your program will be able to retrieve any one of these strings at any time. To do that, each string needs to have some sort of unique identifier that your program can use to reference it. Such an identifier is called a *key*. Any one key is paired with one string. The string is considered the value of the key, so the result is dubbed a *key-value pair*.

The key can be any sequence of case-sensitive characters enclosed in quotation marks. For clarity, you might want to make each key a word somewhat descriptive of the key's value, but that isn't a requirement. Follow the key with an equals sign, and then type or paste in the value, which is the string itself. Enclose the string in quotation marks and the key-value pair is complete.

The following is a Localizable.strings file that holds two strings (two key-value pairs):

```
{
"RouletteWheel" = "The standard American roulette wheel is divided into 38 slots,
numbered 1 to 36 plus 0 and 00.";
"RouletteColors" = "Even numbered slots are red and odd numbered slots are black.
The 0 and 00 slots are green."
}
```

As shown in the preceding code snippet, a semicolon separates key-value pairs, and the entire contents of the file must begin with an opening brace and end with a closing brace. To add a return to a string, don't manually use the Return key. If you do and the string is subsequently retrieved and displayed, the return character symbol, not an actual occurrence of a return, will be displayed. To avoid this outcome, use \r within the string of the key-value pair to indicate a return.

Figure 8.7 shows a Localizable.strings file that holds one string containing several returns. Look ahead to Figure 8.9 to see how that one string looks when retrieved and displayed in a window.

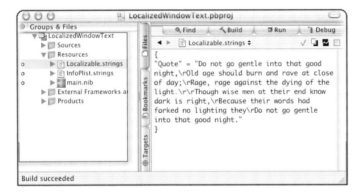

Figure 8.7 A Localizable.strings file with one key-value pair in it.

Using the Text from a Localizable.strings File

When your project holds a Localizable.strings file, your code can make use of any or all the strings in that file. Your program does that by retrieving and then displaying the string.

Retrieving a String

Use the Core Foundation routine `CFCopyLocalizedString` to obtain a reference to a string located in the Localizable.strings file. This call to `CFCopyLocalizedString` obtains the string associated with the key-value pair that has the key `RouletteWheel`:

```
CFStringRef  theString;

theString = CFCopyLocalizedString( CFSTR( "RouletteWheel" ),
            CFSTR( "Short definition of the appearance of the wheel
used in the gambling game of chance roulette." );
```

After the preceding code snippet executes, *The standard American roulette wheel is divided into 38 slots, numbered 1 to 36 plus 0 and 00.* will be the text referenced by `theString`. By default, `CFCopyLocalizedString` examines the file named Localizable.strings, so

there's no need to specify where the string of interest is located. The first argument to
`CFCopyLocalizedString` is the key from the key-value pair of interest; you use the
`CFSTR` macro to pass this key as a `CFString`. The second argument is a comment that
might help the translator should this string need to be translated to a different language. You would pass `NULL` as the second argument if you didn't want to use additional descriptive information.

For clarity, it's always nice to use constants wherever possible, and the key is no
exception. The next snippet skips the comment argument to `CFCopyLocalizedString`
and uses a constant in place of the actual key:

```
#define   kRouletteWheelDescKey    "RouletteWheel"

theString = CFCopyLocalizedString( CFSTR(kRouletteWheelDescKey), NULL );
```

Displaying the String

At this point, you have a string from the Localizable.strings file saved as a `CFString`
object, ready to be displayed in a window. You've been at this point before. In the
"Text Input Fields and Source Code" section of Chapter 5, "Controls," the
`SetControlData` routine was used to place the text of a `CFString` object in a text input
control. You can use that same technique here as well.

To set up an area in a window to which you can write, you can open your project's
main.nib file and add a text input field to a window. You can do that by dragging the
text input item from the palette to a window (the text input field is the framed white
box located at the left edge of the palette). Size the text input field appropriately. In
Figure 8.8, I've made the text input field occupy most of a small window. The text
input field is a control that requires a signature and control ID to enable it to be
accessed. Choose Show Info from the Tools menu, select Control from the pop-up
menu, and enter a signature and ID.

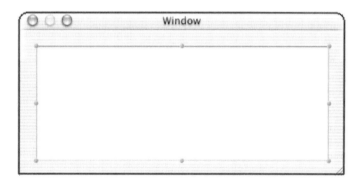

Figure 8.8   A window resource with a text input field.

Your code needs access to the text input field to display text in the field. A call to
`GetControlByID` returns a handle to the control specified by the signature and ID that
comprise a `ControlID` variable:

```
#define     kTextFieldSignature         'Ltxt'
#define     kDylanThomasQuoteControlID      1

ControlHandle   quoteTextEdit;
ControlID       quoteControlID = { kTextFieldSignature,
                                   kDylanThomasQuoteControlID };

GetControlByID( window, &quoteControlID, &quoteTextEdit );
```

Now use the `CFString` text retrieved by a call to `CFCopyLocalizedString` as an argument to `SetControlData`:

```
SetControlData( quoteTextEdit, kControlEntireControl,
                kControlEditTextCFStringTag, sizeof( CFStringRef ),
                &theString );
```

The `SetControlData` arguments consist of the handle to the control to access, a constant representing the control part to access, a constant specifying the type of data
involved, the byte size of the incoming text, and a pointer to the incoming text.

Finish up your code with a call to `DrawOneControl` to redraw the text input field
with the newly added text in place. Figure 8.9 shows the results. Note how the use of
`\r` in the string value in the Localizable.strings file translates to line breaks in the displayed text.

```
DrawOneControl( quoteTextEdit );
```

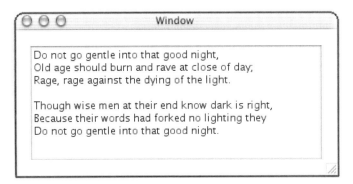

Figure 8.9   A program that displays text retrieved from a Localizable.strings file.

Creating a Localized Localizable.strings File

In this chapter's "Localized Resource Files" section, you saw that you can create localized versions of a project's main.nib resource file to create different language interfaces

for an application. The same is true for the Localizable.strings file. You can create local-ized versions of this text-holding file so that your application displays window content in different languages.

Clicking the arrow to the left of Localizable.strings in the Groups & Files list of the project window reveals all versions of the Localizable.strings file. As it does for the main.nib file, Project Builder automatically names the first version of Localizable.strings "English" (again assuming that you're running Mac OS X with English as the selected language). To create a duplicate Localizable.strings file named for a different language, follow steps similar to those used to create a localized main.nib file:

1. Click Localizable.strings in the Groups & Files list of the project window to highlight this group.
2. Choose Show Info from the Project menu.
3. Click the Localization & Platforms drop-down list and click Add Localized Variant.
4. Enter the name of the new locale (such as German) in the sheet that appears.
5. Click the OK button to create the new file.

Project Builder creates a new Localizable.strings file with the appropriate name and adds it to the Localizable.strings group.

The new Localizable.strings file will hold the same key-value pairs found in the original, English version of the file. It's up to you (or to the translator you've hired) to make the necessary translations. When doing so, don't translate the keys. Recall that the key is used in your source code, and you don't want to have to alter your source code to handle each language. The key serves only as a means for your program to locate a particular string in the Localizable.strings file. The key itself is never displayed by your application, so it doesn't need to be translated.

Figure 8.10 shows the translation from English to German of the one string from the Localizable.strings file pictured back in Figure 8.7. Note that both keys have the same value; *Quote* appears as the key in both cases.

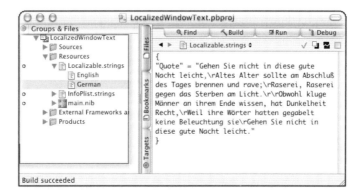

Figure 8.10   The translated string from a project's Localizable.strings file.

> **Note**
>
> The AltaVista search site (`http://www.altavista.com`) includes a link to their language translation page (`http://world.altavista.com`). Here you type or paste a word or words into a text box, choose a translation (such as English to German) from a menu, and click the Translate button. Your text is quickly translated and the resulting translation is displayed above the original text. I've included this note to let you know about this interesting "quick and dirty" means of translating text. I've also included this note to warn you that I don't know German, and that I used this AltaVista method to translate the Dylan Thomas quote used in this chapter from English to German. It's unlikely that AltaVista's web page can compete with a real, live, professional translator, so I can't vow for this translation's accuracy!

The LocalizedWindowText Program

The purpose of the LocalizedWindowText program is to demonstrate how a program retrieves and displays text stored in a Localizable.strings resource file.

Running the program results in the window shown back in Figure 8.9. There you see that the window displays the Dylan Thomas quote that's appeared throughout this chapter.

To provide the program with a place to display the quote, a text input field is added to the main.nib file's one window resource. To match the constants that will be defined in the source code, give the text input field a signature of `Ltxt` and an ID of 1. Back in Figure 8.8, you see the main.nib file's one window with the text input added to it.

Creating the string to display in the window is fairly simple. In the project, create the first Localizable.strings file, as described in this chapter's "Storing Text in a Localizable.strings File" section. Add a single key-value pair to this file. Give the key a value of "Quote" to match the key constant that will be defined in the source code. You can use the same text pictured back in Figure 8.7, but of course, you don't have to do so.

Your next step is to include the braces at the start and end of the file. Then, you need to make sure to enclose both the key and the value (the string) in quotation marks. Save the file and then create a second, localized version of it using the steps listed in this chapter's "Creating a Localized Localizable.strings File" section. This new file has the original string in it. You can take the time to actually make the translation of this text, or you can use this as a simple test program and simply edit the string so that it differs from the original. With two versions of the Localizable.strings file in your project, it's time to write the code.

Example 8.1 shows the complete listing for LocalizedWindowText program. The listing is especially short because the program doesn't define or install any event handlers. When the program runs, a window opens and a string is displayed in it; the user doesn't need to make any menu selections or click a button to make anything happen. In this example, all the window-opening code has been placed in its own application-defined routine. For clarity, you might consider having such a routine for each type of window your program opens.

Example 8.1 **LocalizedWindowText Source Code**

```
#include <Carbon/Carbon.h>
#define   kTextFieldSignature          'Ltxt'
#define   kDylanThomasQuoteControlID      1
#define   kQuoteTextKey               "Quote"

void OpenNewQuoteWindow( void );


int main( int argc, char* argv[] )
{
   OpenNewQuoteWindow();

   RunApplicationEventLoop();

   return( 0 );
}


void OpenNewQuoteWindow( void )
{
   IBNibRef        nibRef;
   WindowRef       window;
   OSStatus        err;
   ControlHandle   quoteTextEdit;
   ControlID       quoteControlID  = { kTextFieldSignature,
                                       kDylanThomasQuoteControlID };
   CFStringRef     theString;

   err = CreateNibReference( CFSTR("main"), &nibRef );
   err = SetMenuBarFromNib( nibRef, CFSTR("MainMenu") );
   err = CreateWindowFromNib( nibRef, CFSTR("MainWindow"), &window );
   DisposeNibReference( nibRef );

   ShowWindow( window );

   GetControlByID( window, &quoteControlID, &quoteTextEdit );

   theString = CFCopyLocalizedString( CFSTR( kQuoteTextKey ), NULL );

   SetControlData( quoteTextEdit, kControlEntireControl,
                   kControlEditTextCFStringTag, sizeof( CFStringRef ),
                   &theString );

   DrawOneControl( quoteTextEdit );
}
```

For More Information

The following web sites provide extra information about some of this chapter's topics:

- **QuickDraw text:**
  `http://developer.apple.com/techpubs/macosx/Carbon/text/QuickDrawText/`
  `quickdrawtext.html`

- **String-related bundle services:**
  http://developer.apple.com/techpubs/macosx/CoreFoundation/BundleServices/
  bundleservices_carbon.html

QuickTime Movies and File Handling

At THIS POINT, YOU KNOW ALL about interface elements such as windows, controls, and menus, and you have a firm grasp on how your program recognizes and handles a variety of types of events. So it's on to the fun stuff. In this chapter, you'll see how your program opens and plays a QuickTime movie. QuickTime is movie-playing software that is part of the system software of every Macintosh in your target audience.

It's possible for a program to cause a QuickTime movie to spring forth from (seemingly) nowhere. However, it's more likely that a movie-playing application will enable the user to select the file that holds the movie to play. Giving the user the power to open a QuickTime movie file, or any other type of file, involves the Open dialog box. We'll look at the Open dialog box first in this chapter.

Files and Navigation Services

A *file* is a sequence of bytes stored on physical media, such as a hard drive, and a *directory* is another name for a folder. A *volume* can be an entire physical storage device or it can be part of the device (the result of formatting the device to consist of multiple volumes). For a program to access a file, it needs to know the file's name, the directory in which the file is located, and the volume on which that directory resides. In certain circumstances, a program that's to open a file includes these values (the file name and location) directly within its code, but that's a scenario few programs use. In addition, this hard-coding of file information prevents the user from choosing what file to open, and it also sets up an application failure should the user move or delete the sought-after file.

A better way to handle the situation is to call Navigation Services routines to make use of the Open dialog box. By displaying the Open dialog box, you enable a user to select the file to open. Handling file opening in this way also forces the system to do the work of determining a file's name and location, and it leaves it to the system to convey this important file information to your program.

The Open dialog box provides the user with a standard interface for opening a file. This same Open dialog box is used by any real-world application. You can see it by choosing Open from the File menu of programs such as Apple's TextEdit or by looking at Figure 9.1.

Navigation Services is part of the Carbon API that makes is possible for your programs to include standard dialogs such as the Open dialog box. In addition, it is an important and useful part of the Carbon API. It routines provide interface consistency for the user and removes the burden of file location determination from the programmer. In this chapter, you'll see how to make use of Navigation Services, so brace yourself for a barrage of information about key Navigation Services routines.

Implementing an Open Dialog Box

You'll make use of a number of Navigation Services routines to display and handle an Open dialog box that is similar to the one TextEdit and other Mac OS X applications use. To do that, your code will perform the following:

1. Create and display the standard Open dialog box.

2. Become aware of the user's action in the Open dialog box.

3. Respond to the user's action (for instance, open the appropriate file if the user clicks the Open button).

4. Clean up by disposing of the Open dialog box when appropriate.

The overall look and behavior of an Open dialog box usually is the same. Such a dialog box includes Cancel and Open buttons and a list view of the folders and files on the user's machine. The general behavior of this type of dialog box is the same from one implementation to another as well; the user navigates through the file list, clicks the name of a file to open within the list, and then clicks the Open button to open the selected file. To promote this consistent look and behavior, Navigation Services defines the NavDialogCreationOptions data structure as the following:

```
struct NavDialogCreationOptions {
    UInt16              version;
    NavDialogOptionFlags  optionFlags;
    Point               location;
    CFStringRef         clientName;
    CFStringRef         windowTitle;
```

```
CFStringRef          actionButtonLabel;
CFStringRef          cancelButtonLabel;
CFStringRef          saveFileName;
CFStringRef          message;
UInt32               preferenceKey;
CFArrayRef           popupExtension;
WindowModality       modality;
WindowRef            parentWindow;
char                 reserved[16];
};
typedef struct NavDialogCreationOptions NavDialogCreationOptions;
```

Figure 9.1 A typical Open dialog box (as displayed in TextEdit).

The NavDialogCreationOptions structure defines the features (such as size and location) of an Open dialog box. The Navigation Services routine NavGetDefaultDialogCreationOptions is used to fill the fields of a NavDialogCreationOptions structure with default values. Use this routine by declaring a variable of type NavDialogCreationOptions and then passing that variable's address as the routine's one argument:

```
OSStatus                  err;
NavDialogCreationOptions  dialogAttributes;

err = NavGetDefaultDialogCreationOptions( &dialogAttributes )
```

After setting the values of the members of a structure to default values, you can customize the structure by changing the value of any individual member. For instance, to make the Open dialog box take over the application and disallow other application actions to take its place, the value of the dialog box's `NavDialogCreationOptions` `modality` member can be set to the Apple-defined constant `kWindowModalityAppModal`:

```
dialogAttributes.modality = kWindowModalityAppModal;
```

You've seen how a program includes an application-defined event handler routine that's associated with a window or other object. The Open dialog box also needs an application-defined event handler routine associated with it. This event handler will be called by the system when the user dismisses the Open dialog box. Navigation Services creates, displays, and runs the Open dialog box, but it is this event handler that should perform the actual work of opening a user-selected file. Like other event handlers, this Open dialog box event handler can have a name of your choosing, but it must include arguments of specific types. Here's the prototype for such a routine:

```
pascal void MyNavEventCallback(
                    NavEventCallbackMessage callBackSelector,
                    NavCBRecPtr             callBackParms,
                    void*                   callBackUD );
```

In a moment, you'll pass a pointer to this event handler to the Navigation Services routine that creates the Open dialog box. The pointer should be of type `NavEventUPP`. The *UPP* in NavEventUPP stands for *universal procedure pointer*, which is a pointer that is capable of referencing procedures, or routines, in different executable formats. In this case, a `NavEventUPP` can point to a routine that is in native Mac OS X executable format or in pre-Mac OS X executable format. You'll also need this pointer elsewhere in your program, so declaring this pointer globally makes sense:

```
NavEventUPP    gNavEventHandlerPtr;
```

Use the Navigation Services routine `NewNavEventUPP` to set this routine pointer variable to point to the Open dialog box event handler:

```
gNavEventHandlerPtr = NewNavEventUPP( MyNavEventCallback );
```

Now it's time to make a call to the Navigation Services routine `NavCreateGetFileDialog` to create the Open dialog box. This routine requires seven arguments, many of which can typically get set to `NULL`. Here's the function prototype:

```
NavCreateGetFileDialog(
    const NavDialogCreationOptions *  inOptions,
    NavTypeListHandle                 inTypeList,
    NavEventUPP                       inEventProc,
    NavPreviewUPP                     inPreviewProc,
    NavObjectFilterUPP                inFilterProc,
    void *                            inClientData,
    NavDialogRef *                    outDialog );
```

Using the previously declared `dialogAttributes` and `gNavEventHandlerPtr` variables, here's how a call to `NavCreateGetFileDialog` could look:

```
NavDialogRef    openDialog;

err = NavCreateGetFileDialog( &dialogAttributes, NULL,
                              gNavEventHandlerPtr, NULL, NULL,
                              NULL, &openDialog );
```

The `inOptions` parameter is a pointer to the set of Open dialog box features that was returned by a prior call to `NavGetDefaultDialogCreationOptions`. In the preceding code snippet, `dialogAttributes` holds that set of default values, with the exception of the modality that was altered after `NavGetDefaultDialogCreationOptions` was called.

The `inTypeList` is a list of file types to display in the Open dialog box's browser; pass `NULL` to display all file types.

The `inEventProc` parameter is the procedure pointer that points to the Open dialog box's event handler routine. In the preceding snippet, the global UPP variable `gNavEventHandlerPtr`, which was assigned its value from a call to `NewNavEventUPP`, is used.

The next three arguments each can be set to `NULL`. The `inPreviewProc` parameter is a pointer to a custom file preview routine. The `inFilterProc` parameter is a pointer to a custom file filter routine. The `inClientData` parameter is a value that gets passed to either of the just-mentioned custom routines (if present). The preceding snippet uses `NULL` for each of these three arguments.

The last argument is a pointer to a variable of type `NavDialogRef`. After `NavCreateGetFileDialog` executes, this argument will hold a reference to the newly created Open dialog box.

`NavCreateGetFileDialog` creates an Open dialog box, but it doesn't display or control it. To do those chores, call the Navigation Services routine `NavDialogRun`:

```
err = NavDialogRun( openDialog );
```

`NavDialogRun` handles the user's interaction with the Open dialog box, so you don't need to write any code to follow the user's actions as he or she uses the dialog box to browse for a file to open. When the user clicks the Cancel or Open button, the application-defined event handler associated with this Open dialog box is called. In doing this, Navigation Services passes on information about the event that initiated the event handler call.

As you'll see a little later in this chapter, the event handler takes care of the opening of the selected file and the dismissing of the Open dialog box. Control then returns to the code that follows the call to `NavDialogRun`. That code should look something like this:

```
if ( err != noErr )
{
   NavDialogDispose( openDialog );
   DisposeNavEventUPP( gNavEventHandlerPtr );
}
```

If `NavDialogRun` completes without an error, your work is done. If there *was* an error, the variable `err` will have a nonzero (non-`noErr`) value. Your code should call the Navigation Services routines `NavDialogDispose` to dispose of the Open dialog box reference and `DisposeNavEventUPP` to dispose of the pointer to the Open dialog box event handler.

Whew. That covers the process of displaying and running the Open dialog box. Now it's time to take a look at all the code as it might appear in an application-defined routine that is used to enable a user to choose a file to open:

```
void DisplayOpenFileDialog( void )
{
    OSStatus                 err;
    NavDialogRef             openDialog;
    NavDialogCreationOptions dialogAttributes;

    err = NavGetDefaultDialogCreationOptions( &dialogAttributes );

    dialogAttributes.modality = kWindowModalityAppModal;

    gNavEventHandlerPtr = NewNavEventUPP( MyNavEventCallback );

    err =  NavCreateGetFileDialog( &dialogAttributes, NULL,
                                   gNavEventHandlerPtr, NULL, NULL,
                                   NULL, &openDialog );

    err = NavDialogRun( openDialog );

    if ( err != noErr )
    {
        NavDialogDispose( openDialog );
        DisposeNavEventUPP( gNavEventHandlerPtr );
    }
}
```

Open Dialog Box Event Handler

After the user of an Open dialog box makes a final decision (by clicking the Cancel or Open button), the Open dialog box event handler is automatically invoked. When the system invokes this handler, the system passes information about the event initiated by the user's action:

```
pascal void MyNavEventCallback(
                        NavEventCallbackMessage callBackSelector,
                        NavCBRecPtr             callBackParms,
                        void*                   callBackUD )
```

Your event handler uses the information in the `callBackSelector` argument to determine the action with which to deal. The bulk of the event handler consists of a `switch` statement that determines which of the primary dialog box-related tasks needs handling:

```
switch ( callBackSelector )
{
```

```
   case kNavCBUserAction:
      // further determine which action took place (open or save)
      // handle the action (open or save selected file)
      break;

   case kNavCBTerminate:
      // clean up after the now-dismissed dialog
      break;
}
```

The main two tasks handled in the `switch` consist of a user action
(kNavCBUserAction), such as the request to open a file, and the memory clean up
(kNavCBTerminate), which is in response to the dismissal of the dialog box.

To respond to a user action, call the Navigation Services routine
`NavDialogGetReply`. Pass this routine a reference to the dialog box that initiated the
event and a pointer to a reply record. `NavDialogGetReply` will fill the reply record
with information about the user's action (such as the file to open). The `context` field
of the event handler argument `callBackParms` holds the dialog reference. Declare a
variable of type `NavReplyRecord` to be used as the reply record:

```
OSStatus        err;
NavReplyRecord  reply;
NavUserAction   userAction = 0;

err = NavDialogGetReply( callBackParms->context, &reply );
```

Now call `NavDialogGetUserAction`, passing this routine a reference to the affected dialog box. Once again, the context field of the `callBackParams` event handler argument
is used. `NavDialogGetUserAction` tells your program the exact action the user took. In
the case of an Open dialog box, you're looking for a user action of
kNavUserActionOpen. Note that similar code is used to handle a Save dialog, and in
such a case, you'd look for a user action of kNavUserActionSaveAs. Finish with a call
to `NavDisposeReply` to dispose of the reply record.

```
userAction = NavDialogGetUserAction( callBackParms->context );

switch ( userAction )
{
   case kNavUserActionOpen:
   // open file here using reply record information
   break;
}
err = NavDisposeReply( &reply );
```

> **Note**
> The preceding code snippet includes one very vague comment. Obviously, some code needs to actually
> open the user-selected file, yet I've waved that chore off with a single comment. That's because the par-
> ticulars of opening a file are specific to the type of file to open; a move file, a graphics file, and an appli-
> cation-defined file all require different code to be transformed from data on media to data in memory
> and finally to information displayed in a window. Later in this chapter, we'll jump into the general steps,
> and the detailed code, for opening one type of file: a QuickTime movie file.

You can put the just-described Open dialog box event handler code into a routine that looks like the one shown here:

```
pascal void MyOpenDialogEventCallback(
                          NavEventCallbackMessage callBackSelector,
                          NavCBRecPtr             callBackParms,
                          void*                   callBackUD )
{
   OSStatus         err;
   NavReplyRecord   reply;
   NavUserAction    userAction = 0;

   switch ( callBackSelector )
   {
      case kNavCBUserAction:
          err = NavDialogGetReply( callBackParms->context, &reply );
          userAction = NavDialogGetUserAction( callBackParms->context );

          switch ( userAction )
          {
             case kNavUserActionOpen:
             // open file here using reply record information
             break;
          }
          err = NavDisposeReply( &reply );
          break;

      case kNavCBTerminate:
          NavDialogDispose( callBackParms->context );
          DisposeNavEventUPP( gNavEventHandlerPtr );
          break;
   }
}
```

The MyOpenDialogEventCallback routine is generic enough that it should work, with very little alteration, in your own file-opening program. Now all you need to do is replace the routine's one comment with a call to an application-defined function designed to open a file of the appropriate type. In the next section, you see how to write such a routine. The code for the application-defined function OpenOneQTMovieFile opens a QuickTime movie file. The OpenPlayMovie example then uses the MyOpenDialogEventCallback routine with a call to OpenOneQTMovieFile.

QuickTime Movies

A sound knowledge of the fundamentals of developing an interface for your Mac OS X program is of great importance, but you didn't choose to learn about Mac programming for the sole purpose of creating windows that include a few buttons. You most certainly also want to know how your own program can include at least *some* multimedia capabilities.

Unfortunately, Mac OS X programming for sound playing, sound recording, and smooth animation are worthy of their own programming book. So, what can I show you in just half a chapter? Well, I can show you one multimedia topic that best showcases Mac OS X multimedia in action: QuickTime. By giving your program the ability to play QuickTime movies, you can add high-resolution graphics, animation, and sound playing to your program.

> **Note**
>
> QuickTime is now cross-platform software, but it started out as an extension of Mac-only system software.

In this section, you see how to use the previously discussed Navigation Services routines to present the user with an Open dialog box that lets him or her choose a QuickTime movie file to open. After that file is open, you use Carbon API routines (which are grouped into the Movie Toolbox area of the Carbon API) to play the movie.

Opening a QuickTime Movie File

This chapter's "Files and Navigation Services" section provides all the details for presenting the user with a standard Open dialog box. It also shows how to respond to a user's selection of a file that is listed in that dialog box.

In this part of the chapter, you'll be using that information to give the user the power to pick a QuickTime movie file to display. Specifically, I'll jump into descriptions of the techniques and Movie Toolbox routines that your program will use to get QuickTime movie file data that exists on the user's disk into a format that's ready to play as a movie in a window. The result will be an application-defined routine named `OpenOneQTMovieFile`. Then, after you've developed this routine, you can insert it into the `kNavUserActionOpen` case label section of the `switch` statement in the `MyOpenDialogEventCallback` routine that was developed earlier in this chapter.

Transferring Movie File Data to Memory

Scan back just a bit in this chapter and you'll see the heading "Opening a QuickTime Movie File." Look ahead a little and you'll see the heading "Playing a QuickTime Movie." In broad terms, these are the two steps a program performs so that a user can view a movie. However, each step is more involved that it would first appear. For instance, in the case of opening a movie file, what's actually taking place is the opening of that file (so its data can be accessed), the copying of that file's movie data content into memory (where it can be referenced by the application), and the closing of the file (because its contents are no longer needed). The goal of what's loosely described as the opening of a file is actually the transferring (or copying) of a file's data into memory.

To open a file, your program needs to know the file's name and location. If the user selected the file in the Open dialog box, that dialog box's event handler gets the required information from the `NavReplyRecord` variable. Recall from this chapter's

"Open Dialog Box Event Handler" section that the Open dialog box event handler called `NavDialogGetReply` to fill a `NavReplyRecord` with information about the user-selected file to open:

```
NavReplyRecord   reply;

err = NavDialogGetReply( callBackParms->context, &reply );
```

With years of computer programming experience comes an appreciation for a programming task as simple as adding two numbers; the job's simplicity ensures there's little or no chance of error. This is in contrast to a task such as file handling, which can be fraught with peril! The task involves selecting a file, opening it, copying its contents to memory, and then accessing that memory to make use of the data within. One flipped bit in this process can really play havoc on a program or even the drive itself!

In an attempt to avoid intimacy with the debugger, file-handling code often makes judicious use of error checking. To increase the explanation-to-code ratio in this book, I've provided descriptions of some basic error-handling techniques in Chapter 2, "Overview of Mac OS X Programming," and then for the most part, kept error-handling code to a minimum in the subsequent chapters. Now, however, is no time to be stingy with error checking, so in upcoming snippets, you'll see a little extra precautionary code, starting right here:

```
OSStatus    err;
AEDesc      newDescriptor;
FSRef       movieRef;

err = AECoerceDesc( &reply->selection, typeFSRef, &newDescriptor );

err = AEGetDescData( &newDescriptor, ( void * )( &movieRef ),
                     sizeof( FSRef ) );
```

The Apple Event Manager routine `AECoerceDesc` accepts data of one type (the first argument), manipulates it to another type (specified by the second argument), and saves the results in a new variable (the third argument). The usage of this routine verifies that the `reply` variable that holds the user-selected file is in the format of an `FSRef`. After the call to `AECoerceDesc` completes, your program is assured of having an `FSRef` within the variable `newDescriptor`. The Apple Event Manager routine `AEGetDescData` then is called to retrieve the `FSRef` from the `newDescriptor` variable.

At this point, the program has an `FSRef` (the variable `movieRef`) that holds information about the user-selected file. Thus, we're *almost* ready to open the QuickTime movie file. However, we need to make one quick detour. Some of the Carbon API routines are older (they existed as original Macintosh Toolbox API routines), and some are newer (they were created to handle Mac OS X tasks for which no original Macintosh Toolbox routine existed). The newer file-handling Carbon API routines that require information about a file accept that information in the form of an argument of type `FSRef`. In contrast, original file-handling Toolbox routines that became part of the Carbon API look for this same information in the form of an argument of type

FSSpec. In addition, opening a QuickTime movie file requires the use of one of these older FSSpec-accepting routines. Fortunately, for situations such as this, the routine FSGetCatalogInfo function can be used to convert an FSRef to an FSSpec:

```
FSSpec   userFileFSSpec;

FSGetCatalogInfo( &movieRef, kFSCatInfoNone, NULL, NULL,
                  &userFileFSSpec, NULL );
```

FSGetCatalogInfo is a workhorse of a utility routine in that it can be used to obtain all sorts of information about a catalog file. (A catalog file is a special file used to keep information about all the files and directories on a volume.) You can use FSGetCatalogInfo to obtain information such as the reference number of the volume on which a file resides or the parent directory ID of a file. You also can use FSGetCatalogInfo to simply obtain an FSSpec for a file for which you already have an FSRef. That's what I'm interested in here. Of most importance in this usage of FSGetCatalogInfo is the first argument, which is a pointer to the FSRef to convert, and the fifth argument, which is a pointer to an FSSpec variable that FSGetCatalogInfo is to fill with the file system specification. The only other non-NULL value is the second argument. This argument normally is used to specify which of many pieces of information about a file or directory are to be returned. I don't need any of this information, so the constant kFSCatInfoNone is used here.

Now it's time to open the file. The Movie Toolbox routine OpenMovieFile does that. The first OpenMovieFile argument is a file system specification. You can use the one returned by the call to FSGetCatalogInfo. After OpenMovieFile opens the specified filem it provides your program with a reference number for that file. That reference number is your program's means of (you guessed it) referring to that file in subsequent calls to Movie Toolbox routines. The next argument is a pointer to a variable in which OpenMovieFile places this reference value. The last argument is a permission level for the opened file. A program that opens a movie for playing but that won't enable the altering of the movie contents should use the constant fsRdPerm.

```
OSErr    err;
FSSpec   userFileFSSpec
short    movieRefNum;

err = OpenMovieFile( &userFileFSSpec, &movieRefNum, fsRdPerm );
```

Caution

Besides fsRdPerm, other permission constants include fsWrPerm (to enable writing) and fsRdWrPerm (to enable reading and writing). In my simple examples, the permission level isn't crucial. That is, you can change it to, say, fsRdWrPerm, and the user still won't be able to cut any frames from an opened movie. However, in your full-blown application, permissions might be of importance. If your program includes a functioning Edit menu that supports the cutting and pasting of multiple data types, you might not want to give the user the ability to alter the frames of a movie. In such an instance, you'll want to make sure that movie files are opened with the fsRdPerm constant rather than with one of the constants that enables file writing.

After opening a movie file, that file's data needs to be loaded into memory. A call to the Movie Toolbox routine `NewMovieFromFile` does this:

```
Movie    movie = NULL;
short    movieResID = 0;

err = NewMovieFromFile( &movie, movieRefNum, &movieResID,
                        NULL, newMovieActive, NULL );
```

After `NewMovieFromFile` completes, the first argument holds a reference to the movie (a variable of type `Movie`). To create this movie, `NewMovieFromFile` needs the movie file reference number that was returned by the prior call to `OpenMovieFile`. You should pass this as the second argument. `NewMovieFromFile` also needs the ID of the movie data in the file in question. Although a single file typically holds one movie, it can hold multiple movies. Thus, it's necessary to specify which of a file's movies is to be used. A value of 0 as the third argument tells `NewMovieFromFile` to use the first movie in the file. Thus, even if there is only one movie in the file, this value of 0 does the job.

When `NewMovieFromFile` exits, it fills in the fourth argument (`movieName`) with the name of the movie resource that was used to create the movie. Note that this isn't the name of the file that holds the movie; it's the name of a resource within the file. That's usually not of importance, so your program can pass `NULL` here. The fifth argument is used to provide supplemental information to `NewMovieFromFile`. Using the constant `newMovieActive` specifies that the new movie should be active; a movie needs to be active for it to be played. The last argument tells whether `NewMovieFromFile` had to make any changes to the data in the file. This shouldn't occur, so again a value of `NULL` typically suffices.

The call to `OpenMovieFile` opened the file in preparation for access to it. `NewMovieFromFile` is the routine that accessed the file. Now, with the movie data safe in memory and a `Movie` variable referencing that data, the file can be closed:

```
CloseMovieFile( movieRefNum );
```

`CloseMovieFile` needs to know which file to close. The reference number returned by `OpenMovieFile` provides that information.

Displaying a Movie in a Window

At this point, a movie is in memory and accessible by way of a `Movie` variable. Now the movie needs to be associated with a window. There's nothing special about a window that holds a movie; you just create a new window resource in your program's main.nib file. You can make the window any size you want. Your code resizes this window to match the size of the movie that eventually gets displayed within the window. With the window resource defined, include the standard window-creation code in your code:

```
WindowRef   window;
OSStatus    err;
IBNibRef    nibRef;
```

```
err = CreateNibReference( CFSTR("main"), &nibRef );
err = CreateWindowFromNib( nibRef, CFSTR("MovieWindow"), &window );
DisposeNibReference( nibRef );
```

Now, for the link between the movie and the window, call `SetPortWindowPort` to make the window's port the active port. Then, call the Movie Toolbox routine `SetMovieGWorld` to associate the movie with the currently active port:

```
SetPortWindowPort( window );

SetMovieGWorld( movie, NULL, NULL );
```

The `GWorld` in `SetMovieGWorld` refers to a graphics world, which is a complex memory drawing environment used in the preparation of images before their onscreen display. The first `SetMovieGWorld` argument is the movie to associate with a port. The second argument is the port; pass `NULL` here to tell `SetMovieGWorld` to associate the movie with the current port, which is the window named in the call to `SetPortWindowPort`. The last argument is a handle to a `Gdevice`, which is a structure describing a graphics device. A value of `NULL` here tells `SetMovieGWorld` to use the current device.

Now determine the size of the open movie and use those coordinates to resize the window to match the movie size:

```
Rect    movieBox;

GetMovieBox( movie, &movieBox );
OffsetRect( &movieBox, -movieBox.left, -movieBox.top );
SetMovieBox( movie, &movieBox );
SizeWindow( window, movieBox.right, movieBox.bottom, TRUE );
ShowWindow( window );
```

Pass `GetMovieBox` a movie and the routine returns a rectangle that holds the size of the movie. This might be all you need, or it might not be. Although the returned rectangle does hold the size of the movie, it's possible that the top and left coordinates of this rectangle each might not be 0. In such a case, looking at `movieBox.right` for the movie's width and `movieBox.bottom` for the movie's height would provide erroneous information. For instance, a `movieBox.left` value of 50 and a `movieBox.right` value of 200 means that the movie has a width of 150 pixels. A call to the QuickDraw routine `OffsetRect` simply offsets the `movieBox` rectangle such that its left and top coordinates each have a value of 0. A call to `SetMovieBox` makes the new, offset values the boundaries for the rectangle that defines the size of the movie.

Although the movie rectangle has been adjusted, the window that's to display the movie has not. A call to `SizeWindow` does that. Pass `SizeWindow` the window to resize, along with the new width and height to use in the size change. The last argument is a Boolean value that tells whether an update event should be generated. The call to `ShowWindow` finally reveals the movie-holding window to the user.

To ensure that the window displays a frame of the movie, call `MoviesTask`. This Movie Toolbox routine does just that. Pass the movie to use in the frame display as the first argument and a value of 0 as the second argument. This 0 value tells `MoviesTask` to service (update) each active movie. If your program can display more than one movie at a time, `MoviesTask` will jump to each open movie, displaying one new frame in each. Precede the call to `MoviesTask` with a call to `GoToBeginningOfMovie`. This Toolbox routine rewinds the movie to its first frame. Although a newly opened movie will most likely be set to the movie's first frame, a call to this routine ensures that that will be so:

```
GoToBeginningOfMovie( movie );
MoviesTask( movie, 0 );
```

Playing a QuickTime Movie

The movie's now open and displayed in a window. Let's play it from start to finish:

```
StartMovie( movie );

do
{
   MoviesTask( movie, 0 );
} while ( IsMovieDone( movie ) == FALSE );
```

Contrary to its name, `StartMovie` doesn't start a movie. Instead, it prepares the specified movie for playing by making the movie active and setting the movie's playback rate. To actually play a movie, call `MoviesTask` within a loop. Each call to `MoviesTask` plays a frame of the movie. Because your program won't know how many frames are in the movie to play, rely on a call to the Movie Toolbox routine `IsMovieDone` to determine when the frame-playing loop should terminate. Pass `IsMovieDone` a movie and the routine returns a value of `TRUE` if the last frame has been reached or `FALSE` if there's one or more frames left to play.

> **Note**
> Related to the running of a movie is the movie controller. It is the thin, three-dimensional control that runs along the bottom of a window displaying a QuickTime movie. The movie controller is under the user's control, and it enables the user to run, pause, or step forward or backwards through the movie displayed in the window. For more information on movie controllers, see the URL listed at the end of this chapter.

OpenPlayMovie Program

The purpose of OpenPlayMovie is to demonstrate how the Navigation Services routines are used to display the standard Open dialog box. It also shows how to respond to a user-selected file when that file is a QuickTime movie.

OpenPlayMovie starts by opening a window that includes a single line of text, as shown in Figure 9.2. When you follow that window's instructions, you see the standard Open dialog box. Use the file lists to move about your drive or drives to find a QuickTime movie. When you click the Open dialog box's Open button, a new window displaying the first frame of the movie appears. Choose Play Movie from the Movie menu and the movie plays from start to finish. You can choose Play Movie as often as you wish.

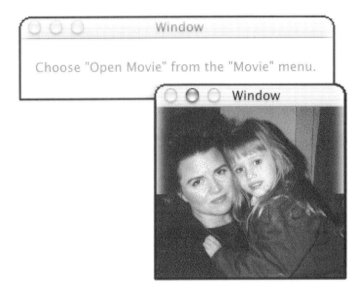

Figure 9.2   Windows displayed by the OpenPlayMovie program.

Nib Resources

The main.nib window in the project's main.nib file includes two windows, as shown in Figure 9.3. By default, Interface Builder sets a new window to be resizable, and it gives the window a small resize control in the lower-right corner of the window. The OpenPlayMovie program eliminates this resize control from the movie-playing window. The control would obscure a small part of one corner of the movie if it were present.

You can use Interface Builder to set a window so that it can't be resizable. To do that, click the MovieWindow window in main.nib (see Figure 9.3), choose Show Info from the Tools menu, display the Attributes pane, and then *uncheck* the Resizable checkbox. While you're there, uncheck both the Close and the Zoom checkboxes so that the window won't be closeable or zoomable.

The Movie menu includes two items: Open Movie and Play Movie. The Open Movie item has a command of Opmv. Assign it that command from the Attributes pane of the item's Info window. The Play Movie item has a command of PLmv. Play Movie item is initially disabled. Click that item, choose Show Info from the Tools menu, and, from the Attributes pane, uncheck the Enabled checkbox. Because the program's code will be accessing the Movie menu, this menu needs an ID. You can give the Movie menu a menu ID of 5 by clicking Movie in the menu window, choosing Show Info from the Tools menu, and entering 5 in the Menu ID field.

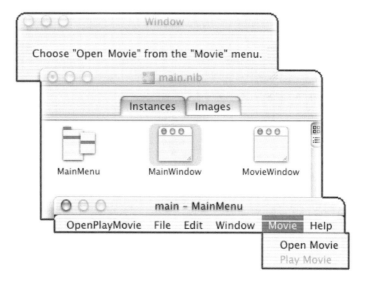

Figure 9.3   The OpenPlayMovie nib resources.

Source Code

The QuickTime function prototypes aren't included in a project by default, so you'll need to include QuickTime.h along with Carbon.h:

```
#include <Carbon/Carbon.h>
#include <QuickTime/QuickTime.h>
```

Define a constant to match the commands assigned to the Open Movie and Play Movie menu items in the nib resource. Also, define constants to match the Movie menu ID and the menu placement of the two items in the Movie menu:

```
#define  kOpenMovieCommand      'OPmv'
#define  kPlayMovieCommand      'PLmv'
#define  kMovieMenuID              5
#define  kMovieMenuOpenItemNum     1
#define  kMovieMenuPlayItemNum     2
```

OpenPlayMovie declares three global variables. The procedure pointer gNavEventHandlerPtr is used in setting up the Open dialog box event handler, gMovie will reference the movie after it's opened, and gMovieMenu will hold a handle to the

Movie menu so that the menu's items can be enabled and disabled:

```
NavEventUPP    gNavEventHandlerPtr;
Movie          gMovie = NULL;
MenuHandle     gMovieMenu;
```

Almost all the main routine is the same as in past examples. Additions of note include a call to EnterMovies (a Movie Toolbox initialization routine that's required before a program makes use of other Movie Toolbox routines) and a call to GetMenuHandle (to obtain a handle to the Movie menu):

```
int main( int argc, char* argv[] )
{
    IBNibRef           nibRef;
    WindowRef          window;
    OSStatus           err;
    EventTargetRef     target;
    EventHandlerUPP    handlerUPP;
    EventTypeSpec      appEvent = { kEventClassCommand,
                                    kEventProcessCommand };

    EnterMovies();

    // set up menu bar, open window, install event handler

    gMovieMenu = GetMenuHandle( kMovieMenuID );

    RunApplicationEventLoop();

    return( 0 );
}
```

OpenPlayMovie demonstrates some simple menu adjustment techniques that make it possible to force the program to enable only one movie to be opened. When the program launches, the Open Movie item is enabled and the Play Movie item is disabled, as specified in the menu resource in the nib file. If a menu item doesn't make sense at a particular moment in the running of a program, it should be disabled. When the program launches, no movie is open, so the Play Movie item isn't applicable. That's why it's initially disabled. The program enables a user to select a movie to open, so the Open Movie item starts out enabled. The toggling of the state of these two items takes place in the application's event handler.

The following snippet comes from MyAppEventHandler and shows the code that responds to a command issued by the user's choosing of the Open Movie menu item:

```
case kOpenMovieCommand:
    DisplayOpenFileDialog();
    if ( gMovie != NULL )
    {
        DisableMenuItem( gMovieMenu, kMovieMenuOpenItemNum );
        EnableMenuItem( gMovieMenu, kMovieMenuPlayItemNum );
    }
    result = noErr;
    break;
```

Handling an Open Movie menu item selection begins with a call to the application-defined `DisplayOpenFileDialog` routine. The global `Movie` variable `gMovie` was initialized to a value of `NULL` to signify that no movie is open. If the user opens a movie, `gMovie` references that movie and will have a value other than `NULL`. In that case, `MyAppEventHandler` disables the Open Movie item and enables the Play Movie item. That makes it impossible for the user to attempt to open a second movie, and it makes possible the playing of the now-open movie. If the user clicks the Cancel button in the Open dialog box, `gMovie` will retain its `NULL` value and the two menu items will retain their initial state. This enables the user to again choose Open Movie to open a movie.

In your more sophisticated movie-playing programs, you might allow the display and playing of multiple movies. In that case, you can expand on the technique discussed here by allowing the closing of movie windows and the toggling of the Play Movie item from enabled to disabled when all such movie windows are closed. One way to do that is to intercept window-closing events. When a window closes, check whether it was the last movie window. (You could keep a global movie window counter that increments and decrements as movies are opened and closed.) In Chapter 3, "Events and the Carbon Event Manager," the MyCloseWindow example introduces the topic of window closing events. (The program sounds a beep when the user clicks a window's Close button.) In Chapter 4, "Windows," the MenuButtonCloseWindow example elaborates on this technique. Finally, in Chapter 6, "Menus," you learn how to enable and disable menu items.

If the user chooses Play Movie, the application-defined `PlayOneMovie` routine is called. Note that there's no need for any menu-item disabling or enabling here. If this item is enabled, it means a movie window is open and can be played. If no movie window is open, this item will be disabled and the `kPlayMovieCommand` can't be generated by the program!

```
case kPlayMovieCommand:
    PlayOneMovie( gMovie );
    result = noErr;
    break;
```

In response to the user's choosing Open Movie, the program calls `DisplayOpenFileDialog`. This application-defined routine was developed in this chapter's "Implementing an Open Dialog Box" section. The OpenPlayMovie source code listing (Example 9.1) shows this routine. The event handler, or callback routine, that `DisplayOpenFileDialog` installs is the application-defined routine `MyOpenDialogEventCallback`.(This is another routine discussed at length in the "Implementing an Open Dialog Box" section. Refer to those pages for more information on this callback function.) Here I'll point out that if the system invokes this routine with a user action of `kNavUserActionOpen`, the callback routine invokes the application-defined function `OpenOneQTMovieFile` to open the user-selected movie file.

The `OpenOneQTMovieFile` routine is basically a compilation of the code discussed in this chapter's "Transferring Movie File Data to Memory" section. `AECoerceDesc` makes sure that the `NavReplyRecord` filled in by the Open dialog box is valid, `AEGetDescData` retrieves an `FSRef` from that reply record, and `FSGetCatalogInfo` converts the `FSRef` to an `FSSpec` for use in opening the movie file:

```
void  OpenOneQTMovieFile( NavReplyRecord *reply )
{
    AEDesc      newDescriptor;
    FSRef       movieRef;
    WindowRef   window;
    OSStatus    err;
    FSSpec      userFileFSSpec;
    IBNibRef    nibRef;

    err = AECoerceDesc( &reply->selection, typeFSRef, &newDescriptor );

    err = AEGetDescData( &newDescriptor, ( void * )( &movieRef ),
                         sizeof( FSRef ) );

    FSGetCatalogInfo( &movieRef, kFSCatInfoNone, NULL, NULL,
                      &userFileFSSpec, NULL );

    gMovie = GetMovieFromFile( userFileFSSpec );
```

The application-defined routine `GetMovieFromFile` (discussed next) opens the movie file and assigns `gMovie` a reference to the movie. A new window then is opened, its port is set to the current port, and the application-defined routine `AdjustMovieWindow` (discussed shortly) resizes the window and associates the movie with the window. `OpenOneQTMovieFile` ends with a call to `AEDisposeDesc` to dispose of the `AEDisc` created earlier in the routine:

```
    err = CreateNibReference( CFSTR("main"), &nibRef );
    err = CreateWindowFromNib( nibRef, CFSTR("MovieWindow"), &window );
    DisposeNibReference( nibRef );

    SetPortWindowPort( window );

    AdjustMovieWindow( gMovie, window );

    AEDisposeDesc( &newDescriptor );
}
```

`GetMovieFromFile` is a short routine that makes three Movie Toolbox calls. `OpenMovieFile` opens the user-selected file. `NewMovieFromFile` loads the movie data to memory and returns a reference to the movie. `CloseMovieFile` closes the movie file. This chapter's "Transferring Movie File Data to Memory" section discusses each routine.

```
Movie  GetMovieFromFile( FSSpec userFileFSSpec )
{
    OSErr   err;
    Movie   movie = NULL;
    short   movieRefNum;
```

```
short      movieResID = 0;

   err = OpenMovieFile( &userFileFSSpec, &movieRefNum, fsRdPerm );

   err = NewMovieFromFile( &movie, movieRefNum, &movieResID,
                           NULL, newMovieActive, NULL );

   CloseMovieFile( movieRefNum );

   return ( movie );
}
```

AdjustMovieWindow combines the code discussed in this chapter's "Displaying a Movie in a Window" section to create a routine that calls SetMovieGWorld to associate the open movie with the recently opened window and to resize the window to match the size of the movie.

```
void  AdjustMovieWindow( Movie movie, WindowRef window )
{
   Rect   movieBox;

   SetMovieGWorld( movie, NULL, NULL );

   GetMovieBox( movie, &movieBox );
   OffsetRect( &movieBox, -movieBox.left, -movieBox.top );
   SetMovieBox( movie, &movieBox );

   SizeWindow( window, movieBox.right, movieBox.bottom, TRUE );
   ShowWindow( window );

   GoToBeginningOfMovie( gMovie );
   MoviesTask( gMovie, 0 );
}
```

At this point, a movie file has been opened and the first frame of the movie is displayed in a window. To play the movie, the user chooses Play Movie from the Movie menu. Doing that initiates a command that the application event handler handles by calling PlayOneMovie. This routine bundles the code discussed in this chapter's "Playing a QuickTime Movie" section, with the result being the playing of the movie from start to finish:

```
void  PlayOneMovie( Movie movie )
{
   GoToBeginningOfMovie( movie );

   StartMovie( movie );

   do
   {
     MoviesTask( movie, 0 );
   } while ( IsMovieDone( movie ) == FALSE );
}
```

Example 9.1   OpenPlayMovie Source Code

```
#include  <Carbon/Carbon.h>
#include  <QuickTime/QuickTime.h>

#define   kOpenMovieCommand       'OPmv'
#define   kPlayMovieCommand       'PLmv'
#define   kMovieMenuID            5
#define   kMovieMenuOpenItemNum   1
#define   kMovieMenuPlayItemNum   2

Movie          GetMovieFromFile( FSSpec userFileFSSpec );
void           AdjustMovieWindow( Movie movie, WindowRef window );
void           PlayOneMovie( Movie movie );
void           DisplayOpenFileDialog( void );
void           OpenOneQTMovieFile( NavReplyRecord *reply ) ;
pascal OSStatus MyAppEventHandler( EventHandlerCallRef handlerRef,
                               EventRef event, void *userData );
pascal void    MyOpenDialogEventCallback(
                           NavEventCallbackMessage callBackSelector,
                           NavCBRecPtr             callBackParms,
                           void*                   callBackUD );

NavEventUPP   gNavEventHandlerPtr;
Movie         gMovie = NULL;
MenuHandle    gMovieMenu;


int main( int argc, char* argv[] )
{
   IBNibRef        nibRef;
   WindowRef       window;
   OSStatus        err;
   EventTargetRef  target;
   EventHandlerUPP handlerUPP;
   EventTypeSpec   appEvent = { kEventClassCommand,
                                kEventProcessCommand };

   EnterMovies();

   err = CreateNibReference( CFSTR("main"), &nibRef );
   err = SetMenuBarFromNib( nibRef, CFSTR("MainMenu") );
   err = CreateWindowFromNib( nibRef, CFSTR("MainWindow"), &window );
   DisposeNibReference( nibRef );

   ShowWindow( window );

   target = GetApplicationEventTarget();
   handlerUPP = NewEventHandlerUPP( MyAppEventHandler );
   InstallEventHandler( target, handlerUPP, 1, &appEvent, 0, NULL );

   gMovieMenu = GetMenuHandle( kMovieMenuID );
```

continues

Example 9.1   Continued

```
    RunApplicationEventLoop();

    return( 0 );
}


pascal OSStatus MyAppEventHandler( EventHandlerCallRef handlerRef,
                                   EventRef event, void *userData)
{
    OSStatus    result = eventNotHandledErr;
    HICommand   command;

    GetEventParameter( event, kEventParamDirectObject, typeHICommand,
                       NULL, sizeof (HICommand), NULL, &command);

    switch ( command.commandID )
    {
        case kOpenMovieCommand:
            DisplayOpenFileDialog();
            if ( gMovie != NULL )
            {
                DisableMenuItem( gMovieMenu, kMovieMenuOpenItemNum );
                EnableMenuItem( gMovieMenu, kMovieMenuPlayItemNum );
            }
            result = noErr;
            break;

        case kPlayMovieCommand:
            PlayOneMovie( gMovie );
            result = noErr;
            break;
    }
    return result;
}


void DisplayOpenFileDialog( void )
{
    OSStatus                 err;
    NavDialogRef             openDialog;
    NavDialogCreationOptions dialogAttributes;

    err = NavGetDefaultDialogCreationOptions( &dialogAttributes );
    dialogAttributes.modality = kWindowModalityAppModal;

    gNavEventHandlerPtr = NewNavEventUPP( MyOpenDialogEventCallback );


    err = NavCreateGetFileDialog( &dialogAttributes, NULL,
```

```
                             gNavEventHandlerPtr, NULL, NULL,
                             NULL, &openDialog );

   err = NavDialogRun( openDialog );
   if ( err != noErr )
   {
      NavDialogDispose( openDialog );
      DisposeNavEventUPP( gNavEventHandlerPtr );
   }
}


pascal void MyOpenDialogEventCallback(
                             NavEventCallbackMessage callBackSelector,
                             NavCBRecPtr             callBackParms,
                             void*                   callBackUD )
{
   OSStatus        err;
   NavReplyRecord  reply;
   NavUserAction   userAction = 0;

   switch ( callBackSelector )
   {
      case kNavCBUserAction:
         err = NavDialogGetReply( callBackParms->context, &reply );
         userAction = NavDialogGetUserAction( callBackParms->context );
         switch ( userAction )
         {
            case kNavUserActionOpen:
               OpenOneQTMovieFile( &reply );
               break;
         }
         err = NavDisposeReply( &reply );
         break;

      case kNavCBTerminate:
         NavDialogDispose( callBackParms->context );
         DisposeNavEventUPP( gNavEventHandlerPtr );
         break;
   }
}


void  OpenOneQTMovieFile( NavReplyRecord *reply )
{
   AEDesc      newDescriptor;
   FSRef       movieRef;
   WindowRef   window;
   OSStatus    err;
   FSSpec      userFileFSSpec;
   IBNibRef    nibRef;
```

continues

Example 9.1 Continued

```
    err = AECoerceDesc( &reply->selection, typeFSRef, &newDescriptor );

    err = AEGetDescData( &newDescriptor, ( void * )( &movieRef ),
                            sizeof( FSRef ) );

    FSGetCatalogInfo( &movieRef, kFSCatInfoNone, NULL,
                      NULL, &userFileFSSpec, NULL );

    gMovie = GetMovieFromFile( userFileFSSpec );

    err = CreateNibReference( CFSTR("main"), &nibRef );
    err = CreateWindowFromNib( nibRef, CFSTR("MovieWindow"), &window );
    DisposeNibReference( nibRef );

    SetPortWindowPort( window );

    AdjustMovieWindow( gMovie, window );

    AEDisposeDesc( &newDescriptor );
}


Movie  GetMovieFromFile( FSSpec userFileFSSpec )
{
    OSErr    err;
    Movie    movie = NULL;
    short    movieRefNum;
    short    movieResID = 0;

    err = OpenMovieFile( &userFileFSSpec, &movieRefNum, fsRdPerm );

    err = NewMovieFromFile( &movie, movieRefNum, &movieResID,
                            NULL, newMovieActive, NULL );

    CloseMovieFile( movieRefNum );

    return ( movie );
}


void  AdjustMovieWindow( Movie movie, WindowRef window )
{
    Rect    movieBox;

    SetMovieGWorld( movie, NULL, NULL );

    GetMovieBox( movie, &movieBox );
    OffsetRect( &movieBox, -movieBox.left, -movieBox.top );
    SetMovieBox( movie, &movieBox );
```

```
      SizeWindow( window, movieBox.right, movieBox.bottom, TRUE );
      ShowWindow( window );

      GoToBeginningOfMovie( gMovie );
      MoviesTask( gMovie, 0 );
}


void  PlayOneMovie( Movie movie )
{
   GoToBeginningOfMovie( movie );

   StartMovie( movie );

   do
   {
      MoviesTask( movie, 0 );
   } while ( IsMovieDone( movie ) == FALSE );
}
```

For More Information

The following web sites provide extra information about some of this chapter's topics:

- **Navigation Services:**
  http://developer.apple.com/techpubs/macosx/Carbon/Files/NavigationServices/navigationservices.html

- **QuickTime technologies:**
  http://developer.apple.com/techpubs/quicktime/quicktime.html

- **QuickTime API:**
  http://developer.apple.com/techpubs/quicktime/qtdevdocs/RM/frameset.htm

- **Movie controllers:**
  http://developer.apple.com/techpubs/quicktime/qtdevdocs/RM/frameset.htm

10

Bundles and Icons

On the desktop, your application's icon suggests that your program is just that—an application file. It's not, however. What appears to the user to be an application is really a bundle consisting of several files and folders. In this chapter, you see how to examine the contents of an application bundle and discover the purpose of the various files and folders that comprise that bundle. You'll also learn how to register a contributor code.

Your application can open multiple windows of a variety of types, with each window displaying text, graphics, and controls. Your program can check for errors, post alerts, and even play QuickTime movie files. In short, your program can do quite a bit when it's running.

However, although your application might perform amazing tricks while executing, it's just another plain, generic icon from the desktop. In this chapter, you'll change that. You'll see how to create an icon and associate it with your application.

With Aqua, Apple introduces an entirely new scheme for displaying icons and the result is that you can design large, high-resolution icons. If you're artistic, or know someone who is, now is the best time to create a truly unique, photo-quality icon that really reflects the nature or purpose of your application.

Applications, Bundles, and Packages

An application that you see as an icon on your Mac's desktop is not an application. It is an *application bundle*, which is a file package that holds folders and files. One of the files in this package is the application itself. The other folders and files support the application file, and they can include image and sound files, multiple versions of nib files (each localized for a different language), files that hold strings localized for different languages, and other files.

The Application Bundle

The application bundle is a file package that holds a self-sufficient binary file that's launchable from the desktop. An application bundle is what a developer usually creates.

> **Note**
>
> There are other types of bundles as well. Frameworks and plug-ins are bundles that can be dynamically loaded and used by applications. The purpose for creating such bundles is reusability. Such a bundle usually has some general purpose and thus can be included with more than one application.

Placing an application and all the files it uses into a single package and then giving that package a single icon on the desktop is a new, important, and clever scheme. It hides the plethora of files so that the end user doesn't get confused or inadvertently delete support files. It also makes the transfer of an application from one computer to another easy in that the program's files are assured to arrive together when the user copies what he or she thinks is a single application file.

The desktop hides the true nature of an application, but it also makes it relatively easy to view the contents of an application package. To do that, press and hold the Control key, and then click an application icon. Choose Show Package Contents from the contextual menu. In Figure 10.1, I'm doing it with the CheckboxDemo program from Chapter 5, "Controls," but you can do this for any application.

Choosing Show Package Contents opens a new Finder window that displays a single folder named Contents. Yes, this folder holds the entire contents of the application bundle you've selected. Figure 10.2 shows the contents of the Contents folder.

In Figure 10.2, you see that the Contents folder holds three files and two folders. Project Builder placed all these items in this folder when the application was built. The following subsections discuss these in detail.

Info.plist

This is an *information property list* that holds application bundle information that's of use to the Finder. For instance, among the information in Info.plist file is the specification that this bundle is an application (a bundle doesn't have to be a standalone application) and that the name of the executable in this bundle is CheckboxDemo. The information in the Info.plist file is in extensible markup language (XML) format. It *can* be hand-edited, but it's a much better idea not to. Instead, leave it to Project Builder to put together this file's information from various settings within the project from which the application gets built.

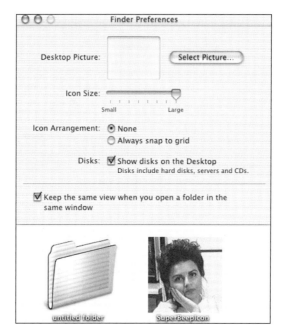

Figure 10.1 Displaying the contents of an application bundle.

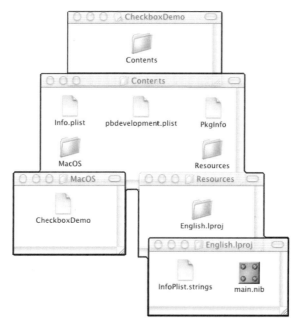

Figure 10.2 The folders and files that make up a typical application bundle.

pbdevelopment.plist

This is an information property list that's of use only to Project Builder. It exists only when a development version of an application is built. When you're at the point where your development is complete, and you're satisfied with the resulting application, you build your deployment version. The building is accomplished by checking the Deployment option under the Targets tab in the project (see Figure 10.8). When a deployment version of an application is built, that application bundle won't include a pbdevelopment.plist file.

PkgInfo

This file holds the bundle type and creator code for the application. An application has a bundle type of APPL and a unique creator code of the developer's choosing. See this chapter's "Registering a Creator Code" section for more information.

MacOS

This is a folder that holds the executable itself. This book's examples each include a single executable, but it's possible to create an application bundle that holds more than one executable. The primary example of such a situation is for a project that's building two versions of the same program. One version would run on Mac OS X and one would run on Mac OS 9. Such a project would actually create two separate executables, with each being launchable on its respective operating system version.

Resources

This folder holds all the resources used by the application. These resources are themselves within another folder in the Resources folder. In Figure 10.2, that folder is named English.lproj.

   If you create localized versions of your application (different versions for different human languages), the Resources folder will hold other folders as well (such as Japanese.lproj). Minimally, the two items in one folder within the Resources folder are the main.nib file and the InfoPlist.strings file. Both are part of every nib-based Project Builder project. The main.nib file has been discussed throughout this book. The InfoPlist.strings file is described in the following section.

InfoPlist.strings Resource File

One of the files that ends up in an application bundle is the InfoPlist.strings resource file. This file is noteworthy because it holds a string that appears in the interface of the program that gets built from the project. If you click the Resources folder under the Groups & Files heading in a project, you'll see the file listed along with the main.nib

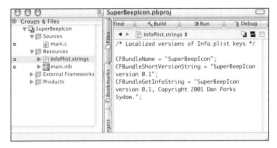

resource file. To view the contents of the InfoPlist.strings file, click its name. Figure 10.3 shows this file for this chapter's SuperBeepIcon example program.

Figure 10.3   The InfoPlist.strings resource file.

The InfoPlist.strings file holds a collection of key-value pairs. In XML, such a collection of pairings is referred to as a *dictionary*. In each new project, Project Builder includes an InfoPlist.strings file that holds three key-value pairs. Each key (, `CFBundleName`, `CFBundleShortVersionString`, and `CFBundleGetInfoString`) has a string assigned to it.

In Figure 10.3, you see that I've edited the Project Builder supplied strings to include references to the name of the project's application and to include proper copyright information. Of most importance here is the `CFBundleName` key. The value you assign to this key is used in the Application menu of your program. In Figure 10.3, you see that the InfoPlist.strings file for the SuperBeepIcon project includes a `CFBundleName` of *SuperBeepIcon*. At the top of Figure 10.4, you see the nib menu resource from this same project. In this case, the name of the Application menu is TestProgram, but when the program is built and executed, the Application menu takes on the name *SuperBeepIcon* (as shown in the lower part of Figure 10.4).

The occurrences of SuperBeepIcon in the Application menu name, in the Hide SuperBeepIcon item, and in the Quit SuperBeepIcon item name come from the `CFBundleName` value in the project's InfoPlist.strings file. It's important to note that the one menu item name that doesn't automatically get assigned the `CFBundleName` value is

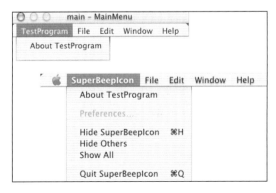

the About item. You're responsible for supplying this item with the proper name in the nib menu resource.

Figure 10.4   A nib menu resource (top) and the resulting application menu (bottom).

One other item of interest in the InfoPlist.strings file is the `CFBundleGetInfoString` key. The value of this key appears as the version information in the Info window that's displayed when the user clicks the application on the desktop and then chooses Show Info from the File menu. As shown in Figure 10.5, the value of this key can be set from under the Application Settings tab when the Targets tab is selected in the project window. As of this writing, in fact, the Get-Info string field under the Application Settings tab is the place to define the version information for your program. It is this string that appears in the Info window.

Figure 10.5   The Get-Info string in a project is used as the version string in the Finder's Show Info window.

Registering a Creator Code

Every file has a four-character type. The value, unsurprisingly, specifies the type of the file. An application always has a type of APPL. (Other common file types are TEXT for a text file and PICT for a picture file.) Every file can also have a four-character creator code, which is a unique value belonging to one and only one application. In the case of an application file, the creator code is an identifier of the application itself. In the case of a file created by an application, the creator code identifies the file as belonging to (or created by) the application with the same creator code.

As an example of a creator code, consider Apple's SimpleText text editor application. The resource editor ResEdit can be used to ascertain the type and creator code of any file. At the top of Figure 10.6, you see that ResEdit reports that for SimpleText, the file type is APPL (it's an application) and the creator code is ttxt (a unique four-character value registered to this one application).

Now consider a file created by SimpleText. I launched SimpleText and created a new file, which I named ReadMe.txt. After closing that file, I viewed it in ResEdit. The results are shown at the bottom of Figure 10.6. In that figure, you see that a file created by SimpleText has a type of TEXT (it's a text file) and a creator code of ttxt (it was created by the application with this same creator code— SimpleText).

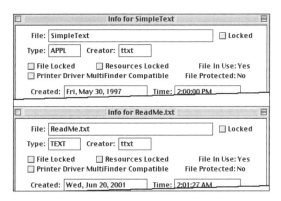

Figure 10.6   The file type and creator of the SimpleText application (top) and of a file created by the SimpleText application (bottom).

An application's creator code is used by the Finder to associate files created by that application to that application. This system makes it possible for a double-click on a file to result in the launching of the creating application and the opening of the clicked-on file.

Registering a Creator Code With Apple

At Apple's developer site (`http://developer.apple.com`), you'll find a link to a technical support area (`http://developer.apple.com/products/techsupport/`) that includes links to pages that offer information about specific programming topics. The *Registrations* link takes you to a page (`http://developer.apple.com/dev/cftype`) that includes information about registering a creator code (or application signature) for your own application. Click the *Find* link to move to a page that lets you enter one or more creator codes and then search to see which are available.

In Chapter 5, I mentioned that I had registered a creator code for one of this book's example programs. Figure 10.7 shows the result of my search to see whether the creator code *SPRB* was available. It was, so the next step was to register the code with Apple. Clicking the *Register new creator/file types* link (see Figure 10.7) is how the registration is done.

The registration is short and simple. You enter a little information, such as your name and mailing address, and then you click the Submit button. That's it. If the creator code availability search told you that your code of interest was available, you now can consider it yours. Absolute confirmation is supplied in a couple of days. That's about how long it takes to receive a confirmation email notice from Apple.

Figure 10.7 Searching at Apple's site for the availability of a creator code.

Assigning a Creator Code to Your Program

After you've found an unused creator code and registered it with Apple, you can assign that creator code to your application. That's done from within Project Builder. Open the project that's used to build your application and click the Targets tab in the column of tabs in the project window. Click the target in the Targets area (the SuperBeepIcon target is selected in Figure 10.8), and then click the Application Settings tab from the row of tabs. As shown in Figure 10.8, you then can set the application's signature. Just type it into the Signature field. In this figure, you can see that I'm using the SPRB creator code that I've registered with Apple. Leave the Type field set to APPL. It stands for *application*, which is the type of file you're creating.

Figure 10.8 Associating a creator code with an application in a project.

With the signature set in the project, each build you perform results in an application with the specified signature.

Application Icons

From the desktop, every application is displayed as an icon. Each real, shipping application has its own unique icon, one that displays an image that might provide a hint about the nature of the application. For instance, the TextEdit text editor application that is bundled with Mac OS X has an icon that looks like a piece of paper with writing on it and with a pen laid across it.

When you build an application in Project Builder, that application is given a generic icon. By now, you should be familiar with this application default icon, but if you need to take a look at it, look at the icon for the BasicShapes program on the far left side of Figure 10.9. Although every application needs an icon, you probably won't want to go through the work of creating a unique icon for your short test programs. Thus, this Project Builder-supplied icon turns out to be a handy solution. When the time comes to build a "real" version of your program, though, you'll want to associate a "real" icon with that program. In this section, you see how to do that.

Application and Document Icons

On the desktop, an icon represents a folder or a file. If the icon represents a file, it can be for an application or a document created by an application. Figure 10.9 shows icons for four applications and two types of documents.

Figure 10.9 Application icons (top) and document icons (bottom).

The four icons in the top row of Figure 10.9 are application icons, while the two icons in the lower row are document icons. The leftmost icon in the top row of Figure 10.9 is the generic icon assigned to any program that doesn't explicitly define its own icon. Looking back at this book's examples reveals that every example project builds an application that sports this icon.

The next two icons in the top row of the figure are the icons for real programs. TextEdit is Apple's text editor that comes bundled with Mac OS X, while Internet Explorer is, of course, Microsoft's web browser program.

The last icon in the top row is the icon I've created for one of this chapter's example programs. In the bottom row, the leftmost icon is the one TextEdit assigns to its documents, while the rightmost icon is the one Internet Explorer assigns to its Hypertext Markup Language (HTML) documents.

Apple recommends that every application have a custom icon that provides some visual clue as to the purpose of the program. The icon for Apple's TextEdit application conforms to that guideline. The icon for Microsoft's Internet Explorer doesn't (at least *I* can't make out much of a correlation between a lowercase *e* and a program used to browse the World Wide Web [WWW]).

You'll find that numerous applications *don't* abide by Apple's guideline. Rather than provide feedback on the nature of the program, an application's icon might instead include some image that's already firmly set in the public eye. It also might be some version or adaptation of the software company's name or logo. In that spirit of rebellion, the icon I've created for this chapter's SuperBeepIcon program (shown at the far right of Figure 10.9) has nothing to do with sound or beeping.

> **Note**
>
> Other reasons that I chose to use a digitized image from my camcorder as the basis for an application icon include the fact that I don't have anywhere near the level of artistic skills necessary to create an interesting, professional-looking icon, and because I'm too cheap to pay a graphic designer to do the work of designing such an icon!

The following three sections discuss the steps you'll perform to assign an icon to an application. In short, those steps are as follows:

1. Create an image in a graphics program and save it as a .pict or .tiff file.

2. Convert that graphic file to an icon file.

3. Include the icon file in a Project Builder project.

4. Within Project Builder, specify that this icon file be associated with the application that results from performing a build.

Creating an Image for an Icon

New to Mac OS X is the 128×128 pixel icon size. This very large pixel size means an icon can be designed with a lot of detail and look much better than ever before. Also new to Mac OS X is powerful scaling technology that enables a large icon to be accurately scaled down.

Typically, you'll create a large 128×128 pixel icon and leave it to the system to scale it to the size the user prefers for the display of desktop icons. However, if you find that your large icon loses important detail in scaling, you can design intermediate-sized icons that assist the system in scaling. Those other sizes are 64×64 pixels, 32×32 pixels, and 16×16 pixels. In this chapter, I'll create just one icon—the 128×128 pixel size—and leave it to the system to handle all icon scaling.

In the design of an icon you (or, more likely, a graphic designer) can use any graphics program that provides the desired results. If you're using a digitized image, you can use a graphics program to simply crop the image to isolate the portion of interest and then scale that image to 128×128 pixels. If your image is to be designed from scratch or if it is to be an collage or adaptation of clip art, you'll use graphics programs such as Adobe Photoshop, Adobe LiveMotion, and so forth.

When you have an image with which you're satisfied, save it in a file of type .pict or .tiff. For this chapter's SuperBeepIcon example program, I saved some output from my camcorder to my iMac and copied one frame to the Clipboard. I then launched a graphics program (the shareware program GraphicConverter, which is discussed in Chapter 2, "Overview of Mac OS X Programming"), created a new, empty document 128×128 pixels in size, and pasted that image into the document. I dragged the pasted image around until the portion of the image of interest was centered in the document, and then I saved the document as a .pict file. That gave me a 128×128 pixel *image*, but it didn't give me a 128×128 pixel *icon*. There's one more program to run to accomplish that conversion.

Saving an Image as an Icon

After you create an image that's to be used as an icon, you need to import that image into the Icon Composer application. Icon Composer is another free development application from Apple. You'll find it in the Applications folder inside the Developer folder on your Macintosh.

With your image created and saved as a 128×128 pixel .pict or .tiff file, launch Icon Composer. Choose Import Image from the File menu. As shown in Figure 10.10, the window that appears enables you to move to the folder that holds the image that's to be converted to an icon. Move to that folder now. Choose Thumbnail 32bit data from the Import To pop-up menu located at the bottom of the window, and then select the file of interest. Your actions tell Icon Composer that the file you're about to select holds an image that's to be used as a 128×128 pixel icon. Now double-click the name of the file that holds the image.

Figure 10.10   Importing an image into Icon Composer.

After you select a file, Icon Composer responds by placing that file's image into the Thumbnail box at the bottom of the icon window, as shown in Figure 10.11. Note that if it turns out that the file you saved as a 128×128 pixel image varies by even one pixel in either dimension, Icon Composer will ask you if you want the image scaled. Go ahead and let Icon Composer do this. The change won't be noticeable, unless your image is in fact of a size that varies quite a bit from the 128×128 pixel size of a thumbnail.

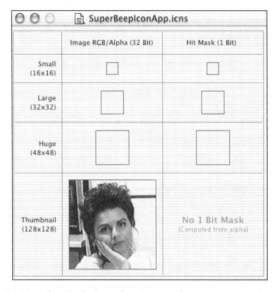

Figure 10.11   The displaying of an imported image in Icon Composer.

Now choose Save from the File menu. The file name can be of your choosing, but don't add an extension to the name. When you click the Save button, Icon Composer will add an extension of .icns to the name you entered. Save the file to the project folder.

Adding the Icon File to Your Project

Before the contents of a file can be used by a project, that file needs to be added to the project. In the Chapter 2 example of HelloWorldPict, you saw this was the case for including a picture in a program window. The same holds true for an icon. After using Icon Composer to convert an image to an icon and saving that icon to a file, you need to add the resulting file to a project. Open the Project Builder project that's to use the icon and click the Resources folder in the Groups & Files list in the project window (that selection determines where the added file will end up). Now choose Add Files from the Project menu. Select the .icns file to use and click the Open button. When prompted to specify which targets to add the file to, click the Add button.

Figure 10.12 show how the SuperBeepIcon project (discussed ahead) looks after an Icon Composer file named SuperBeepIconApp.icns has been added to it. For organizational purposes, the icon file typically is kept in the Resources folder, although it doesn't have to be there for the icon to become associated with the application. If the icon file doesn't end up in the Resources folder, simply drag it there now.

Figure 10.12   Adding an icon file to a project.

Adding the .icns file to the project is one of two steps to getting a project to recognize the file's icon. Now you need to name the same file in the Application Settings of the project. Begin by clicking the Targets tab in the column of tabs in the project window. Click the target in the Targets area (the SuperBeepIcon target is selected in Figure 10.13). Click the Application Settings tab from the row of tabs. Now scroll down to the Icons section and type the name of the .icns file in the Icon file text box. In Figure 10.13, you see that the file name matches the name of the .icns file added to the project back in Figure 10.12.

Figure 10.13   Associating an icon file with an application in a project.

At this point, the icon in the .icns file will replace the generic icon that Project Builder uses when no icon is specified. Now when you build the application from this project, the resulting application will display the icon that's in the .icns file.

Viewing the Results

When you build an application from a project that includes a .icns file, that application displays the icon at the desktop. Unless you've specified otherwise in Project Builder, building an application from a Project Builder project places the executable in the build folder in the project folder, so you'll look in that folder to see the application.

In Figure 10.14, you see the result of associating the icon shown in Figure 10.11 with the project shown in Figures 10.12 and 10.13. If your application isn't sporting the new icon, don't be alarmed. It might just mean that your desktop isn't updating promptly. If you built the application once without the new icon, the desktop might still associate the generic application icon with your program. Try this to remedy the situation: click the application icon in the build folder and copy the application to another folder. The duplicate application should now have the new icon.

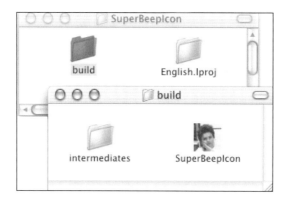

Figure 10.14   The newly added icon is displayed on the desktop.

The size of the icon your program uses is adjustable by the user. Because you've created a large, detailed icon, the desktop is capable of accurately scaling that icon to a smaller size. To test this, you can copy the application from its folder directly to the desktop and then choose Preferences from the desktop menu. Drag the Icon Size slider control to different settings and watch the application icon (and all other icons on the desktop) change in size. Figure 10.15 shows desktop icons being increased to their largest size.

SuperBeepIcon Program

The purpose of the SuperBeepIcon program is to illustrate how a custom icon is associated with an application.

If you haven't already guessed, the preceding sections have walked you through this example. I used the Chapter 5 RadioButtonGroup project as the starting point for this example's project, nib resources, and source code. However, you can use *any* existing or new project because the resources and source code are entirely unimportant in the associating of an icon to an application. In the following short sections, I'll summarize how to create an icon and associate it with your application.

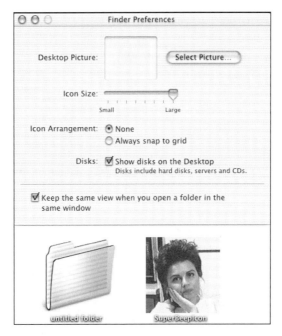

Figure 10.15   Resizing icons (including your application's icon) on the desktop.

Create a 128×128 Pixel Image

To practice the adding of an icon to an application, you can start out easy. Focus on the process of creating and adding the icon to your program. Don't initially get caught up in the particulars of creating an intricate image. After you know how to add an icon to a program, you can easily repeat the steps later after you've obtained the best possible icon for your application.

Begin by launching your favorite graphics program and opening a 128×128 pixel document. If your graphics program doesn't let you specify an initial document size by pixels, open a new document and resize, or trim, it to this size. Then add some simple graphics to it, such as a couple colored rectangles. This is a test, so any graphics will do for now. Now save the document as either a .pict or .tiff file.

Convert the Image File to an Icon File

Convert the graphic image to an icon by importing it into Icon Composer. Launch the Icon Composer program and choose Import Image from the File menu. Select the Thumbnail 32bit data item from the Import To pop-up menu located at the bottom of the window. Then choose the graphics file to import. Choose Save from the File menu and provide a name for the file. Leave off the file name extension, as Icon Composer will append a .icns extension to the name you supply.

Add the Icon File to the Project

Open the project of interest in Project Builder and choose Add Files from the Project menu. Select the .icns file to use. Click the Open button and then, when prompted to specify to which targets to add the file, click the Add button. Now specify the name of this same file in the project's application's settings. Click the Targets tab, click the target in the Targets area, and then click the Application Settings tab. Scroll down to the Icons section and enter the name of the .icns file in the Icon file text box.

Build the Application

The next time, and every subsequent time, that you build an application from the project, that application will bear the icon you've added to the project.

For More Information

For more information about this chapter's topics, visit any of the following web sites:

- **Creator code registration:** `http:// developer.apple.com/tools/`
- **Icon software:** `http://developer.apple.com/ue/resources.html`
- **Icon routines:**
  `http://developer.apple.com/techpubs/macosx/Carbon/HumanInterfaceToolbox /IconServUtili/iconservicesandutilities.html`

11

Porting Mac OS 8/9 Code to Mac OS X

IF YOU HAVE SOME MAC OS PROGRAMMING EXPERIENCE, you'll want your previous programming efforts to run on Mac OS X. Fortunately, without any modification, most of your Mac applications will make the transition. Unfortunately, they'll run only in the Classic environment of Mac OS X. That is, when a user of one of your Mac OS 8/9 applications copies that program to his or her Macintosh running Mac OS X and then launches that application, the program automatically runs under Mac OS 9. There will be no Aqua interface, no protected memory, and no other features that are integral to Mac OS X. If you want users of your previously developed efforts to experience your program as a native Mac OS X application, you need to port its code to Mac OS X.

Adding new Mac OS X features, such as support of the new Carbon Event Manager, to your program can take a fair amount of programming effort. However, the benefits of Mac OS X make those efforts worthy of the time expended. In addition, before you jump into a full-scale conversion, you can alter your older project's code to be Mac OS X compatible and then recompile that project's code to develop a native Mac OS X application. Doing that means a double-click on your application's icon launches the program in Mac OS X, places that application's code in its own protected memory space, and paints the Aqua look on the program's interface elements. After you've reached that point, you then can decide which new Mac OS X features to add to your program. After you decide which features that you want to add, you can read this chapter to find out the basic steps for turning your Mac OS 8 or Mac OS 9 code into an application that's launched in the Mac OS X space!

Carbon Dater: Getting Ready for Carbon

You'll want to have a plan before jumping in and making changes to the code of your existing Mac OS 8/9 application. In particular, you'll want to know which Macintosh Toolbox routines are no longer supported and which are supported for now but might not make the cut to Carbon. (Remember that the Carbon API isn't yet finalized.) To this end, Apple supplies developers with the Carbon Dater. If you're porting code to Mac OS X, this free, easy-to-use utility is a must.

Carbon Dating Your Code

Carbon Dater is a small application available for downloading from Apple (http://developer.apple.com/macosx/carbon/dater.html). After obtaining the Carbon Dater.sit folder and unstuffing it, drag and drop your application onto the Carbon Dater - Drop App here file that resides in the Carbon Dater folder. Note that you're inputting the actual application you've built, not its source code or the project from which the application was built.

The Carbon Dater application analyzes your application's code and takes note of the Macintosh Toolbox routines your application calls. It then compiles those routine names in a list. The Carbon Dater can also recognize some coding practices that you might use that might not be supported by Carbon. These practices are saved along with the function name list and stored collectively in a single text file. When Carbon Dater is finished, this text file is created and given the name of your application with an extension of .CCT (for Carbon Compatibility Test).

The contents of the text file aren't in a format that's of much use to you. The file's contents are ready, however, for more analysis and formatting by Apple. You'll attach this text file (preferably compressed using the Aladdin StuffIt program that's included with Mac OS X) to an email message and send it to Apple at CarbonDating@apple.com. You don't need to supply a subject or include any text in the body of the message. The .CCT file is all that Apple needs. Don't worry about this being a time-consuming process; no human intervention is needed on Apple's end. The file is analyzed and a Carbon compatibility report in Hypertext Markup Language (HTML) format is generated and sent to you through email, usually within hours.

Reading the Carbon Dater Report

When you receive Apple's Carbon compatibility report, open it in your web browser of choice. Figure 11.1 shows a part of one such report.

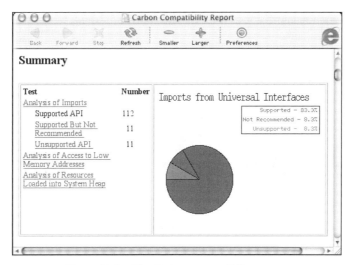

Figure 11.1   The Carbon compatibility report.

Apple notes each Macintosh Toolbox routine that your application calls and compares each one to the Carbon API. The result is that every function call is categorized as Supported API, Supported But Not Recommended, or Unsupported API.

If a call to a Macintosh Toolbox routine is supported, you know that this original Toolbox routine now exists in the Carbon API. A good 70 percent of more of the Macintosh Toolbox functions are part of Carbon. Such routines are fully supported, so you don't have to make any changes to those calls, and the Carbon compatibility report offers no more information on them.

If a call to a Macintosh Toolbox routine is unsupported, you know that this original Toolbox routine is not a part of the Carbon API. If you leave such a call in your source code and rebuild your application targeting Mac OS X (as occurs when building a project in Project Builder), a compilation error will occur. You need to replace such a call with its newer Carbon API counterpart. If no such Carbon routine exists, you need to rewrite your code to eliminate the one Toolbox call and replace it with calls to perhaps two or more Carbon routines that collectively provide your program with the result that was provided by the one call to the original Toolbox routine. Because the unsupported routine necessitates a code change, the Carbon compatibility report offers suggestions and tips on what you can do.

Figure 11.2 shows a couple memory-related comments that might be found in a Carbon compatibility report. The figure also shows an example of how an unsupported function is listed. Here you see that `MaxApplZone`, a routine commonly used to allocate an appropriately sized block of heap memory for an application, isn't supported. Mac OS X memory management is set up differently than in previous versions of the Mac OS, and no such call is needed. Here the solution is simple; Apple states that you might want to omit this call from the source code.

If a call to a Macintosh Toolbox routine is supported but not recommended, you still can use this original Toolbox routine, but it might not work at a later date. The Carbon API is a work in progress, and some original Macintosh Toolbox routines that now are part of the Carbon API could be replaced in the future. Here Apple is strongly hinting that your best move is to replace such calls now so that your program won't break in the future. Because the supported routines might become obsolete, the Carbon compatibility report offers feedback regarding alternate routines you can use.

Figure 11.3 shows a couple memory-related tips in a Carbon compatibility report, along with an example of how a Supported But Not Recommended routine is listed. Here you see that `MoreMasters`, which is a routine used to reserve memory for a new block of master pointers, is supported. Note, however, that its use isn't recommended. The report provides a better way of doing things: replace the call to `MoreMasters` with a call to the newer routine `MoreMasterPointers`.

> **Note**
>
> A master pointer is fixed in memory and points to a relocatable block of memory.

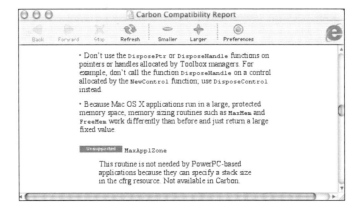

Figure 11.2   An unsupported routine listed in the Carbon report.

You'll want to focus on the routines in the Carbon compatibility report that are Unsupported or Supported But Not Recommended. However, you'll also want to read the report from start to finish. Apple includes plenty of commentary on major and minor porting issues that are of concern to any developer.

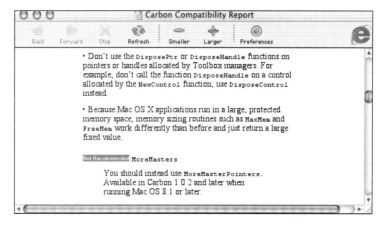

Figure 11.3   A supported but not recommended routine listed in the Carbon report.

Tips for Handling Major Porting Issues

The larger and more complex your application, the more "gotchas" you'll encounter as you move the code from Mac OS 8/9 to Mac OS X. The following sections contain tips on dealing with those gotchas.

Start with PowerPC Code

Macintosh computers initially made use of 68K processors. These processors are from the Motorola 68000 family. All Macs shipped in the last few years now include a PowerPC processor. If your application was developed within the last few years, it probably is already PowerPC-native. That's the starting point for moving to Mac OS X. If you've come across some old code that you'd like to update that isn't already PowerPC-native, check it on Mac OS 8/9 first.

Update Header Files

After ensuring that your code compiles and runs under Mac OS 8/9, don't immediately start altering your code for Mac OS X. Instead, make sure that you're using the latest version of the Universal Interface header files. These files include the latest prototypes for the Carbon API routines.

The Universal Interface files are available as a single download from Apple and as a part of the Carbon SDK (Software Developer's Kit). Apple occasionally updates both files, and the latest version of each is available for downloading at `http://developer.apple.com/sdk` page.

When using Project Builder, use a single `#include` statement to give your project access to the Carbon framework:

```
#include <Carbon/Carbon.h>
```

The examples in this book use the #include statement. Doing so eliminates the need to include individual header files (such as Dialogs.h). More importantly, it ensures that your project has direct access to the Carbon framework.

> **Note**
> Individual header files might not work properly in the project because there isn't a direct correlation between the individual header files and the Mac OS X frameworks.

Eliminate Direct Access to Opaque Structures

In the past, a programmer could view the makeup of structures such as WindowRecord and DialogRecord. Programmers would sometimes directly access the fields of these structures or use routines that made assumptions about the ordering or size of fields in these records. Consider this code snippet:

```
WindowPtr    window;

GetNewWindow( 128, nil, (WindowPtr)-1L );
SetPort( window );
```

After creating a window from a WIND resource, the preceding code then calls SetPort to make the new window's port the current port. In the past, this code compiled properly and executed properly because WindowPtr was the same as GrafPtr. The GrafPort (graphics port) of a window was the first field in the window's record, so a pointer to the window and a pointer to the window's graphics port pointed to the same place.

Unfortunately, things have changed. Windows and dialogs are now opaque structures, so you shouldn't attempt direct access to structure fields, and you can't use routines that do the same. Instead, you should rely on new Carbon API casting routines that exist specifically to perform these access tasks for you. For instance, to make a window's port the current port, create the window and then use the GetWindowPort routine:

```
SetPort( GetWindowPort( window ) );
```

Other casting functions of interest are listed in the Dialogs.h and MacWindows.h Universal Interface files. These functions include the following:

```
DialogPtr  GetDialogFromWindow( WindowPtr window );
WindowPtr  GetWindowFromPort( CGrafPtr port );
WindowPtr  GetDialogWindow( DialogPtr dialog );
CGrafPtr   GetWindowPort( WindowPtr window );
```

Use New Carbon Technologies

The new Carbon Event Manager is an improvement on the original Event Manager. Chapter 3, "Events and the Carbon Event Manager," covers the Carbon Event Manager at length. Apple recommends that you use the newer Carbon Event Manager routines in your Mac OS X application, but it's not a requirement. The use of a couple other new technologies is required, though. In addition, if your Mac OS X program opens or saves files, it must use Navigation Services routines in place of the original Standard File Package routines. If your Mac OS X program enables printing, it needs to use Carbon Printing Manager routines in place of the Classic Printing Manager functions. Printing is an involved topic that's beyond the scope of this book.

Note

Chapter 9, "QuickTime Movies and File Handling," introduces Navigation Services and provides an example of its use in opening a QuickTime movie file.

For More Information

The following web sites offers more information on some of the topics presented in this chapter:

- **Carbon Dater download:**
  http://developer.apple.com/macosx/carbon/dater.html
- **Carbon specification:** http://developer.apple.com/techpubs/carbon/
- **Mac OS X porting information:**
  http://developer.apple.com/technotes/tn/tn2003.html
- **Universal Interfaces download:** http://developer.apple.com/sdk/
- **SDK download:** http://developer.apple.com/macosx/carbon/index.html

Carbon API Summary

As YOU PROGRAM FOR MAC OS X, you might find yourself occasionally forgetting a few of the basics. For instance, you might forget which Carbon API routine is used to obtain a reference to a menu (it's `GetMenuHandle`), or you might forget the order or data types of the arguments of a commonly used routine, such as `SetRect`. (The arguments are all integers, and the order is left, top, right, and bottom.) See how handy an API summary can be?

In this appendix, you'll find the basics. Keep in mind that the Universal Interface header files are the definitive references to Carbon API routine prototypes. From any Project Builder project, you can select Show Batch Find from the Find menu and search for a Carbon API routine. Project Builder returns a list of files in which the routine is found. Among those files will be the universal interface file that holds the function's prototype. For instance, a batch search for *SetRect* reveals that the function prototype is listed in the QuickDraw.h file. When you click that file name, its contents are displayed in the Project Builder window.

The sections of this appendix loosely follow the order of appearance of the topics in this book. For instance, you find Interface Builder functions, such as CreateNibReference, before QuickDraw functions, such as SetRect, because the Interface Builder material is introduced in Chapter 2, "Overview of Mac OS X Programming," and QuickDraw is covered in Chapter 7, "QuickDraw Graphics."

Include Files

A Project Builder project typically requires just one include file, but in some cases, it could require others. The two header files discussed in the following sections are the most commonly used in Project Builder projects.

Carbon.h: Access to the Carbon Framework

A Project Builder project needs to include the Carbon.h file to provide the project with access to the entire Carbon framework. (You'll recall that the Carbon framework is a set of libraries and resources that together implement Carbon.) All Mac OS X projects will include this file:

```
#include <Carbon/Carbon.h>
```

QuickTime.h: Access to the QuickTime Movie Toolbox

If your project makes use of QuickTime routines, include the Carbon.h file and include the QuickTime.h header file:

```
#include <QuickTime/QuickTime.h>
```

Common Data Types and Functions

The Carbon API defines many data types and routines not found in ANSI C (ANSI being the American National Standards Institute, the standardization body that develops standards for many things, including programming languages such as C). Some are used only in specific programming tasks; others are used throughout the Carbon API. The following sections describe some of the more important of the commonly used types and functions.

OSStatus: Function Execution Status

The OSStatus type is a 32-bit integer that holds an error value, sometimes referred to as an error code. Several Carbon routines have a return value of this type. If a Carbon routine returns an OSStatus value of 0, no error occurred in the execution of the routine. If a nonzero value is returned, your application knows an error occurred and can respond accordingly. For clarity in checking for errors, the Carbon API defines the constant noErr as 0:

```
OSStatus   err;

err = RoutineName( argument );
if ( err != noErr )
    // handle the error here
```

Note that if a routine has a return type of OSStatus and your program has minimal error checking (as in the case of a small experimental program), you can choose to not only ignore the returned value, but also to not even accept the returned value. Thus, the preceding snippet could be written like the following:

```
RoutineName( argument );
```

require_noerr: **Handling an Error**

The Debugging.h header file defines standard exception handling macros, including require_noerr. After invoking a Carbon API routine that returns an error status, you can call require_noerr to determine if the Carbon API routine executed without error:

```
require_noerr(error, label)
```

Pass require_noerr the OSStatus value returned by a previously called Carbon API routine, such as CreateWindowFromNib. The second require_noerr argument is a label to which execution should jump if an error did in fact occur, as shown in the following code:

```
OSStatus    err;

err = CreateWindowFromNib(nibRef, CFSTR("MainWindow"), &window);
require_noerr( err, CantCreateWindow );

// other code here

CantCreateWindow:
    return err;
```

Core Foundation

Core Foundation is the part of Carbon that includes routines that provide basic, or core, functionality to a program. Of most interest here is CFSTR, which is a macro used to generate a string object that can be passed to many other routines.

Many Carbon routines that require a string as an argument accept a reference to a CFString object (a CFStringRef) rather than to an actual string. The CFSTR routine converts a string to such an object and returns a reference to that object, as shown in the following code:

```
CFStringRef  dateStrRef = CFSTR("Today's date is:");
```

Interface Builder Manager (Nib Files)

The Nib Manager is the collection of routines used to access nib files and to work with the resources within such files. All the routine names that include *Nib* (such as CreateWindowFromNib) are Nib Manager routines.

> **Note**
>
> The function prototypes for the Interface Builder Manager routines are found in the IBCarbonRuntime.h header file.

A resource is (typically) an interface element such as a window or menu. Resources are created in Apple's Interface Builder application and stored in a nib (Next Interface Builder) file. Interface Builder archives resource information in XML format. XML (extensible markup language) is a markup language for documents containing structured information. Interface Builder displays this information graphically so that it's easy to create and edit. The details of how Interface Builder stores this information is typically unimportant to the programmer; that's the reason Interface Builder exists!

IBNibRef

To make use of the resources in a nib file, a program needs to first open that file. Doing that supplies the program with a nib file reference value that the program can subsequently use to access the contents of the opened file:

```
IBNibRef   nibRef;
```

CreateNibReference: **Opening and Accessing a Nib File**

Call `CreateNibReference` to open a nib file so that resources within that file can be unarchived and used by the program:

```
OSStatus CreateNibReference( CFStringRef inNibName,
                             IBNibRef *  outNibRef );
```

Pass the routine the name of the nib file to open, less the .nib extension. `CreateNibReference` returns a file reference, which is a variable of the data type `IBNibRef`, to be used in calls to subsequent Interface Builder Manager routines.

```
OSStatus   err;
IBNibRef   nibRef;

err = CreateNibReference( CFSTR("main"), &nibRef );
```

DisposeNibReference: **Closing a Nib File**

When the program has finished accessing the contents of a nib file, the program closes that file by calling `DisposeNibReference`:

```
void DisposeNibReference( IBNibRef inNibRef );
```

Pass `DisposeNibReference` the nib file reference received from the earlier call to the nib file opening routine, which was `CreateNibReference`:

```
OSStatus   err;
IBNibRef   nibRef;

err = CreateNibReference( CFSTR("main"), &nibRef );
// access nib file here
DisposeNibReference( nibRef );
```

SetMenuBarFromNib: Creating a Menu Bar from a Nib Resource

Create a menu bar in Interface Builder and save it in the project's main.nib file. Your program then unarchives that menu bar resource and displays the menu bar by calling SetMenuBarFromNib:

```
OSStatus SetMenuBarFromNib( IBNibRef    inNibRef,
                            CFStringRef inName );
```

Pass SetMenuBarFromNib the nib file reference received from the earlier call to the nib file opening routine CreateNibReference. The second argument is the name of the menu bar resource, as defined in the nib file.

```
OSStatus   err;
IBNibRef   nibRef;

err = CreateNibReference( CFSTR("main"), &nibRef );
err = SetMenuBarFromNib( nibRef, CFSTR("MainMenu") );
```

CreateWindowFromNib: Creating a Window from a Nib Resource

Create a window in Interface Builder and save it in the project's main.nib file. Your program then unarchives that window resource by calling CreateWindowFromNib. Note that the result is a window that can be referenced, but that window is not made visible. Follow the call to CreateWindowFromNib by a call to the Window Manager routine ShowWindow to display the window.

```
OSStatus CreateWindowFromNib( IBNibRef    inNibRef,
                              CFStringRef inName,
                              WindowRef * outWindow );
```

Pass CreateWindowFromNib the nib file reference received from the earlier call to the nib file opening routine CreateNibReference. The second argument is the name of the window resource, as defined in the nib file. In the third argument, CreateWindowFromNib returns a reference to the opened window.

```
OSStatus   err;
IBNibRef   nibRef;
WindowRef  window;

err = CreateNibReference( CFSTR("main"), &nibRef );
err = CreateWindowFromNib( nibRef, CFSTR("MainWindow"), &window );
ShowWindow( window );
```

Event Manager

An application needs an event loop that watches for events and reports those events to the program. The Event Manager defines event type constants and event-related routines. The function prototypes for the Event Manager routines are found in the CarbonEvents.h header file. The following sections describe the most commonly used event-related constants and routines.

Event Class and Kind Constants

Each event type has an event class and an event kind. Some event types also have event parameters (also called event attributes). The number, and purpose, of an event's parameters depends on the event type in question. Become familiar with the contents of the CarbonEvents.h header file. The more times you read through it, the better understanding you'll have of the various types of events.

All the event classes are defined in a single enumerated list of constants:

```
enum { kEventClassMouse        = 'mous',
       kEventClassKeyboard     = 'keyb',
       kEventClassTextInput    = 'text',
       kEventClassApplication  = 'appl',
       kEventClassAppleEvent   = 'eppc',
       kEventClassMenu         = 'menu',
       kEventClassWindow       = 'wind',
       kEventClassControl      = 'cntl',
       kEventClassCommand      = 'cmds',
       kEventClassTablet       = 'tblt',
       kEventClassVolume       = 'vol ' };
```

An event type is defined by combining an event class with an event kind. All the event classes are listed in the preceding code. The following bulleted list contains select, commonly used event kinds. There are hundreds of event kinds—far too many to list here. Again, refer to the CarbonEvents.h header file for more detailed information, and refer to the "EventTypeSpec: Event Type Specification" section of this appendix for an example of combining an event class and event kind to define an event type.

- **Mouse event kinds:**

  ```
  kEventMouseDown
  kEventMouseUp
  kEventMouseMoved
  kEventMouseDragged
  kEventMouseWheelMoved
  ```

- **Application event kinds:**

  ```
  kEventAppActivated
  kEventAppDeactivated
  kEventAppQuit
  kEventAppLaunchNotification
  kEventAppLaunched
  kEventAppTerminated
  kEventAppFrontSwitched
  ```

- **Window event kinds:**

  ```
  kEventWindowUpdate
  kEventWindowDrawContent
  kEventWindowActivated
  kEventWindowDeactivated
  kEventWindowShowing
  ```

```
kEventWindowHiding
kEventWindowShown
kEventWindowHidden
kEventWindowBoundsChanging
kEventWindowBoundsChanged
kEventWindowResizeStarted
kEventWindowResizeCompleted
kEventWindowDragStarted
kEventWindowDragCompleted
kWindowBoundsChangeUserDrag
kWindowBoundsChangeUserResize
kWindowBoundsChangeSizeChanged
kWindowBoundsChangeOriginChanged
kEventWindowClickDragRgn
kEventWindowClickResizeRgn
kEventWindowClickCollapseRgn
kEventWindowClickCloseRgn
kEventWindowClickZoomRgn
kEventWindowClickContentRgn
kEventWindowClickProxyIconRgn
kEventWindowCollapse
kEventWindowCollapsed
kEventWindowCollapseAll
kEventWindowExpand
kEventWindowExpanded
kEventWindowExpandAll
kEventWindowClose
kEventWindowClosed
kEventWindowCloseAll
kEventWindowZoom
kEventWindowZoomed
kEventWindowZoomAll
kEventWindowDrawFrame
kEventWindowDrawPart
```

- **Menu event kinds:**

```
kEventMenuBeginTracking
kEventMenuEndTracking
kEventMenuChangeTrackingMode
kEventMenuOpening
kEventMenuClosed
kEventMenuTargetItem
kEventMenuMatchKey
kEventMenuEnableItems
kEventMenuDispose
```

- **Command event kinds:**

```
kEventProcessCommand
kEventCommandProcess
kEventCommandUpdateStatus
```

- **Control event kinds**:

```
kEventControlInitialize      = 1000,
kEventControlDispose         = 1001,
kEventControlHit             = 1,
kEventControlHitTest         = 3,
kEventControlDraw            = 4,
kEventControlApplyBackground = 5,
kEventControlApplyTextColor  = 6,
kEventControlSetFocusPart    = 7,
kEventControlGetFocusPart    = 8,
kEventControlActivate        = 9,
kEventControlDeactivate      = 10,
kEventControlSetCursor       = 11,
kEventControlClick           = 13,
kEventControlTrack           = 51,
kEventControlSetData         = 103,
kEventControlGetData         = 104,
kEventControlValueFieldChanged = 151,
kEventControlBoundsChanged   = 154,
```

EventTypeSpec: Event Type Specification

You can use the following code to declare a variable of type `EventTypeSpec` and assign it an event class and an event type to define one type of event for which your program wants to be notified:

```
struct EventTypeSpec{ UInt32    eventClass;
                      UInt32    eventKind };
typedef struct EventTypeSpec  EventTypeSpec;
```

The following code defines an event type to be used to watch for the occurrence of a command event, such as an event triggered by a menu selection or a click on a button.

```
EventTypeSpec   eventType = { kEventClassCommand,
                              kEventProcessCommand };
```

The `EventTypeSpec` is then passed to a Carbon Events routine such as `InstallEventHandler`.

GetWindowEventTarget: Obtain an Event Target Reference

An event has a target, which is something that the event acts on or affects. This target often is a window, but it also can be the application itself. Before installing an event handler routine, obtain a reference to the target—as is being done here:

```
EventTargetRef GetWindowEventTarget( WindowRef inWindow );
```

The one argument passed to `GetWindowEventTarget` is the window that's to be considered the target. The returned `EventTargetRef` later will be used in the installation of the application-defined event handler routine (see the "InstallEventHandler: Installing an Event-Handler" section of this appendix for more information).

```
WindowRef      window;
EventTargetRef  target;

target = GetWindowEventTarget( window );
```

GetApplicationEventTarget returns a target for the application itself, as shown in the following code. There are no arguments.

```
EventTargetRef GetApplicationEventTarget( void );
```

Other event target reference routines include GetControlEventTarget and GetMenuEventTarget, as shown in the following code:

```
EventTargetRef GetControlEventTarget(ControlRef inControl);

EventTargetRef GetMenuEventTarget(MenuRef inMenu);
```

NewEventHandlerUPP: Obtaining a Pointer to an Event-Handling Routine

You'll define your own event handler routine to handle the occurrence of one or more types of events for which your program is watching. Your program will need a special type of pointer to that routine—a universal procedure pointer. The NewEventHandlerUPP routine provides your program with such a pointer:

```
EventHandlerUPP NewEventHandlerUPP(EventHandlerProcPtr userRoutine);
```

Pass NewEventHandlerUPP the name of your application-defined event-handling routine and NewEventHandlerUPP returns an EventHandlerUPP. This variable gets passed to InstallEventHandler (see the "InstallEventHandler: Installing an Event-Handler" section of this appendix). For a program with an event-handler named MyEventHandler, the call to NewEventHandlerUPP looks like this:

```
EventHandlerUPP   handlerUPP;

handlerUPP = NewEventHandlerUPP( MyEventHandler );
```

InstallEventHandler: Installing an Event Handler

After defining an event type, creating an event target, coming up with a name for the written (or soon-to-be-written) event handler routine, and creating a pointer to the event handler, you're ready to install the event handler routine. Installing the event handler makes the Carbon Event Manager aware of the routine that's to be invoked at the occurrence of an event of a particular type. The following is the prototype for the InstallEventHandler routine:

```
OSStatus InstallEventHandler( EventTargetRef      target,
                              EventHandlerUPP     handlerProc,
                              UInt32              numTypes,
                              const EventTypeSpec* typeList,
                              void*               userData,
                              EventHandlerRef*    handlerRef );
```

As shown in the preceding code, the first argument is the target, as returned by the appropriate target-returning function, such as `GetWindowEventTarget` or `GetApplicationEventTarget`. The second argument is a pointer to the event handler routine to install, as returned by a call to `NewEventHandlerUPP`. The third argument, `numTypes`, is the number of event types to which this one event handler can respond. The next argument, `typeList`, is a pointer to the event type or event types that this event handler routine handles. This is a variable of type `EventTypeSpec` (or an array of elements of this type).

Continuing our discussion, note that the `userData` argument is used to pass a pointer to any information that might be of use to the event handler. This most often is a pointer to the window that might be affected by the event. Finally, the last argument can be a pointer to an event handler reference, which is a value that the Carbon Event Manager fills in for use by your program. Because your program needs to use this value only if your program will be dynamically changing the event types that make use of the event handler routine, a value of `NULL` is usually used here.

The following snippet calls `InstallEventHandler` to install an event handler routine named `MyEventHandler`. This event handler's job is to process a command (typically resulting from a menu item selection or a click on a button).

```
WindowRef       window;
EventTargetRef  target;
EventHandlerUPP handlerUPP;
EventTypeSpec   eventType = { kEventClassCommand,
                              kEventProcessCommand };

target = GetWindowEventTarget( window );
handlerUPP = NewEventHandlerUPP( MyEventHandler );

InstallEventHandler( target, handlerUPP, 1, &eventType,
                     (void *)window, NULL );
```

MyEventHandler: Writing an Event-Handling Routine

An event handler is an application-defined routine that exists to handle the occurrence of one or more types of events. The prototype of this routine is always the same:

```
pascal OSStatus MyEventHanlder( EventHandlerCallRef nextHandler,
                                EventRef            theEvent,
                                void*               userData );
```

In the preceding code, `MyEventHandler` is a placeholder. It's a name of the programmer's choosing. Your event handler can have any name that makes sense for your program.

The body of the event handler routine is application-specific. There is no one routine that is "right" or that handles every type of event. However, there are a few generalities to consider. To handle a command (an event generated by a menu selection or button click), the event handler will follow this format:

```
#define    kTheCommand    'myCd'
```

```
pascal OSStatus MyEventHandler( EventHandlerCallRef  handlerRef,
                                EventRef             event,
                                void *               userData )
{
   OSStatus    result = eventNotHandledErr;
   HICommand   command;

   GetEventParameter( event, kEventParamDirectObject, typeHICommand,
                      NULL, sizeof (HICommand), NULL, &command );

   switch ( command.commandID )
   {
      case kTheCommand:
         MyCommandHandlingRoutine( (WindowRef)userData );
         result = noErr;
         break;
   }
   return result;
}
```

In Interface Builder, define a four-character command for an interface element such as
a button. In code, define a constant of the same character value. Then, have the event
handler handle that particular command by invoking an application-defined routine
that carries out the particulars of how this one event type is to be handled.
(`MyCommandHandlingRoutine` is such a routine in the preceding code example.) If a
window is affected by the event, that window should be stored in the `userData` argument of the event handler.

GetEventParameter: **Extracting Details About an Event**

An event can have information other than its class and kind associated with it. This
extra information is held in the event's parameters. A parameter has an event parameter
name and an event parameter type. The handling of some event types requires that the
event's parameter information be known. A call to `GetEventParameter` in the event
handler routine reveals that information, as shown in the following code:

```
OSStatus GetEventParameter( EventRef          inEvent,
                            EventParamName    inName,
                            EventParamType    inDesiredType,
                            EventParamType *  outActualType,
                            UInt32            inBufferSize,
                            UInt32 *          outActualSize,
                            void *            outData);
```

Here's a typical call to `GetEventParameter` in the context of an event handler routine:

```
pascal OSStatus MyEventHandler( EventHandlerCallRef  handlerRef,
                                EventRef             event,
                                void *               userData )
{
```

```
OSStatus    result = eventNotHandledErr;
HICommand   command;

GetEventParameter( event, kEventParamDirectObject, typeHICommand,
                   NULL, sizeof (HICommand), NULL, &command );

// rest of event handler code here
}
```

The first argument is the event from which the parameter data is to be extracted. You use the event argument that's passed to the event handler routine. kEventParamDirectObject and typeHICommand are the name and type of the parameter of interest. If the event kind is kEventCommandProcess (see the "EventTypeSpec: Event Type Specification" section of this appendix), the parameter of interest most likely will have a name of kEventParamDirectObject and a type of typeHICommand. These values come from CarbonEvents.h.

The fourth GetEventParameter argument holds the actual type, and it should match the value of the third argument. Pass NULL if this isn't of interest to you. The fifth argument is the size of the buffer that is to hold the parameter value that GetEventParameter returns. Use sizeof with the data type of the expected return value. The sixth argument gets filled in with the actual size of the returned data. Pass a value of NULL here if this information isn't needed. The last argument is a pointer to the memory that will receive the parameter data.

The important information returned by GetEventParameter is found in the command argument. Examine the commandID field of this structure to determine the four-character command that is part of the event:

```
switch ( command.commandID )
{
    case kTheCommand:
        // handle this particular command
```

RunApplicationEventLoop: **Executing an Event Loop**

Call RunApplicationEventLoop to start your program's event loop. RunApplicationEventLoop suspends the application's execution until an event occurs. When an event occurs, the Event Manager system software returns information about that event to your program.

```
void RunApplicationEventLoop( void );
```

Call RunApplicationEventLoop after your program has set up a menu bar and opened a window:

```
OSStatus    err;
IBNibRef    nibRef;
WindowRef   window;

err = CreateNibReference( CFSTR("main"), &nibRef );
```

```
err = SetMenuBarFromNib( nibRef, CFSTR("MainMenu") );
err = CreateWindowFromNib( nibRef, CFSTR("MainWindow"), &window );
ShowWindow( window );
DisposeNibReference( nibRef );

RunApplicationEventLoop();
```

Window Manager

A window is created using the Interface Builder Manager routine `CreateWindowFromNib`. After that, application control of the window is achieved through Window Manager routines. The function prototypes for the Window Manager routines are located in the MacWindows.h header file. The following sections describe commonly used window-related data types and functions.

WindowRef: Referencing a Window

A window is referenced by way of a variable of type `WindowRef`. A `WindowRef` is a pointer to a window object. Your program obtains such a reference to a window at the time the window is created.

Creating a Window

A window is created by calling `CreateWindowFromNib` to unarchive a window resource stored in a nib file. Refer to the "Interface Builder Manager (Nib Files)" section of this appendix for more information.

ShowWindow: Showing a Hidden Window

A window created by calling `CreateWindowFromNib` is initially hidden (invisible). In addition, a window that has been the object of a call to `HideWindow` will be hidden. In either case, call `ShowWindow` to make the window visible. Pass `ShowWindow` a reference to the window that it should make visible:

```
WindowRef   window;

ShowWindow( window );
```

HideWindow: Hiding a Visible Window

A window is made visible by calling ShowWindow. To hide (make invisible) a window, call HideWindow. Pass `HideWindow` a reference to the window that it should make invisible:

```
WindowRef   window;

HideWindow( window );
```

Control Manager

A control is created as an item in a window resource in a nib file. Accessing that control from source code is achieved by using Control Manager routines. The function prototypes for the Control Manager routines are located in the Control.h header file. The next sections describe the main control-related types and routines.

ControlHandle / ControlRef: Referencing a Control

A variable of the type `ControlHandle` is used to reference a control, such as a radio button. Call the Control Manager routine `GetControlByID` to obtain a handle to a control:

```
ControlHandle    myRadioButtonGroup;
```

Note that the `ControlHandle` data type is defined as type `ControlRef`, so your code can use variables of these two types interchangeably.

ControlID: Specifying a Control

Your project defines a control as an item in a window resource in a nib file. That control is given a control ID, which is the combination of a signature and an ID. Together, the values specify one and only one control. Your code declares a variable of type `ControlID` to specify one control. Like the control item in the nib resource file, the `ControlID` variable consists of a signature and an ID.

```
#define  kControlSignature      'Xapp'
#define  kRadioGroupControlID     101

ControlID   myRadioGroupControlID = { kControlSignature,
                                      kRadioGroupControlID };
```

GetControlByID: Obtaining a Handle to a Control

To obtain a handle to a control, call the `GetControlByID` routine:

```
OSStatus GetControlByID( WindowRef          inWindow,
                         const ControlID *  inID,
                         ControlRef *       outControl );
```

The first argument to `GetControlByID` is a reference to the window that holds the control. The second argument is a pointer to the control's ID, as set up in a variable of type `ControlID`. The final argument is a control reference that's filled in when `GetControlByID` returns. Use this `ControlRef` variable in calls to other Control Manager routines, such as a call to `GetControl32BitValue`.

```
OSStatus       err;
WindowRef      window;
ControlHandle  myRadioButtonGroup;
ControlID      myRadioGroupControlID = { kControlSignature,
                                         kRadioGroupControlID };
```

```
err = GetControlByID( window, &RadioGroupControlID,
                      &myRadioButtonGroup );
```

GetControl32BitValue: Obtaining a Control's Value

After calling `GetControlByID`, your program has a handle to one control. Your program can use this handle to access the control. Accessing a control often means getting, or setting, the control's value. A call to `GetControl32BitValue` is made to obtain the value of a control:

```
SInt32 GetControl32BitValue( ControlRef theControl );
```

The following snippet obtains the value of a radio group control. For this type of control, the value represents the item number of the radio button that is currently on:

```
SInt32     controlValue;

controlValue = GetControl32BitValue( myRadioButtonGroup );
```

After the control's value is obtained, take the appropriate action based on the returned value. For instance, in the case of a radio button group, a switch statement is used to carry out the task at hand:

```
switch ( controlValue )
{
   case 1:
      // handle the first, or top, radio button being the one that's on
      break;
   case 2:
      // handle the second from top radio button being the one that's on
      break;
}
```

Menu Manager

A program's menu bar is created using the Interface Builder Manager routine `SetMenuBarFromNib`. After that, application control of the menu bar and its menus and items is achieved through Menu Manager routines. The function prototypes for the Menu Manager routines are located in the Menus.h header file. The following sections describe the most commonly used menu-related types and functions.

MenuRef: Referencing a Menu

A menu and its items are referenced by way of a variable of type `MenuRef`. A `MenuRef` is the same as the older `MenuHandle` data type, so these two types can be used interchangeably.

Creating a Menu Bar

A menu bar is created by calling `SetMenuBarFromNib` to unarchive a menu bar resource stored in a nib file. Refer to the "Interface Builder Manager (Nib Files)" section of this appendix for more information.

GetMenuHandle: Accessing a Menu

Before altering the state of a menu or menu item, changing a menu item's characteristics, and performing similar tasks, your program needs a handle or reference to the affected menu. Call `GetMenuHandle` to obtain a handle or reference:

```
MenuRef GetMenuHandle( MenuID menuID );
```

When editing the project's menu bar in Interface Builder, assign the menu an ID. Use this ID in the call to `GetMenuHandle`:

```
#define   kCalculateMenuID    106

MenuRef   gCalculateMenu;

gCalculateMenu = GetMenuHandle( kCalculateMenuID );
```

Disable/EnableMenuItem: Disabling and Enabling Menus

To disable a menu item, call `DisableMenuItem`. To enable a menu item, call `EnableMenuItem`. Both are shown in the following code:

```
void DisableMenuItem( MenuRef        theMenu,
                      MenuItemIndex  item);
void EnableMenuItem( MenuRef         theMenu,
                     MenuItemIndex   item);
```

Pass either routine a handle (reference) to the menu that holds the item to alter. You also pass the number of the item to alter. For instance, to disable the first item in a menu, pass a value of 1 for that item number:

```
#define   kCalculateMenuID    106

MenuRef   gCalculateMenu;

gCalculateMenu = GetMenuHandle( kCalculateMenuID );

DisableMenuItem( gCalculateMenu, 1 );
```

To disable an entire menu (the menu title and all menu item s in that menu), call `DisableMenuItem` with a value of 0 as the number of the item to disable. To enable and entire menu, call EnableMenuItem with a value of 0 as the number of the item to enable. The following code shows both actions:

```
DisableMenuItem( gCalculateMenu, 0 );

EnableMenuItem( gCalculateMenu, 0 );
```

FMGetFontFamilyFontName: Obtaining a Reference to a Family of Fonts

To change the font of a menu or menu item, you first need to obtain a reference to the family of the font to use. Note that a font exists as a family in that there are different sizes, and in some cases, different faces, associated with one font.) To get this reference, call `FMGetFontFamilyFontName`:

```
FMFontFamily FMGetFontFamilyFromName( ConstStr255Param inName );
```

Pass `FMGetFontFamilyName` the name of the font of interest (Arial, Geneva, Times, and so forth), and the routine returns the font family reference associated with this name. This reference then is used as an argument to font-altering routines such as `SetMenuFont`. For legacy reasons, some API routines expect a string argument to be formatted as a Pascal string. `FMGetFontFamilyName` is such a routine. When passing a font name, preface the name with \p and enclose the string in quotation marks. The following code example returns a reference to the Verdana family of fonts:

```
FMFontFamily   fontFamily;

fontFamily = FMGetFontFamilyFromName( "\pVerdana" );
```

SetMenuItemFontID: Changing the Font of a Menu Item

The `SetMenuItemFontID` routine is used to change the font of a single menu item. Use `SetMenuFont` to change the font of all items in a menu.

```
OSErr SetMenuItemFontID( MenuRef inMenu,
                         SInt16  inItem,
                         SInt16  inFontID );
```

Pass `SetMenuItemFontID` a reference (a handle) to the menu that holds the affected menu item. Then, pass the item number of the item. In this case, the first item in a menu will have an item number of 1, the second item will have an item number of 2, and so forth. Finally, pass the font family reference for the font to use. The following snippet sets the second menu item of the File menu to Times:

```
#define   kFileMenuID    101
#define   kOpenMenuItem    2

MenuRef        fileMenu;
FMFontFamily   fontFamily;

fileMenu = GetMenuHandle( kFileMenuID );

fontFamily = FMGetFontFamilyFromName( "\pTimes" );
SetMenuItemFontID( fileMenu, kOpenMenuItem, fontFamily );
```

SetMenuFont: Changing the Font of an Entire Menu

To change the font of all items in a menu, call `SetMenuFont`, as shown in the following code:

```
OSStatus SetMenuFont( MenuRef   menu,
                      SInt16    inFontID,
                      UInt16    inFontSize );
```

Pass `SetMenuFont` a menu reference (handle), a font family reference (obtained from a call to `FMGetFontFamilyFromName`), and a constant specifying the point size of the font. For instance, to change the font of all the items in the File menu to 24 point Arial, you'd use the following code:

```
#define   kFileMenuID         2
#define   kMenuFontPointSize   24

MenuRef       fileMenu;
FMFontFamily  fontFamily;

fileMenu = GetMenuHandle( kFileMenuID );

fontFamily = FMGetFontFamilyFromName( "\pArial" );

SetMenuFont( fileMenu, fontFamily, kMenuFontPointSize );
```

QuickDraw

Drawing to a window involves the Carbon API routines that are grouped in an area called QuickDraw. The function prototypes for the QuickDraw routines are located in the QuickDraw.h header file. The next sections describe commonly used QuickDraw routines.

SetPortWindowPort: Specifying the Window to Draw To

QuickDraw drawing routines draw to a port, which is a graphics environment capable of maintaining its own set of graphical information. Every window has its own port, as does the screen itself. Before drawing, call `SetPortWindowPort` to tell QuickDraw in which port (which window) to draw.

```
void SetPortWindowPort(WindowRef window);
```

MoveTo and *Move*: Specifying the Starting Point for Drawing

Before drawing, specify in which window to draw by using `SetPortWindowPort`, and specify where within that window content area drawing is to take place. Call `MoveTo` to specify a starting location relative to the upper-left corner of the window in which drawing is about to occur:

```
void MoveTo( short   h,
             short   v );
```

Pass `MoveTo` the number of pixels to move relative to the left side of the window and the number of pixels to move relative to the top of the window. To specify that drawing start 20 pixels from the left side and 60 pixels from the top of the content area of a window, call `MoveTo` like this:

```
MoveTo( 20, 60 );
```

The `Move` routine is similar to `MoveTo` in that it specifies a starting point for drawing. `Move`, though, uses the current starting point as its reference.

```
void Move( short   h,
           short   v );
```

`Move` moves the starting location a number of pixels horizontally and vertically from the current location. Consider this snippet:

```
MoveTo( 20, 60 );
Move( 10, 40 );
```

The call to `MoveTo` sets the drawing starting location 20 pixels from the left side and 60 pixels from the top of the window's content area. The call to `Move` then moves the starting location from that position to a location that is 10 more pixels to the right and 40 more pixels down. The result of executing the preceding code snippet is a starting location 30 pixels from the left of the window (20 + 10) and 100 pixels down from the top of the window (60 + 40).

LineTo and *Line*: Drawing Lines

To draw a line, call the `LineTo` routine:

```
void LineTo( short   h,
             short   v);
```

`LineTo` draws a line from the current drawing starting point (see the "MoveTo and Move: Specifying the Starting Point for Drawing" section of this appendix) to the specified end point. Pass `LineTo` the horizontal pixel end point relative to the left side of the window to which to draw and the vertical pixel end point relative to the top of that window. For instance, to draw a horizontal line 100 pixels in length, starting at a point 20 pixels from the left and 50 pixels from the top of a window, use this code:

```
MoveTo( 20, 50 );
LineTo( 120, 50 );
```

Note in the preceding snippet that the vertical starting point established by `MoveTo` and the vertical end point established by `LineTo` are both 50 pixels from the top of the window. Thus, the line is horizontal.

To draw a line of a specified length without regard for the starting point, call `Line`, as shown in the following code:

```
void Line( short   h,
           short   v);
```

Line is similar to LineTo in that it draws a line, but Line draws the line without specifying an end point. For instance, a call to Line(100, 0) draws a horizontal line 100 pixels in length, regardless of the location of the current drawing starting point.

SetRect: Defining the Boundaries of a Rectangle

A rectangle is an important shape in that it is used to define rectangles, squares, ovals, circles, and round rectangles. To define the coordinates of a rectangle, call SetRect, as shown in the following code:

```
void SetRect( Rect *  r,
              short    left,
              short    top,
              short    right,
              short    bottom );
```

Pass SetRect a pointer to a Rect variable, along with the four rectangle-defining coordinates. The order is left, top, right, and bottom. Each coordinate is specified in pixels, with the top-left corner of the window serving as the origin. The following snippet defines a rectangle 100×50 pixels. The rectangle's top-left corner is stationed 30 pixels from the left edge and 70 pixels from the top of the window.

```
Rect   theRect;

SetRect( &theRect, 30, 70, 130, 120 );
```

SetRect does not draw a rectangle; it only establishes the rectangle's boundaries. To frame the rectangle, call FrameRect.

FrameRect: Framing (Drawing) a Rectangle

After establishing the boundaries of a rectangle using SetRect, frame that rectangle by calling FrameRect, as shown in the following code:

```
void FrameRect( const Rect * r );
```

After you pass FrameRect a pointer to a rectangle, FrameRect draws a frame around that rectangle:

```
Rect   theRect;

SetRect( &theRect, 30, 70, 130, 120 );
FrameRect( &theRect );
```

Of course there are many, many other QuickDraw drawing routines you'll want to know about, so make sure to peruse the QuickDraw.h header file. In fact, you'd be wise to spend some time browsing and searching through any of the header files to learn about other Carbon API routines not covered in this appendix.

B

UNIX and the Terminal

IF YOU'RE MOVING TO MAC OS X from a UNIX background, you might have already discovered how to use your Macintosh to use UNIX to enter commands, create source code files, and build applications. Someone like you might be able to skip this appendix. You should be aware, though, that UNIX in Mac OS X does vary in some ways from other UNIX implementations—so you might want to at least skim this appendix regardless of your level of expertise in UNIX.

On the other hand, if you're a long-time Macintosh user who is light on UNIX experience, you might never have created or edited a text file in UNIX, and you probably never ran a compiler from the command line. You might not even know how to go about using a command line interface. If any of this sounds like you, read this appendix. In just a few pages, you'll be moving through directories, writing source code, and compiling that code—all from the UNIX command line.

UNIX and the UNIX Shell

Darwin is Apple's name for the lowest level, or foundation, of the Mac OS X. A big part of Darwin is *Berkeley Standard Distribution (BSD)*. It is a popular version of UNIX. BSD provides file system support, network services, multiprocessing support, and other important operating system services.

326 Appendix B   UNIX and the Terminal

BSD also supports the *shell* environment. A shell is a command-line interface that provides a means for a computer user to perform system tasks. By typing UNIX commands in the shell, a Mac OS X user can perform a multitude of tasks, including moving, renaming, and copying files, running applications, and compiling source code files.

A person new to UNIX might think of the shell as UNIX itself, but that would be a false assumption. The shell is an application that enables indirect access to UNIX. The word "indirect" is important here. Enabling direct access to the core-level code that makes up an operating system (OS) would be dangerous. A user could corrupt OS code and file data. To counteract this possibility, the aptly named shell provides a "wrapper" around the OS kernel. In that respect, the shell is similar to the *Finder*. The Finder enables a user to perform many of the same tasks as does a shell, but it won't let a user directly alter OS code. The Finder is a shell. It just happens to be a graphics-based shell rather than a text-based command line shell.

Most Mac OS X users won't be aware of the UNIX underpinnings of Mac OS X, and they won't be aware of the shell that enables access to the UNIX part of Mac OS X. However, many power-users, and many programmers, will know (or will want to know) about UNIX and the shell. In Mac OS X, you get to the shell by running the Terminal application. You'll find the Terminal in the Utilities folder of the Applications folder. You run the Terminal as you do any other Mac application—you double-click its icon.

If you're familiar with UNIX command line environments, you might be interested to know that, by default, the Terminal uses a tcsh shell. Other shells, including csh and bash, can be used as well. However, if shell environments types are meaningless to you, don't worry! To get started with the Terminal, you don't need to know the details of the environment. You need only know a few simple UNIX commands!

UNIX Commands

A UNIX shell (the Terminal is a UNIX shell) is a command-line interface that lets a user interact with UNIX by typing commands. Knowing commands means knowing UNIX.

To run a command, you enter it in the shell. A command often requires that you either know the path to a particular directory or that you move into a particular directory. Of course, to do anything useful with commands, you need to know at least a few of the most important commands.

Entering Commands

Working with a shell is a cyclical process. The following three steps are repeated over and over again:

1. Shell presents the user with a prompt.
2. User enters a command and presses the Return (or Enter) key.
3. Shell executes (carries out) the command.

In Figure B.1, you see a Terminal window in front of a Mac OS X Finder window. (You can have more than one Terminal window open at a time if you feel so inclined.) I've left the Finder window in the figure simply to emphasize that in Mac OS X, the Terminal is simply another application and that using the Terminal to work with UNIX doesn't monopolize your Mac's resources. While using the Terminal, you're free to click another application's window and interact with that application.

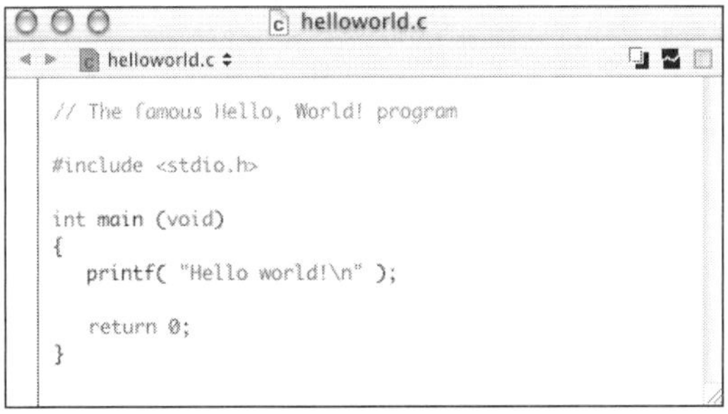

Figure B.1   Entering a command in the Terminal.

A Terminal prompt includes the username you use when you log into your Mac. Note that when you start up Mac OS X, you log in, but you need not also log into UNIX itself when you start the Terminal. In Figure B.1, the prompt is [localhost:~] dansydow%. The dansydow part of the prompt comes from the fact that I log into my Mac with a username of dansydow.

Figure B.1 provides an example of executing a UNIX shell command. At the first prompt, I typed the pwd command and then pressed the Enter key. The pwd command is the *print working directory* command. Executing it results in the display of the current directory, which is the directory in which you're currently working. After the command is executed, the prompt reappears and is set to receive the next command.

Directory Tree and Paths

The *pathname*, which is the listing of the location of a file or folder relative to other folders, is important to many UNIX commands. When organizing files, Mac users are accustomed to the concept of *folders*. UNIX users refer to these same entities as *directories*. The difference in terms is simply a matter of custom, and the two terms are interchangeable.

As it turns out, a directory (or folder) is simply a file that contains a table listing of the files contained within it. In keeping with the concept of giving just about every element a graphical presentation, the Macintosh OS displays such a file with the look of a folder. Because the Macintosh interface is graphical, the exact pathname of a file or folder (the chain of folders that leads to a file or folder nested within other folders) isn't too important. The user just double-clicks folders to work "down" to the folder or file of interest. In contrast, the UNIX interface is textual, so pathnames become more important. The UNIX user relies on the pathname to know where he or she is presently working.

In a pathname, a directory name is preceded by a slash. Consider the example shown in Figure B.1, where the pathname is given as this:

```
/Users/dansydow
```

Figure B.1 shows that the shell replies to the `pwd` command by showing that I'm currently working in the directory named dansydow, which itself is in a directory named Users. The slash that precedes Users refers to the root, or main, directory. The root directory is the drive on which Mac OS X was installed (typically a hard drive), so it's not represented by a directory name, as are all directories on the drive.

The organization of folders and files can be viewed as a hierarchical tree, as shown in Figure B.2. In this figure, I show a very small subset of the folders on my computer's hard drive. In this figure, the drive itself is considered the root directory.

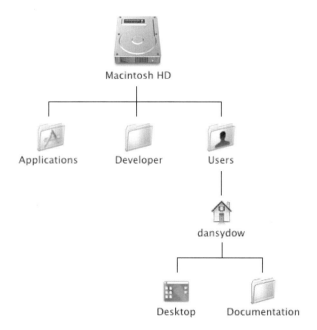

Figure B.2 A simple directory tree.

Referring to Figure B.2, you can determine the pathname of a number of directories. You've already seen that the dansydow directory has this pathname:

```
/Users/dansydow
```

The Documentation directory that lies within the dansydow directory has the following pathname:

```
/Users/dansydow/Documentation
```

As one last example, consider that the Applications directory has this pathname:

```
/Applications
```

Moving into a Directory

To access a file, one needs to be in the folder that holds the file. For instance, to run a program, you move into the folder that holds the program itself and then double-click the program's icon. A Mac user moves within a folder to access a file (or another folder) by double-clicking a folder or, new to Mac OS X, by clicking a folder name to view its contents in a Finder window.

A UNIX user also needs to move into a folder to access its contents. To do that, the cd (change directory) command is used. To use the cd command, you use cd followed by the name of the target directory.

Referring to the tree shown in Figure B.2, let's assume I'm currently in the dansydow directory and I want to move into the Documentation directory located within dansydow. To do that at the prompt in the Terminal window, I'd type the following:

```
cd Documentation
```

If I followed that cd command with the pwd command to view the directory in which I'm working, the Terminal window would respond with the following:

```
/User/dansydow/Documentation
```

OK, that covers moving "down" the tree. That is, you've just seen how to access a subdirectory (a directory within another directory). However, you'll also want to know how to move "up" the tree. That is, if you're currently in the Documentation directory, how do you move up out of it and back into the dansydow directory? Again, the cd command is used. To move up the tree, you don't need to remember where you came from. Instead, you need only follow the cd command with two periods (..). This always moves you into the parent directory, which is the directory that holds the directory in which you're currently working. Continuing with our example, typing cd.. followed by a pwd command results in the Terminal window responding with the following:

```
/User/dansydow
```

Common Commands

A UNIX shell such as Terminal understands numerous commands—far too many to cover in this appendix. However, knowledge of just a handful of these commands enables you to do quite a bit with UNIX, and it give you a good base from which to explore working with UNIX further. Table B.1 lists a number of commonly used UNIX commands. Following the table are detailed descriptions of some of the more interesting commands.

B.1   **Commonly Used UNIX Commands**

Command	Result
pwd	Prints working (current) directory
cd	Changes directory (moves to new current directory)
ls	Lists contents of current directory
mkdir	Makes a new directory
rmdir	Removes an existing directory
mv	Moves or renames a file (moves a file from one name to another)
rm	Removes a file
cp	Copies a file
man	Displays onscreen help for a specific command
apropos	Lists commands related to the keyword following apropos
who	Shows who is logged into the system
pico	Runs the pico text editor
gcc	Compiles C source and builds an application
g++	Compiles C++ source and builds an application

pwd

As you move about from directory to directory, it's quite possible to get "lost," so you need a command that, in essence, tells you where you are. To see where you are, you can print the working (or current) directory by using the pwd command:

    pwd

cd

Use the change directory (cd) command to move from the current working directory to a new working directory. To move down one level (to move to a directory within the current directory), type cd followed by the directory name:

    cd directoryname

To move up one level (to move to the parent directory, which is the directory that houses the current directory), type cd followed by two periods:

    cd..

ls

To view the contents of the current directory, use the list contents (`ls`) command:

```
ls
```

mv

To rename a file, you "move" it from its old name to the new name that you specify. First, use the `cd` command to move into the directory that holds the file to rename. Then enter the `mv` command followed by the original filename, which in turn is followed by the new filename. After executing the command, you can enter an `ls` command to verify that the filename has been changed:

```
mv oldfilename newfilename
```

cp

To create a duplicate of an existing file, use the `cp` command. Move into the directory that holds the file to copy, and then enter the `cp` command. Follow the `cp` with the name of the file to copy and the name of the file that should hold the copy:

```
cp originalfilename newfilename
```

man

One particularly nice feature of UNIX is that user manuals are available online. If you need help with any UNIX command, type the `man` command followed by the name of the command about which you need information. For instance, if you want to view reference material on the change directory (`cd`) command, type the following:

```
man cd
```

The documentation for a command often occupies more than one screen. To display the next screen of information, press the space bar. To display the previous screen of information, press the B key (for "back"). Press the Q key to "quit" displaying information (or just press the V key until you reach the end of the online manual).

apropos

This command is especially useful for those new to UNIX. Enter the `apropos` command (*apropos* being a French word loosely translating to "with regard to or concerning") followed by a keyword of your choosing. The Terminal then will return a list of UNIX commands related to the keyword. Find the command that most closely matches the action you have in mind, and then use the `man` command to get more information on the command's use:

```
apropose keyword
```

As an example, if you weren't sure how to copy a file, you could use `apropos copy` and the Terminal would return a list of copy-related commands. In that list would be the cp command and its description of "copy files," which sounds like the command to use. Next, you enter man cp to get a description of how the cp command works. Then, go ahead and use the cp command to copy the file of interest.

pico

There are several easy-to-use text editors available for UNIX; pico is one of them, and it's included with Mac OS X. To run a program in UNIX, you type the program name. For pico, follow the program name with the name of the file to edit. If you're editing an existing file, use the cd command to move to the directory that holds the file to edit, and then enter pico, followed by the name of the file to edit. If you're creating a new text file, use the cd command to move to the directory in which you want the new file to reside, and then enter pico followed by the name that the new file should have.

```
pico filename
```

gcc **and** *g++*

UNIX has a number of freely available C and C++ compilers. Mac OS X includes a compiler based on the GNU C compiler. Use the gcc command to compile and build a program from a C source code file. Use the g++ command for a C++ source code file.

For either gcc or g++, you should use -o (that's the minus sign followed by the letter *o*) and a program name. The *o* is for "output," and it tells the compiler what name you're specifying for the program that results from the running of the compiler. The last operand to gcc or g++ is the name of the source code file to be compiled. For gcc, this filename should have a *.c* extension. For g++, this filename should have a *.cpp* extension. This appendix's "UNIX Programming" section provides more information about compiling a C or C++ source code file in UNIX. Here's the format of both the gcc and g++ commands:

```
gcc -o programname Csourcecodefilename
g++ -o programname C++sourcecodefilename
```

Moving About

For someone moving from a graphical user interface (GUI)-based operating system, such as the Mac OS, to UNIX, learning to move about from directory to directory takes some getting used to. In this section, you'll see an example of how one might use the Terminal and UNIX commands to traverse the file tree. Additionally, you'll get confirmation that a Macintosh program is more than just a single application file. You'll see that a Mac program is actually a bundle that holds several files (including the application itself).

Traversing the Tree

Starting a UNIX session begins with the running of the Terminal program. When you run Terminal, you see a Terminal window like the one shown in Figure B.3. For this figure, I logged into my Mac with a username of dansydow, so the Terminal has included dansydow% in the [localhost:~] dansydow% prompt. Your terminal will display the username you logged in as.

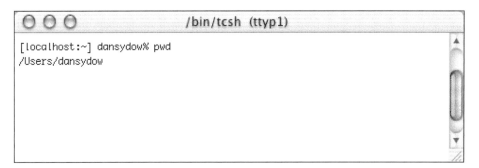

Figure B.3   The Terminal window after entering the print working directory command.

To run a UNIX command, you type the command and press the Return key. A good command to start with is pwd. Entering the pwd command results in the display of the pathname of the current directory (the directory in which you're currently working). Figure B.3 shows that I'm in a directory named dansydow, which itself is in a directory named Users.

You're probably used to viewing directories in a more graphical manner in Mac OS X, so take a look at Figure B.4 to see that the dansydow directory is indeed within the Users directory, which itself is in the root directory (the drive named Macintosh HD).

Figure B.4   The path from home (Macintosh HD) to dansydow.

To see an alphabetical listing of the current (working) directory, type the ls (*list directory contents*) command followed by a press of the Return key. The right-most column in Figure B.4 shows what I see in my dansydow directory. Figure B.5 demonstrates that the `ls` command typed into the Terminal window did indeed list the proper contents of the current directory.

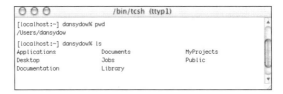

Figure B.5 The Terminal window after entering the ls contents command.

To move down into a directory, use the `cd` command. Follow this command with the name of the directory into which you want to move. In Figure B.6, I've followed the `ls` command with a `cd MyProjects` command. It changes the working directory to the MyProjects directory. After moving inside a directory, the Terminal window again displays the prompt. To list the contents of the directory that's just become the current working directory, type another `ls` command. In Figure B.6, you see the content of the MyProjects directory is two other directories: App1Project and App2Project.

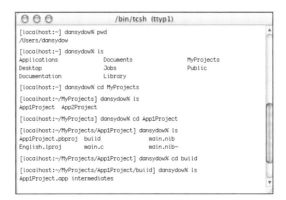

Figure B.6 Displaying the contents of the build directory.

The next steps were to move into the App1Project directory (`cd App1Project`), view its content (`ls`), and then move into the build directory (`cd build`). Look at Figure B.6 to confirm that these actions were taken.

In the last line of Figure B.6, you see two names: App1Project.app and intermediates. Note that in the Finder, intermediates is displayed as a folder, while App1Project is displayed as a file (an application file with no extension appended to its name). As discussed in Chapter 10, "Bundles and Icons," an application is actually a bundle, which is a directory that holds a number of files. The Mac OS X Finder hides this fact from end-users, but the UNIX Terminal doesn't. Refer to Figure B.7 to see how the Mac OS X Finder displays the contents of the build folder.

Figure B.7   The content of the build folder.

In the Terminal window, I can type cd App1Project.app to move into the application directory, which is the directory that the Finder displays as a file! Near the top of Figure B.7, you see that the contents of the App1Project.app directory is another directory—one named Contents. Moving into the Contents directory (cd Contents) and then entering an ls command shows four names: Info.plist, MacOS, PkgInfo, and Resources (see Figure B.8).

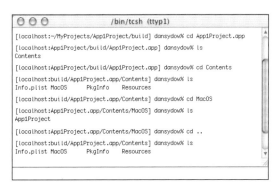

Figure B.8   Commands and their results in the Terminal window.

The actual application file itself is stored in the MacOS directory. Figure B.8 shows the application's name is *App1Project*.

You've seen that to move down into a folder, you type the cd command followed by the name of the directory into which you want to move. To move back out of a directory, type the cd command followed by two periods (cd..). Look at Figure B.8 to see that I typed cd.. to move from the MacOS directory to its parent directory (the Contents directory). Also note that you can follow cd with a space and a hyphen (minus sign) to move to the last directory you visited.

UNIX/Finder Integration

If you aren't completely convinced that Mac OS X is UNIX-based, the following simple exercise should help you become a believer. Here I'll use a UNIX Terminal window to change the name of an existing file, and that file's new name will be displayed in both the UNIX Terminal *and* in a Mac OS X Finder window.

Figure B.9 illustrates the start of the experiment. In a Terminal window, I've moved to my Mac's Documents directory and am about to change the name of a file from myNotes.rtf to myNewNotes.rtf. To do this, I use the UNIX `mv` command to "move" the file to a new name. In the Terminal window, you see the `ls` command was used to display the contents of the Documents directory before the name change. Behind the Terminal window, you see an Aqua Finder window that also is displaying the contents of the Documents folder.

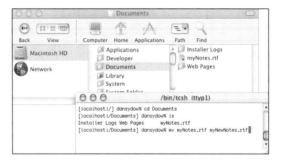

Figure B.9   Changing a filename using the Terminal.

After changing the filename from myNotes.rtf to myNewNotes.rtf, I type the `ls` command to see the contents of the Documents directory in the Terminal window. Sure enough, as shown in Figure B.10, the filename has been changed. In addition, as also illustrated in Figure B.10, when I click the Mac OS X Finder window, the Finder window is updated to display the new filename as well. Obviously, it's true that the Finder knows UNIX!

Figure B.10   A renamed file has its new name displayed in the Aqua Finder.

UNIX Programming

You bought this book to learn to create programs that run on the Mac OS X. After reading this section, though, you'll also be able to use your Macintosh to create programs that can run on your Mac and on any computer running UNIX. These programs are true UNIX applications, so they won't sport the Aqua look, but then, UNIX isn't about a fancy interface anyway.

Get ready—with just several minutes of work, you'll be able to perform command-line UNIX programming, amaze your friends with your cross-platform programming skills, and pad your resume ("Programming Experience By Platform: Mac OS, UNIX")!

Mac OS X and UNIX

As discussed in Chapter 1, "System Components and Programming Technologies," BSD is a variant of UNIX. In Mac OS X, BSD is an important part of the kernel environment. It supports key operating system features, such as preemptive multitasking and memory protection. The work BSD does is invisible to a Macintosh end-user, but BSD is accessible to a programmer. In addition, because BSD is a flavor of UNIX, a programmer working on a Mac running Mac OS X can use the command line to write and build UNIX programs, just like a programmer working on a PC running UNIX.

Back in Figure 1.1 in Chapter 1, you saw the five application environments. In that figure, BSD is shown off to the side. This indicates that there is no relationship between the BSD environment and any other layer of the operating system, with the exception of the Kernel Environment. (In Figure 1.1, note the line running from the BSD box to the Kernel Environment layer.) When you use the BSD programming environment, you're creating a program that doesn't make use of any Macintosh-specific application program interface (API) functions, and you're creating a program that won't be displayed in Aqua. Instead, you use the Terminal to compile source code that runs on BSD.

Writing the C Source Code

To develop a Mac OS X application, it makes sense to use powerful software tools to create resources, write source code, organize files, compile code, and build the stand-alone program. In Chapter 2, "Overview of Mac OS X Programming," you saw that both Apple and Metrowerks offer such programming tools. To develop a UNIX application, though, it's not necessary to use a full-featured integrated development environment. Instead, your work typically can be performed from the command line.

For a very simple exercise in creating a UNIX program on a Mac, start by running the Terminal program. Now you're communicating with BSD. You can create a new text file and enter your program's code by typing `pico filename` at the prompt. I typed `pico helloworld.c`, which ran the pico text editor that is a UNIX editor included with Mac OS X. It then created a new file named helloworld.c.

Figure B.11 shows the complete source code listing for my simple program. You can see that it's nothing more than a few lines of code written in ANSI C. Pressing Ctrl+X (that's the Control key, not the Command key, along with the X key) exits the pico editor. As it exits, pico asks if you want to save your changes. Press the Y key for yes, and you find yourself back at the system prompt.

Figure B.11   Using pico to create a source code file in the Terminal.

Building an Application from the C Source Code

There are several C compilers available for UNIX programmers. A popular one, and one that's included with Mac OS X, is the GNU C compiler (GCC). GCC is what you type to compile your C source code file and to create an executable program. After moving to the directory that holds your source code file, type the following at the prompt:

```
gcc -o hello helloworld.c
```

Typing gcc runs the GNU C compiler. The -o (that's the letter o, not a zero) option, followed by a filename, specifies the name for the output file. In the preceding code snippet, I'm building a program named "hello." The last operand (helloworld.c in this example) is the name of the input source file.

After I press the Return key, the compiler asks if it's okay to continue. Press the Y key and in just a moment, the preprocessing, compilation, assembly, and linking are complete. You can run the program, as I've done in Figure B.12, by typing ./*program-name* (./hello in this example). Preceding the program name with ./ tells the system that the program in question is in the current directory (the directory from which you're currently working). The result of running the program should be the display of the string Hello world! in the Terminal window. As you can see in Figure B.12, we're operating in UNIX, so there's no Aqua look here!

Figure B.12   Running the Hello world program in the Terminal.

Programming in C++

The same GNU C compiler that you just used to compile a C program also can be used to compile a C++ program. In fact, Apple has modified the Free Software Foundation GNU C compiler from which this C compiler is based so that it compiles Objective-C code as well. (Objective-C is the language used to produce Cocoa applications, and is out of the scope of this book.)

To build a program written in C, Apple recommends ending the source code file-name with the .c extension and typing gcc to run the compiler. To build a program written in C++, Apple recommends ending the source code filename with the .cpp extension and typing g++ to run the compiler.

If you've had success with the simple C program, you might want to try building an equally simple C++ program. To do that, create a source code file named hel-loworld.cpp and enter the following code:

```
#include <iostream.h>

int main( void )
{
    cout << "Hello world!" << endl;

    return 0;
}
```

To enable the program to interact with the screen, keyboard, and file system, we include iostream.h in place of stdio.h. The only other change from the C source code listing is the use of cout in place of fprint to generate screen output.

To create the new executable, type g++ in place of gcc. You might also want to choose a different program name (such as hellonew) so that you don't overwrite your previous masterpiece (the hello program resulting from the C source code). At the prompt in the Terminal, your input will look like this:

```
g++ -o hellonew helloworld.cpp
```

As you did for the C program, you can run the resulting C++ program by typing
`./filename` (as in `./hellonew`). The result of running the C++ program is the same as
the result of running the C program—the text *Hello world!* is written to the Terminal.

The UNIX-Aqua Connection

For these simple UNIX examples, I created and edited the source code files using
pico. I just as easily could have used a Macintosh text editor such as TextEdit (or the
editor built into Apple's Project Builder or Metrowerks' CodeWarrior) to perform this
task. Figure B.13 shows a version of my helloworld.c file that I created in Apple's
Project Builder.

```
// The famous Hello, World! program

#include <stdio.h>

int main (void)
{
    printf( "Hello world!\n" );

    return 0;
}
```

Figure B.13   Using a Mac OS X text editor
to create a file to be compiled in the Terminal.

If you're used to working in a graphical interface environment, editing source code
might be easier using a Macintosh text editor. After doing so and then saving your
source code file, the result is as if you'd created and edited the file using a UNIX text
editor such as pico. To compile the file, make sure it's in the desired folder, move to
that directory using the Terminal, and then use the appropriate compile command
(gcc or g++). Keep in mind that UNIX isn't some software unit that's peripheral to
Mac OS X. UNIX is the very core of Mac OS X. When you create a file in the Aqua
Finder, UNIX knows about it. If you view a folder's contents in an Aqua Finder window, use the Terminal to view that same directory's contents using the ls command.
You'll see that both methods yield the same list of files.

Index

A

D

FSGetCatalogInfo routine, 265

FSRef data type, converting to FSSpec data type, 264

FSSpec data type, converting FSRef data type to, 264

functions. *See* routines

G

g++ command (UNIX), 330, 332

GCC (GNU C compiler), 338

gcc command (UNIX), 330, 332

GetApplicationEventTarget routine, 106

GetControl32BitValue routine, 167, 174, 181, 319

GetControlByID routine, 167, 174, 180, 318-319

GetControlData routine, 181-182

GetDefaultOutputVolume routine, 175-176

GetEventParameter routine, 78-79, 315-316

GetIndPattern routine, 231

GetMenuHandle routine, 199, 271, 320

GetMovieBox routine, 267

GetPixPat routine, 235

GetQDGlobalsDarkGray routine, 225

GetWindowEventTarget routine, 312-313

GetWindowPort routine, 220

GetWindowProperty routine, 142-143

global system patterns, 229-231
GlobalPatterns example program, 231-233

global variables, referencing windows, 116-117
GlobalWindows example program, 117-119

GlobalPatterns example program, 231-233

GlobalWindows example program, 117-118
editing nib file, 118
source code, 119

GNU C compiler (GCC), 338

GraphicConverter, 63

graphics environment (QuickDraw)
drawing
lines, 219-220
text, 220-221
GraphicsPortAndPen example program, 221-224

graphics pen, 130

graphics. *See* QuickDraw

GraphicsPortAndPen example program, 221-224

grid (QuickDraw), 218-219

grouping text input fields, 184

groups (Project Builder IDE), 30
External Frameworks and Libraries group, 31
Products group, 31
Resources group, 31
Sources group, 31

GUI. *See* user interface (Aqua)

H

handles, 146

handling errors. *See* error handling

handling events. *See* event handling

header files, 306
Carbon.h file, 306
#include statements, 42
QuickTime.h file, 306
routine prototypes in, 305
updating, porting Mac OS 8/9 code to Mac OS X, 301-302

O

P

VOICES THAT MATTER

HOW TO CONTACT US

VISIT OUR WEB SITE

WWW.NEWRIDERS.COM

On our web site, you'll find information about our other books, authors, tables of contents, and book errata. You will also find information about book registration and how to purchase our books, both domestically and internationally.

EMAIL US

Contact us at: **nrfeedback@newriders.com**

- If you have comments or questions about this book
- To report errors that you have found in this book
- If you have a book proposal to submit or are interested in writing for New Riders
- If you are an expert in a computer topic or technology and are interested in being a technical editor who reviews manuscripts for technical accuracy

Contact us at: **nreducation@newriders.com**

- If you are an instructor from an educational institution who wants to preview New Riders books for classroom use. Email should include your name, title, school, department, address, phone number, office days/hours, text in use, and enrollment, along with your request for desk/examination copies and/or additional information.

Contact us at: **nrmedia@newriders.com**

- If you are a member of the media who is interested in reviewing copies of New Riders books. Send your name, mailing address, and email address, along with the name of the publication or web site you work for.

BULK PURCHASES/CORPORATE SALES

If you are interested in buying 10 or more copies of a title or want to set up an account for your company to purchase directly from the publisher at a substantial discount, contact us at 800-382-3419 or email your contact information to corpsales@pearsontechgroup.com. A sales representative will contact you with more information.

WRITE TO US

New Riders Publishing
201 W. 103rd St.
Indianapolis, IN 46290-1097

CALL/FAX US

Toll-free (800) 571-5840
If outside U.S. (317) 581-3500
Ask for New Riders
FAX: (317) 581-4663

New Riders

WWW.NEWRIDERS.COM

RELATED NEW RIDERS TITLES

ISBN: 0735710201
1100 pages
US$49.99

Inside XML

Steven Holzner

Inside XML is a foundation book that covers both the Microsoft and non-Microsoft approach to XML programming. It covers in detail the hot aspects of XML, such as, DTD's vs. XML Schemas, CSS, XSL, XSLT, Xlinks, Xpointers, XHTML, RDF, CDF, parsing XML in Perl and Java, and much more.

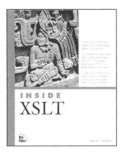

ISBN: 0735711364
640 pages
US$49.99

Inside XSLT

Steven Holzner

In order to work with XML fully you need to be up to speed with XSLT, and this is the book to get you there. Covering everything from creating Xpath expressions to transforming XML to HTML, *Inside XSLT* will have you heading straight down the road to programming efficiency.

ISBN: 0735711178
300 pages with CD-ROM
US$34.99

ebXML: The New Global Standard for Doing Business on the Internet

Alan Kotok, David Webber

To create an e-commerce initiative, managers need to understand that XML is the technology that will take them there. Companies understand that in order to achieve a successful Internet presence they need an e-commerce methodology implemented. Many department managers (the actual people who have to design, build, and execute the plan) don't know where to begin. *ebXML* will take them there.

ISBN: 0735710899
760 pages with CD-ROM
US$49.99

XML, XSLT, Java, and JSP: A Case Study in Developing a Web Application

Westy Rockwell

A practical, hands-on experience in building web applications based on XML and Java technologies, this book is unique because it teaches the technologies by using them to build a web chat project throughout the book. The project is explained in great detail, after the reader is shown how to get and install the necessary tools to be able to customize this project and build other web applications.

ISBN: 0735711143
500 pages
US$44.99

Perl for the Web

Chris Radcliff

Build quick-loading high-performance next-generation websites with the help of this book, which provides all the tools and techniques you need to work in Perl on the web.

ISBN: 073571052X
330 pages with CD-ROM
US$39.99

C++ XML

Fabio Arciniegas

The demand for robust solutions is at an all-time high. Developers and programmers are asking the question, "How do I get the power performance found with C++ integrated into my web applications?" Fabio Arciniegas knows how. He has created the best way to bring C++ to the web through development with XML and in this book, he shares the secrets developers and programmers worldwide are searching for.

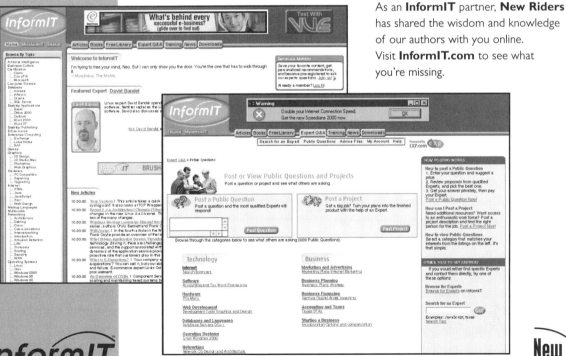

Publishing
the Voices
that Matter

OUR BOOKS

OUR AUTHORS

SUPPORT

NEWS/EVENTS

PRESS ROOM

EDUCATORS

ABOUT US

CONTACT US

WRITE/REVIEW

| web development | graphics & design | server technology | certification |

You already know that New Riders brings you the Voices that Matter.

But what does that mean? It means that New Riders brings you the

Voices that challenge your assumptions, take your talents to the next

level, or simply help you better understand the complex technical world

we're all navigating.

Visit **www.newriders.com** to find:

- ▶ Never before published chapters
- ▶ Sample chapters and excerpts
- ▶ Author bios
- ▶ Contests
- ▶ Up-to-date industry event information
- ▶ Book reviews
- ▶ Special offers
- ▶ Info on how to join our User Group program
- ▶ Inspirational galleries where you can submit
  your own masterpieces
- ▶ Ways to have your Voice heard

WWW.NEWRIDERS.COM

Colophon

One of the largest amphitheaters of the ancient Roman Empire, El Jem of Tunisia, is the image featured on the cover of this book. Situated in eastern Tunisia between the resort town of Sousse and Sfax, the great amphitheater of El Jem is one of the most important Roman monuments in Tunisia. It is recognized as the finest building in classical Africa. Although smaller than the Colosseum in Rome, the El Jem amphitheater is more impressive because it lies unobstructed by modern construction. It was founded during Julius Caesar's reign. Measured at 114 meters wide and 138 meters long, it remains incredibly well preserved and tourists marvel at the architectural and engineering genius of this civilization.

This book was written using Microsoft Word, and laid out in QuarkXPress. The fonts used for the body text are Bembo and MCPdigital. It was printed on 50# Husky Offset Smooth paper at VonHoffmann Graphics Inc., in Owensville, Missouri. Prepress consisted of PostScript computer-to-plate technology (filmless process). The cover was printed at Moore Langen Printing in Terre Haute, Indiana, on 12pt, coated on one side.